The New Testament: A Taster

THE NEW TESTAMENT: A TASTER

Mark J. Keown

MORPHE PUBLISHERS

AUCKLAND

The New Testament: A Taster

Morphe
paperback isbn: 978-0-473-50869-2
ebook isbn: 978-0-473-50868-5
Manufactured in USA February 1, 2020

All translations the authors unless specified.

Contents

Acknowledgments

This book arises from years of teaching an Introduction to the New Testament. Having worked hard to produce my three-volume *Discovering the New Testament* (Lexham), which is still in production at the time of publication of this book, I resolved to write something much more basic that would introduce students and others to the very basics of understanding the New Testament albeit giving links to my other more detailed work. This book is an attempt to do this. I do hope readers are encouraged to explore the New Testament at a deeper level once they taste the possibilities in this short book.

I want to acknowledge God, Father, Son, and Spirit above all for his constant goodness to me and in calling me to this work, what an honor. I thank Laidlaw College and its people for the boundless support and encouragement over the years. Special thanks go to those others who teach New Testament at Laidlaw College who have read and enhanced this material over recent years: Ian Waddington, Julia van den Brink, and Féy Cotter. I also give thanks to the many students who have come through my classes challenging me with great questions and learning with enthusiasm.

I also thank my phenomenal wife and co-worker, the Rev Dr Emma Keown, for her love and support in all I do. I must also mention my lovely daughters, Gracie, Annie, and Esther and my mum Nolarae, all I love deeply and have shaped me. I truly am blessed.

Abbreviations

1 Cor	1 Corinthians
1 En.	1 Enoch
1 Kgs	1 Kings
1QM	War Scroll (DSS)
1 Pet	1 Peter
1 Sam	1 Samuel
1 Thess	1 Thessalonians
1 Tim	1 Timothy
2 Cor	2 Corinthians
2 En.	2 Enoch
2 Kgs	2 Kings
2 Macc	2 Maccabees
2 Pet	2 Peter
2 Sam	2 Samuel
2 Thess	2 Thessalonians
2 Tim	2 Timothy
Ant.	Josephus, *Antiquities of the Jews*
ad	anno domini ("in the year of our Lord")
Asc. Isa.	Ascension of Isaiah
bc	Before Christ
b.Sanh.	Babylonian Talmud Sanhedrin

CD	Damascus Document (DSS)
Dan	Daniel
DSS	Dead Sea Scrolls
Eph	Ephesians
Exod	Exodus
Ezek	Ezekiel
Gen	Genesis
Gal	Galatians
Deut	Deuteronomy
Heb	Hebrews
Hos	Hosea
Isa	Isaiah
Jas	James
Jer	Jeremiah
J.W.	Josephus, *The Wars of the Jews*
Jub.	Jubilees
LEB	Lexham English Bible
Lev	Leviticus
Life	Josephus, *The Life of Flavius Josephus*
lxx	The Septuagint
Matt	The Gospel of Matthew
Neh	Nehemiah
NET	New English Translation
NT	New Testament
Num	Numbers
NZRFU	New Zealand Rugby Football Union
Phil	Philippians
Phlm	Philemon
Prov	Proverbs
Ps	Psalm(s)
Pss. Sol.	Psalms of Solomon
OT	Old Testament
Q	Quelle ("source")

Rev	Revelation
Rom	Romans
RWC	Rugby World Cup
s.a.	see also
Sib. Or.	Sibylline Oracles
Tit	Titus
T.Reu.	Testament of Reuben
Zech	Zechariah
Zeph	Zephaniah

Introduction

The New Testament A Taster is a book written for my biblical studies students. It is a simple introduction to the New Testament for those setting out on the journey of biblical study. While basic and introductory, it enables students to get the gist of some of the underlying ideas which inform biblical scholarship. Throughout, it has links to more detail in my three-volume *Discovering the New Testament* published by Lexham Press and one or two other things I have written posted on Academia. It is designed to whet a reader's appetite for more. It will help students grasp what the NT is, how it can be read more closely, its main themes, and how to apply it to life.

1

Chapter One: The Historical, Religious, and Social Setting of the New Testament

This chapter looks at the background to the NT.

More Detail

Keown, *Discovering the New Testament*, Vol 1, ch. 1–3.

Suggested Bible Readings

Matthew 1–4

Luke 1:4–4:13

The Jewish Background to the NT

The New Testament begins in Israel (or Palestine), or as it was at the time, Judea, Galilee, and Samaria. Its central character, Jesus, was a Jew. The key early figures Peter, Paul, and the other leading apostles and disciples were

Jews. The thought-world was Jewish. As seen by the many OT references and the dominant theme of promise (OT) and fulfilment (NT), the NT is written as a continuation of the Old or First Testament. The NT writers continue Israel's story, which is also the story of the world. So, all the Jewish ideas of Creation, the Fall, Abraham, Exodus, Covenants, Moses, Law, Wilderness, Conquest, Exiles, Restoration, and Hope come to their fulfilment in the NT. Hence, we are looking at Part 2 of the great story of God and his world. To understand the NT, one must be immersed in Israel's story.

Geography

Israel is a Middle Eastern country. It is hot in summer and can be quite cool in winter. At the time of Christ, it was separated into three parts: Galilee to the north, Samaria in the centre, and Judea to the south. Galilee was a mixed region, also called Galilee of the Gentiles. Samaria was the area of the Samaritans, despised by the Jewish population, with their own version of belief in Yahweh. To the north was Cilicia and Phoenicia (Lebanon) and to the east over the Jordan was the Decapolis (ten cities) and Perea. South was Egypt. To the east lay the Great Sea (Mediterranean). The whole area is not large, about the size of Northland in NZ (north of Auckland).

Distinctive geographical features included the Judean desert where Jesus was tempted, mountains on which events occurred (e.g. the Transfiguration), the River Jordan which marked the eastern boundary of the country, and the Sea of Salt (Dead Sea). The main centre was Jerusalem, the capital, where the Temple was, and so the centre of Israel's political, economic, and religious life. Other important centres include Caesarea Maritima on the western coast, which was a main centre for Roman occupation, Sepphoris near Nazareth, Tiberias on the eastern shore of the Sea of Galilee, Caesarea Philippi in the north where Peter confesses Jesus' messiahship, and Jericho, near Jerusalem. The population of Israel at the time was around 2 million with 200,000 to 300,000 in Galilee, 80,000 in Jerusalem (which swelled greatly in festivals), and with 5 million Jews living outside Israel (the so-called Diaspora, Dispersion).

Ethnocentricism

While the Jewish majority had diverse ideas and interests, there are some generalisations that can be made which are important for NT study. They saw themselves as Jews and the rest of the world as Gentiles and tended to be discriminatory against non-Jews. To become a member of God's people, Gentiles needed to Judaize—become Jews through circumcision and other rituals. This becomes important in the story of the gospel spread to Gentiles (below).

Monotheism

Unlike many modern Westerners and like most people in history, Jews (like all ancient peoples) believed in God. Unlike the Greco-Roman world, for them, there was one God, Yahweh, whose name they tended to avoid uttering as it was so sacred. The idea of God having a divine Son was ridiculous. They confessed this every day in the sacred Shema based on Deut 6:4–5.

Temple

Jews loved their religious rituals, especially centred on their cycle of festivals and the central role of the Jerusalem Temple. Solomon originally built the Temple. After its destruction by Babylon and a period of exile, it was rebuilt. God's glory did not descend, and Israel yearned for this. In a sense, Israel was still in exile until this came to pass. The temple was being rebuilt at the time of Jesus by Herod the Great and was finished in the early 60s ad, a few years before it was again destroyed by the Romans. The place heaved during festivals and daily prayer times. With its sacrifices, crowds, and heat, many areas would be very messy and bloody. The festivals, especially the Passover, the Feast of Booths, and Pentecost play important roles in the NT story. These retold the story of Israel and kept them strong in their faith. The Temple becomes vital in the story of Jesus as he challenges its system in his final week, stating that it would be destroyed and rebuilt. This was taken literally and misused to have Jesus killed. What Jesus actually meant was that he was establishing a new Temple, a people of God, a Temple which would surpass the physical space in Jerusalem. In all the Gospels the Temple is a place of debate between Jesus and his opponents. Paul particularly picks up the idea of the people of God as the Temple of God.

Synagogues

There were synagogues scattered throughout the country and in the cities of the Diaspora. These were more like the community centres of the Māori marae than simply places of worship. There, young boys learned the Torah, and memorised huge parts of it, until their coming of age at twelve. The synagogues were not an all-Jewish affair. Especially in the wider Roman world, but also in Israel, there were some Gentiles who were drawn to Judaism. Some converted and became Jewish proselytes. Others would attend worship with limited rights. These were called "worshipers of God" (of God-fearer, devout person) in the NT, e.g. Lydia, Titius Justus (Acts 13:43, 50; 16:14; 17:4, 17; 18:17). The patterns of early Christian worship come from the synagogue which centred on praise, prayer, and preaching.

Prayer

Israel had a formal prayer ritual. Prayers were held in the morning and evening sacrifices. Sometimes people prayed at midday. Each day they recited the Shema, stating that God is one and he is to be loved with all they have. This is the Great Commandment of Jesus' teaching. They also prayed the eighteen benedictions each Sabbath. When absent from Jerusalem, they prayed toward the Temple. Modern patterns of Islamic prayer give us an idea of this kind of thing. Prayers were said at Festivals and on each Sabbath. They were held at the Temple and in Synagogues and were said in the homes over meals and at other important times. Prayer was essential to Jewish life.

Sabbath

Every Saturday, the Sabbath, which ran from darkness on Friday night to Saturday sunset, was a sacred time of worship and rest. Work was strictly forbidden. This becomes important when Jesus is critiqued for healing on the Sabbath and a major source of contention. His claim to be "Lord of the Sabbath" was particularly provocative. Indeed, if you get to travel to Israel, in some more Jewish places like Tiberias on the shore of the Sea of Galilee, you will see that the Jewish world is utterly quiet in this period, with limited travel, and shops and businesses closed.

Circumcision

Aside from the Temple, synagogues, festivals, and Sabbaths, circumcision was very important to Israel. This originated in Gen 17 when Abraham was commanded to circumcise the men in his clan. This became basic to being Jewish. All boys were circumcised when they were 8 days old. Any man who wanted to convert had to be circumcised to be a proselyte (this remains the case today). This requirement became a huge issue when the gospel expanded to Gentiles and was resolved (at least in principle) at the Jerusalem Council (Acts 15).

Religious Purity

Also important were matters of religious purity. Israel's law was premised on keeping oneself ritually clean, which meant avoiding that which contaminates—the dead, the wrong food, Gentiles, the disabled, sinners, the cursed, and so on. Holiness was critical and needed to be maintained. Hence, one ate the right things, washed hands in the right way, avoided dead bodies, kept away from sinners, avoided the marginalised including the ill and disabled (as they are cursed by God), did not enter the homes of Gentiles, women were not to enter holy places while menstruating, and so on. Jesus was challenging concerning these things. He was prepared to touch dead bodies, eat with Gentiles and unclean hands, hang out with the disabled and sinners, go into the home of a Roman, and so on. He challenged this idea directly, calling for inner holiness rather than external cleanliness which is neither here nor there. This made Jesus very popular among those at the margins and equally unpopular among those who wanted to protect the status quo of Judaism.

Language

There were four languages used in first century Israel. Latin had been introduced by the Romans and was the language of the Roman elite and used in their circles. Hebrew was the historical language of Israel, which most of the OT is written in (there is also a small portion written in Aramaic). Hebrew was used in synagogue and temple worship, and in other religious contexts. The main language was Koine Greek, introduced by Alexander the Great when he conquered the region, and the common language of the Greek and then Roman Empires. It was the main language of life, trade, and commerce. Among Jews, Aramaic was the main language of conversation. It is very similar to Hebrew. Young Jews were a multilingual people and would grow up familiar at least with Aramaic and Greek and would learn Hebrew through Scripture. We see this in Paul who speaks to crowds in Aramaic and Hebrew and writes in Greek. Fishermen like Peter, Andrew, and the sons of Zebedee would use Greek in trading. Tax-collectors would also use Greek in their trade. They may also be familiar with Latin. Although some scholars argue

Jesus taught in Greek, his teaching was likely in Aramaic. This means our records of Jesus are translations and shaped by those who crafted the Gospels and our absolute certainty concerning the exact words of Jesus is a little blurred. However, these writers sought to faithfully record his words and the sense of his teaching is clear.

Wealth and Poverty

At the time of Christ, Israel's people were mainly poor, living hand to mouth. The wealthy elite were mainly the Romans and those who supported them, including the leading priests. There were many wealthy landlords who had large chunks of land which were farmed by Israel's struggling poor. The majority struggled; the vagaries of the climate and other natural disasters were a continual threat. They paid Roman taxes, tithes, and temple taxes. In a world with rudimentary health care, they were vulnerable to sickness. The life-expectancy was 35-40 for all people and lower for women, as giving birth was a dangerous time. This makes sense of the enormous crowds coming to Jesus. Here was someone who fed them and healed them.

A Subjugated People Hoping for Deliverance

To grasp Israel's social situation at the time of Jesus, a few things need to be clearly understood. First, after Solomon's reign, Israel had been divided into north and south in the tenth century. The north was Israel. The south Judah. This division remained intact even during the time of Christ.

Secondly, both kingdoms, Israel and Judah, had declined in that time and had become increasingly syncretistic, blending Judaism with foreign religious ideas (e.g. the Baals). They worshiped false gods and neglected the social justice called for in the Mosaic Law. This compromised them deeply and prophets arose to critique the king and other leaders who did not do enough to sort the problem out. Eventually, due to their sin, the northern kingdom was destroyed by Assyria and went into exile in the eighth century. Although the south withstood Assyria, the same thing happened when Babylon destroyed Jerusalem and exiled many from Judah in the sixth century bc.

After these exiles, Israel remained largely a nation under foreign rule, aside from one period in which they had more autonomy. After Judah's exile, the Medo-Persians allowed Judah to return from Babylon and the Temple was rebuilt (read Ezra, Nehemiah, Haggai). It was never as glorious as the first Temple and God's glory did not fill it. Those who returned rebuilt the nation and it was ruled by the Medo-Persians. In the fourth-century bc, Alexander the Great claimed the nation for the Macedonian (Greek) Empire and they ruled it. Then, in the mid-second century bc, led by a Judean family, the Maccabees, there was a revolt. This was to an extent successful, leading to a period of self-rule and determination: the Hasmonean Empire. This period is important when we come to the NT, as it seems many saw John the Baptist and Jesus as deliverers who would complete what the Maccabees sought to do.

In the mid-first century bc, the Romans conquered the area. They had bases in Caesarea Maritima and Jerusalem in particular. Soldiers like Cornelius were stationed in Caesarea and all over the country. In Jerusalem, adjoining to the Temple was the Fortress Antonia, from which Roman soldiers could move quickly into the Temple to suppress uprisings. So, Israel was under Roman rule.

Israel also had the writings of the prophets which predicted a time when God would move and deliver his nation from foreign rule. Indeed, he would not only liberate the nation, be he would ultimately conquer the world. They hoped for a time when all nations would believe in the Jewish God, its males circumcised, with Jerusalem the world's capital, and the Jewish law as the legal basis for all human life. They had a range of expectations concerning what would happen. In some scenarios, God himself simply intervenes in history to seize control. In others, a human or semi-divine agent would bring redemption. The main ideas included the Messiah (the Anointed One, or Christ, a Davidic King), a Son of Man, a Prophet like Moses or Elijah. All would be warrior-figures like Moses, Joshua, David, or Elijah and would be supernaturally empowered. They would raise Israel's armies empowered by God and his angels, and then liberate Israel from the Gentiles. It is likely that Jesus' disciples were full of such hopes and expectations and saw in Jesus the person of a new Joshua, Moses, or David, who would bring to pass this dream. The story of the NT is that he did, but not in the way that was expected. The idea of a crucified Messiah, Son of Man, or Prophet, who would bring redemption through his death was to them an oxymoron. For Israel, any such figure crucified on a tree was cursed by God and definitely not God's saviour (Deut 21:23; Gal 3:13). This problem of a crucified Messiah is a big stumbling block that Paul, especially, defends.

Law

All of Israel's life, including many of the legal expectations placed on the people mentioned thus far, was governed by the laws of Moses. These were extremely important for preserving the status quo, pleasing God, and hopefully bringing redemption. The ten commandments were the heart of the law, but as we read in Exodus, Leviticus, and Deuteronomy, there were a huge range of laws to be kept. Sacrifices needed to be made at the right time. Tithes were expected. Sabbath-keeping and circumcision were obligatory. The festivals were important. The main laws bounded Israel from the nations and are sometimes called boundary markers. Although Israel recognised it was chosen by God through grace, they were bound up in keeping the law. Christianity is set against this legalism and especially the boundary markers. These are reframed in the teaching of Christ, Paul, and the apostles.

Religious Parties

There was a range of religious ideas in Israel at the time of Christ, expressed in different "parties" among the religious elite.

Pharisees

The first group was the Pharisees. While some were priests, most were not. They were religious scholars. They accepted the whole OT canon and also the Halakhah, a written law that was in place to ensure Israel kept God's Torah. They saw themselves as the gatekeepers for Judaism, and they in particular were offended by Jesus who challenged them on issues of eating protocols, Sabbath, and forgiveness (which he claimed authority over). They believed in a Messiah, resurrection, predestination and free will, angels, and demons. In many ways, their theology aligns with Jesus and Paul (who was a Pharisee). But, at the same time, their theology is reframed through Jesus and Paul. Their dream was that Israel would become more holy, and this would bring deliverance. They thus accepted Roman rule as God's judgment. They hoped for better things. The ideas of the Pharisees became the basis of the writings of Israel after the Fall of Jerusalem in ad 70, the Mishnah and other writings. The Scribes were probably linked to the Pharisees—kind of like junior lawyers.

Sadducees

The second group is the Sadducees. They were mainly priests, and many were in the Sanhedrin , the ruling council of seventy-one Jews, under the high priest. They only accepted the Torah, the first five books of the Bible, as authoritative. They did not believe in angels, demons, resurrection, and the Messiah. Hence, they show little interest in Jesus, only really confronting him once over resurrection and marriage. They, however, were very important politically, accepting the Roman rule, and dominating Israel's political scene.

Essenes

A third group is the Essenes. The Essenes are known from the Qumran Community, a group of Jews who lived monastically beside the Dead Sea. Their writings were found between 1946 and 1951, the so-called Dead Sea Scrolls ((DSS). They were dissatisfied with the Jewish religious system of priests and the Temple. They basically opted out, preferring to establish a community in the hope that God would come. They shared their financial resources. They lived in community. Some think John the Baptist was one of them, and some even claim the same for Jesus and others. Yet, such links are tenuous. Their existence does show that Jesus was not the only one who critiqued Israel's religious system. There was much dissatisfaction at the time.

Herodians

It is also important to be aware of the Herodians. Herod the Great was a friend of the Caesars and a puppet or client king with limited control. The Herodians formed an important part of the political elite. He is the one who tried to kill Jesus (Matt 2). He also is responsible for many great buildings including the Temple and Caesarea Maritima. Any visitor to Israel finds evidence of this all over the country. After his death around 4 bc, his sons were given control of different parts of the area. Most important is Herod Antipas who governed Galilee as most references to Herod in the Gospels, including at Jesus' death, refer to him. Other descendants feature in Acts, especially Herod's grandson Agrippa I, who put James to death and then died after declaring himself a god (Acts 12). Then, later in Acts 24–25, there is Agrippa II, who interrogates Paul and is interested in Christian things. These Herodians were corrupt Roman-like rulers who were not widely loved but were given significant political power. Both the Roman Caesars and Herodians stand in stark contrast to the real King Jesus and help us make sense of how radical he is.

Sanhedrin

As noted above, the Romans allowed the Sanhedrin

(sometimes known as the Seventy, or the Ruling Council) to govern the religious world and some aspects of wider life. The Sanhedrin was made up of a ruling group of seventy men, mainly Sadducees, priests, and some Pharisees, plus the High Priest (e.g. Caiaphas), who was appointed by the Romans at the time. They were not permitted to put people to death, hence, they all condemned Jesus but then handed him over to Pilate. At times they violated the law in this area, e.g. the killing of Stephen. Joseph of Arimathea and Nicodemus (John 3), who buried Jesus, were both members of the Sanhedrin. Paul also had some association with it, holding their coats as Stephen was stoned.

Zealots

Some in Israel at the time of Jesus longed for liberation from Roman rule and were prepared to use violent force to achieve their ends. This impulse has its origins in the conquest when Joshua led Israel to victory over the Canaanites and the establishment of the nation in the land. The Maccabean revolt and setting up of the Hasmonean dynasty served as inspiration for a repeat led by the expected one of God. This desire for liberation was seen in the period before and after Jesus in messianic movements. Our main source for this is Josephus, while some are mentioned in the NT. When Herod died in 4 bc, Judas in Galilee, Simon in Perea, and Athronges in Judea claimed kingship. Others arose at the time of the revolt against Rome including Simon bar Giora. Other movements included prophetic claimants to messiahship including Theudas and an Egyptian who are both mentioned in Acts (Acts 5:36; 21:38). Some of the Twelve had such an impulse for revolution. Clearly, this is the case with Simon the Zealot. Judas may have been from the Sicarii (assassins) while the nickname "Sons of Thunder" given to James and John could indicate revolutionary zeal. It is likely the whole group saw Jesus as a new Joshua leading a new Conquest targeting Rome. His death and resurrection led them to reconceive his mission as one of conquest through humility, love. and service. This zealous nationalist tendency led to the revolt against Rome which saw the nation devastated.

An Agrarian World

Other features of Israel's culture and social setting are important, especially compared to ours. First, it was a rudimentary world, pre-industrial, agrarian, with all the challenges that such a context brings. Jesus hung out mainly outside the cities, in the towns and environs. There he mingled with the likes of farmers and fishermen, and his stories about seeds, harvests and fishing are contextually appropriate to life, which was tough. Many were poor. Life was slower too, with no modern gadgets. Walking was the main mode of transport. People ate off the land. It was very basic.

Patriarchy

The ancient world was very patriarchal. Men dominated everything. The main sphere of influence for women was the home. Jewish women were not permitted to learn the Torah. All official positions were held by men, whether Pharisees, Sadducees, leading Essenes, priests, Levites, politicians, or educationalists. Women were chaperoned everywhere. They covered their bodies carefully and guarded their virginity zealously. Menstruation and childbirth made them unclean and meant they needed to be marginalised at such times. They were concerned with matters of women (menstruation, childbirth, and lamenting in death). Society was sharply divided, with a limited association between men and women in wider society. Many criticise early Christianity, and especially Paul, for being patriarchal, but when we realise what the context was like, they were revolutionaries building societies in which women could learn and contribute.

Collective Cultures

The cultures of the ancient world were more collective than individual in orientation. Families were not nuclear (mum, dad, two kids), but were more like the Māori idea of a family. The family leader was the oldest living male. Elders were greatly respected. Power was held by the seniors. This made change very difficult and young upstarts, like Jesus, were problematic. The family links were wide. Genealogy was important. Children were seen and not heard and expected to uphold the family name. Life was about the collective—family, tribe, nation.

Honour-Shame

The ancient cultures were honour-shame based, rather than guilt-freedom based, as ours often are. What mattered was upholding the status quo, maintaining one's honour, and that of the collective (family, tribe, nation). Honour came through upholding religious and social expectations. Shame was to be avoided and came through failure to uphold the expectations of the group, as this brought shame on both the individual and group.

Reciprocity

Reciprocity was vital in these cultures. If one gave, one received. This could be positive, whereby one gave a gift and then expected something in return. This becomes extremely important in NT understandings of reward and retribution. Christianity was counter-cultural in that it is not based on personal reciprocity. Rather, God reciprocates. Hence, if one is on the receiving end of violence, one does not take an eye for an eye. Rather, one responds with blessing and prayer and leaves justice to God. Similarly, if one gives to the needy, one does not expect reciprocation from that person, as God will reward.

Hospitality

Hospitality was extremely important, and life revolved around meals. In this sense, the culture was like a modern Māori or Pasifika culture. When one's own people needed help, it was given. Hence, the shock when Joseph and Mary were rejected in Bethlehem before Jesus' birth. Three whole chapters of Luke happen at meals.

Marriage and Sexuality

Israel had strict laws concerning marriage. Marriage was purely heterosexual. While there is polygamy in the OT, monogamy was the ideal. The key text was Deut 24:1 which forbade divorce except where there is unfaithfulness. This was interpreted by some strictly, others more liberally allowing a man to divorce his wife for almost anything. Jesus was caught up in this debate (Mark 10; Matt 19) and 1 Cor 7 needs to be read with this in mind. A woman could not divorce her husband. The sexual immorality of the pagan world was ridiculed and rejected.

Angels, Demons, Magic, and the Occult

Angels feature in the OT. By the time of Christ, angels and demons were a part of their cosmology. The apocalyptic writings of Israel are full of encounters between angels and demons. Exorcisms were performed. While people believed in God, there was also a vibrant belief in spirits. Magic and sorcery were theoretically forbidden, but there is evidence that some dabbled in such things.

Abortion and Exposure

One of the features of the Roman world was the practice of abortion and exposure whereby a father decided whether a child was kept or left to die (exposed). Abortion was condemned in Jewish writings and although it is not forbidden in the NT, other early Christian writings utterly reject it.

An Oral or Aural Culture

In the modern world, at least up until the digital revolution, we tend to learn through a combination of oral teaching and reading (the book and other written literature). Now, increasingly, we use a combination of oral teaching, reading, and the use of AV resources (as in this course). Back in the day, life was learned primarily through hearing and observing. Life was imparted through teaching through speech and through example. We see this in Jesus, who taught, did ministry, and lived with his disciples passing on the patterns of the Kingdom of God. Sons learned in this way from fathers, as Jesus likely learned to be a carpenter from Joseph. Daughters learned from their mothers. Rabbis passed on traditions. There were writings, held in scrolls, which only the educated could read. These were memorised, processed, and the traditions passed on by those chosen to do this. The Gospels and no doubt the OT traditions, began as oral stories. These were joined together to form Gospels as the apostles neared death. These then became sacred scrolls, copied, and passed on in mainly oral form in churches and across the empire. Eventually, Christians developed the book (the Codex) and full Bibles were created (initially in Greek). Then, these were passed on across the Empire, but until the age of the printing press, life was mainly passed on orally. The printing press brought a revolution in the ability to pass on information as much through reading as through speech. Now we are all living in the dawn of a new digital revolution. God knows where that will take us.

The Greco-Roman setting and today

As ancient cultures were similar in many ways, some of what has been said above also applies to our context. So, such things as the rudimentary nature of the pre-industrial world, patriarchy, collective cultures, honour-shame, reciprocity, and hospitality are very much the same in the wider Greco-Roman world. However, there are many other distinctive features.

Cities

The city was very important across the Roman world. Cities such as Rome, Corinth, Athens, Thessalonica, Ephesus, and Syrian Antioch, were crucial centers for life. Jesus did most of his ministry outside the main centers of Israel other than Jerusalem, which he visited for festivals. Paul, on the other hand, focused on cities in his mission. They were cosmopolitan, more open to change. They had synagogues in many of them, enabling him to start his mission among Jews and Gentiles who gathered there. The gospel could spread fast and penetrate the cities quickly.

While the wealthy had villas, most people lived mainly in Insulae, large apartment blocks. These were densely populated, even more than modern Asian cities like Kolkata. Often, there were shops on the lower level. These would circle the agora, the marketplace and were the centres of life. There were other places people gathered—fountains, baths, gymnasia, and for the Jews, synagogues. Many cities had regular games like the Olympics (e.g. Corinth). The insula was essentially a place for sleeping and storing possessions as life was mostly lived outdoors. Hence, everyone's business was there for all to see.

The cities were large in some instances. Rome is said to have been a city of 1 million people. Thessalonica was 200,000 or so. Others were also large. Corinth was a young city, having been demolished by the Romans in the mid-second-century bc and rebuilt in the mid-first-century bc.

As a young city, it was a haven for people trying to make it big.

Polytheism and Religious Ritual

Unlike Israel's monotheism, the Greeks and Romans believed in a multiplicity of gods and goddesses. They each had a pantheon of twelve which were parallel (e.g. Zeus and Jupiter), but also believed in a wide range of other gods and goddesses and were always open to religions like the mystery religions of the east (e.g. Mithras). They had gods for most parts of life (e.g. Bacchus or Dionysus were the god of wine for Romans and Greeks) and they also worshiped the emperor, the so-called Imperial Cult. There were temples everywhere, dedicated to gods, goddesses, emperors, and their wives. They worshiped with sacrifices and libations led by a range of priests and priestesses. They believed in prophecy, with oracles consulted, e.g. the oracle of Delphi. They were extremely superstitious, into magic and occult, and life was devoted to keeping the gods and the spiritual forces happy. This was done through careful religious rituals. Maintaining the status quo was critical, thus keeping the *Pax Deorum* (peace of the gods) and *Pax Romana* (peace of Rome) was vital. When things went wrong, the gods were consulted. While religions were welcomed, they could be blamed for bad events, upsetting the spirits. Exclusive religions believing in one God, as in Judaism, clashed with Greco-Roman polytheism. Yet, there was also an attraction for many to Judaism with its strong ethics and family life.

Philosophy

Philosophy was critical to the Greeks and Romans. They had an amazing heritage of great thinkers like Plato and Aristotle, who were followed by many others. Many of the ideas which undergird western civilisation come from them. The Greeks, followed by the Romans who were enamoured with them, privileged the mind over the body. It was believed the soul was immortal, from God, and placed in the mind. Philosophy was the path to fully being what one was created to be. Hence, they were extreme rationalists. Emotions were seen negatively as unreliable and women were put down for being too emotional. The body was also seen negatively.

There were different groups among the philosophers: Stoics, Neo-Platonists, Epicureans, and Cynics. Stoics tended to focus on seeking virtue as the main means of happiness. Hence, they tended to be more rigorous in their views. Epicureans went the other way, seeing pleasure as the highest good, found through living modestly, gaining knowledge, and limiting desire. Cynics were traveling preachers who tended to be critical of the state; they begged for a living and often lived in squalor and could be quite disgusting in their behaviour.

One of the great traditions of philosophy is logic and rhetorical argument, taught to all young elite Roman men as they grew up. A lot of modern biblical scholarship considers how NT writers used rhetoric in their writings (rhetorical criticism). There is no doubt that the NT writers used methods and ideas gained from philosophy, although there is ongoing debate concerning to what extent.

Roads and Travel

The Romans were great road builders. For example, they built roads that ran from Rome to the bottom tip of east Italy (Via Appia) and from western Greece (Illyricum) to what we call Istanbul (Byzantium). The roading system was great for trade, communication, and the movement of the military. Paul used these roads as he travelled around the Roman world. They also had a sophisticated shipping system, avoiding travel from mid-Autumn and winter. At times, they made errors as in the great shipwreck journey of Paul in Acts 27. The combination of ship and road meant movement of goods was possible. Huge amounts of food were required for the great city of Rome and this was possible with such a system.

Social Status

The ancient Roman world was very "classist." One was born into one's position. A child of a slave was born into slavery. A member of the elite senatorial or equestrian classes was born into privilege. To be a member of these groups was not easy and depended on being part of an old family with great prestige and wealth. From these classes came Roman leaders, born into privilege and leadership. Old money and the aristocracy were where the power was held. These people controlled politics, were elected to the Senate, and held positions in city leadership. Slaves could gain their freedom by buying it or being gifted it. They then became citizens, which was greatly cherished, for, while there were some slaves who gained good positions, slavery was still not freedom and repudiated.

The status system was linked in with honour and shame.

One sought to gain honour through military service and benefaction (below). Such things helped one move up the Roman social ladder. Finding ways to do this was critical. Hence, boasting was an important art whereby without blowing one's own trumpet too loudly, through others, one sought to climb the social ladder. One also sought to bring down enemies to elevate self. It was a brutal political and social world.

Elite Romans had lots of slaves and so did no menial work. The idea of an elite Roman tentmaking was appalling. Paul, then, although a citizen, would have been on the outside. This may contribute to negative views of him in Corinth (2 Cor 10:10).

Patronage

The Roman world revolved around the wealthy giving to the needy and to cities. This sounds noble, but it was part of a carefully orchestrated system to gain prestige and enhance one's status. So, people made contributions to cities, not just to improve the city, but to enhance their own status. A good example is Erastus mentioned in Rom 16:23 as the Corinthian city treasurer. An inscription has been found in Corinth stating that a piece of road was gifted from a certain Erastus, which some scholars consider may well be the same person. In NZ, we have this kind of dynamic with people making contributions to build libraries, sports facilities, and other civic buildings. This is a great thing, but Christian giving is not to improve one's status, but to improve the situation of others.

There was also personal patronage which functioned under the rules of reciprocity. Rich patrons gave as they willed to people in need. These people would then repay in kind. Sometimes writers received patronage. Some consider Theophilus may have been Luke's patron, paying him as he wrote (Luke 1:3; Acts 1:1). The poor would also gather at the homes of the wealthy in the morning hoping for a handout. Such people would then be expected to support their benefactors in any way they could as they sought prominence. The Emperor was considered the *paterfamilias* and patron of the empire. Without the complex state-sponsored social welfare systems we have today, patronage was critical for maintaining the state. However, it ran a bit like the mafia. If a rich man looked after you, you looked after him, or paid the price.

Marriage and Sexuality

Marriage was seen as the basic unit of life. Unlike Israel, women could divorce husbands and vice versa. Families tended to be much smaller (usually about 2 children), as they exposed and aborted unwanted infants. Sexual immorality was much more prevalent and even encouraged at times of celebration. However, men had far more license than women. Women were expected to be chaste for marriage and men encouraged to 'sow their wild oats'. Homosexuality was seen as legitimate, although it was better to be the dominant male (sodomite) not the one who played the female role (catamite).

The elite, including the royals, were famous for their sexual liaisons. An example is Nero who at one point castrated a boy and married him. Prostitution was a part of the religious system whereby people could worship with sacral prostitutes. This appears to have been an ongoing problem in the Corinthian church. Paul's warnings against sexual immorality across his letters speak to the prevalence of the issue. Alcohol abuse was also a major problem throughout the Roman world, and it is linked to sexual immorality. As western culture moves away from its Judeo-Christian mores, we see our society becoming more and more like this. The early Christians never compromised the ethics taught them by Christ, Paul, Peter, and others as they encountered this. Neither should we.

Resurrection

The Greek distaste for the body meant that they viewed death as a blessed release from the cage of the body. They believed in an afterlife, but this was a spiritual affair and not bodily in any sense. They believed in Hades, a grey world ruled by Hades, the Lord of the dead. Those who lived well, got to live in Elysium but the wicked went into the deeper pit of Tartarus. Those who lived well would experience pleasure and bliss. Remembering the dead was important, and so they lived on. The Jewish idea of resurrection was foreign to them. The body was dispelled at death. It is likely 1 Cor 15 is written to Christians who accept the resurrection of Jesus, but do not accept their own bodily resurrection. The NT is clear, the body is raised as is the whole being and it is freed from sin, decay, and death. As with sexual immorality, even though the surrounding culture rejected resurrection (as in Athens when they laughed at Paul), the Christians never compromised their belief. Over time, many Romans were drawn to this belief. The body is important.

Diaspora

Reference was made earlier in this chapter to the diaspora (dispersion) of Jews around the world. Much like many of the Pasifika cultures where there are more of their people living in places like NZ and Australia than at home, there were around 5 million Jews in the diaspora, and only 2 million in Israel. Under the Empire, Judaism was a legal religion. This was one of the brilliant features of the Romans. They allowed locals and migrants from other cities to maintain their cultures and religions, as long as they were not a threat to the city and state. So, wherever Jews went, and if there were more than ten adult men, they set up synagogues. We see them in almost all the cities Paul visited, aside from Philippi where a group of women met outside the city (Acts 16). The synagogues were the centre of Jewish life in the cities. They tended to live near each other in ethnic enclaves in order to maintain their culture and belief. Older scholars believed that Palestinian Judaism was pure, and diaspora (Hellenistic) Judaism was corrupted. Now this is rejected. Hellenism certainly influenced Judaism, but across the empire Judaism was much the same.

The synagogues of the diaspora are critical for understanding the spread of the gospel. Paul always began his mission in a synagogue knowing there would be Jews, proselytes, and God-worshiping Gentiles present. He always managed to gain a few converts and start a church after they were driven out, as was inevitable. These people familiar with the Jewish Scriptures and ethics would be the leadership for a new church. He would leave them to it and move on. Many of the first converts were Jew and Gentile people who gathered at the synagogue. It meant the gospel could get a foothold in each context and the church could engage in its own mission after he left, and Christianity spread.

Households

As noted earlier, the family was the core unit of the Roman world. Like Israel's families, this meant a wider family than the European nuclear idea. The oldest male was paterfamilias, the head, with significant power. The family included the wife, children, slaves, and sometimes others. The home was also a place of worship, with shrines established. As the church developed and was driven out of the synagogue, the homes of the wealthy became the centres of the church's worship and life. So, we see churches established in the homes of women like Lydia and Nympha, with a married couple of Priscilla and Aquila, and so on. These homes were likely larger villas, with a pool used for washing which became a baptismal, and an atrium which housed up to thirty for worship.

Mealtimes were also important as often at the main evening meal, a speaker (e.g. a philosopher) would be welcomed to speak. It is likely that early Christians spoke on these occasions. The gospel would have moved primarily through family groupings in households and moved from household to household as people were converted. This meant that the church was more like the underground church of China than a modern situation with obvious basilica-like church buildings all over the city as in Auckland or Christchurch. This allowed Christianity to spread subtly and subversively. This was important as when it came to the attention of authorities, it was seen as a threat.

2

Chapter Two: The Four Gospels-their Relationships, and Distinctives

This chapter discusses the four Gospels, their distinctive perspectives, and their relationship. Of special interest is the connections between the three Synoptic Gospels: Matthew, Mark, and Luke. This is called the Synoptic Problem.

More Detail

Keown, *Discovering the New Testament*, Vol 1, ch. 4–9.

Suggested Bible Readings

Luke 1:1–4—note how Luke wrote his Gospel, his sources, his purpose.

Mark 1:1—what is Mark's purpose?

Matt 28:18–20: how does this help us discern Matthew's purpose?

John 20:30–31—what is John's purpose?
Compare Mark 6:30–44 with Matt 14:13–21; Luke 9:10–17; John 6:1–14—note the differences.

Compare Luke 14:15–24 with Matt 22:1–14 (material common to Matthew and Luke)
Matt 25:31–46 (only found in Matthew)
Luke 17:11–19 (only found in Luke)
John 1:1–18 (only found in John)

Introduction

A Gospel is an account of the good news, the *euangelion*. The Bible includes four Gospels: Matthew, Mark, Luke, and John. These are all from the ancient genre of biography, in which the life of a prominent person is narrated. They are narratives. They continue the OT story. Sometimes people today do not get why there are four Gospels. Why not harmonise them into one? In fact, some in the second-century ad had the same problem. Tatian wrote a harmony called the Diatessaron based on John including material from the other four Gospels. When the church debated making this their sacred text, it was roundly rejected. Four Gospels give four views of Jesus. In Jewish thought, two to three witnesses are required to prove a legal point. The four Gospels are then important. Further, early Christians did not see a problem with the four Gospels. They not only gave credibility to the Christian claims, but they give four eyewitness perspectives. Imagine one goes to Eden Park to watch the Blues play the Crusaders in rugby (or an NFL or EPL sports event or similar). Later, you ask a person from each of the four main grandstands to narrate their story of the game. There will be many common things based especially on the main moments. However, there will also be differences in detail, perspective, and some different points made. The four Gospels are like four views of Jesus. They are also written for particular audiences at different times facing different issues. Hence, they have differing emphases, depending on the points the Gospel writer is trying to make. Many sceptics note that there is also a range of other gospels that should be given equal privilege (e.g. the Gospel of Thomas). Well, there are other gospels, but the early church was careful to preserve those that were written early, are based on eyewitness tradition, and preserve the authentic apostolic gospel. These other gospels are clearly much later and not to be trusted.

The Synoptic Problem

A casual observer will notice that the first three Gospels, Matthew, Mark, and Luke, have a lot of similar material. They are thus labelled the Synoptic Gospels. Synoptic is formed by *syn* (with) and *optic* (sight) meaning they can be laid side by side and read at the same time, comparatively. Hence, they can be read in a synopsis.

This commonality has led to huge swathes of scholarship as people try to determine how they are related. Here is a summary of the main views with the final of views the one dominant in scholarship.

1) An Oral-Tradition Relationship: as noted earlier, the Gospels were formed from circulating oral traditions. A few have tried to argue that there is no literary relationship between the Gospels and that their commonalities are due to shared oral traditions. This is seen to be unlikely as the correspondence between the three Gospels is too close to be purely oral.

2) Matthew's Gospel First: the Griesbach Hypothesis, and

one held by some in the early church like Augustine, considers that Matthew was the first Gospel. Mark and Luke are then based on Matthew. Mark abbreviates Matthew. Luke uses Matthew and perhaps Mark and creates his own story, with a few extras. This is a minority view held in modern scholarship.

3) Mark's Gospel First, Matthew Second, Luke Used Both: Some scholars today see Mark as first, followed by Matthew and then Luke. In this view, the Farrar-Goulder Hypothesis, Mark was written at the end of Peter's life by Mark. Matthew used Mark and other material to write his Gospel. Luke used both Mark and Matthew to write his. This is another minority position today, although it is gaining more traction.

4) Mark's Gospel First, Luke Second, Matthew Third: Some reverse the previous, arguing Mark was first, Luke wrote with Mark's Gospel and other sources he found himself in his research, and Matthew wrote using Mark and Luke. This is the Wilke-Hypothesis and is not widely held today.

5) Mark's Gospel First, A Common Source Q (Quelle), Matthew and Luke Wrote Independently using Mark, Q, and Their Own Sources: this is the view that dominates today. It is argued Mark was written toward the end of Peter's life sometime in the 60s to early 70s. Another document exists, which is termed Q (from the German *Quelle*, "Source"). Matthew and Luke wrote their Gospels using a combination of Mark, Q, and their own gathered material. Some see Q as a combination of oral and written sources.

The final view above is the main view in scholarship. Is it important? At one level, not at all. At another level, it is important for the interpretation of Matthew and Luke. If we believe Luke and Matthew used Mark for their version, we can study the way that the two evangelists adapt and use Mark to discern their perspectives. We can see what they left in, left out, and how they reword it to make a point. For example, Luke will often add a detail that Jesus was praying when something happened (e.g. his baptism). We then realise that prayer is very important in Luke's story of Jesus—he wants us to pray! For those who wish to advance in biblical study beyond an introductory level, the Synoptic Problem is important when it comes to exegeting and understanding a passage and the author's intention in telling the story the way they do.

The Distinctives of the three Synoptic Gospels

In this section, each Gospel will be briefly introduced and their distinctives noted. This is very basic material and fuller detail can be gained from Chs. 6–8 in Vol. 1 of *Discovering the New Testament.*

As noted in the previous section, the three Synoptic Gospels are related to each other in some way. Likely, Matthew and Luke used Mark's account as the basis for their Gospels. This can be explained by the pre-eminence of Mark's Gospel, as early church tradition is consistent in stating that Mark's Gospel was put together at the time of Peter's death in the mid-60s and represents Peter's kerygma, his proclamation. As such, the writers of Matthew and Luke used Mark's account due to the Petrine connection. Here, the distinctives of the three Gospels will be briefly outlined.

Mark

Mark's Gospel was likely written in the 60s or 70s ad. Papias, a second-century bishop of Hierapolis, in what we would call western Turkey, notes that Mark was Peter's interpreter who wrote down with some accuracy what he recalled of Peter's proclamation concerning the things done by God. His account is not orderly in a chronological way but is an account arranged for his purposes (Eusebius, *Hist. eccl.* 3.39.15–16). Mark is traditionally understood to be the John Mark of Acts, a member of the early Jerusalem Christian community (Acts 12:12), and a relative of Barnabas (Col 4:10). He travelled with Paul for a period but returned to Jerusalem (Acts 12:25–13:13) and in the aftermath of this, he and Barnabas fell out with Paul and he engaged in mission with Barnabas (esp. Acts 15:36–41). He is connected both with Peter and Paul in Rome in later life (Col 4:10; 2 Tim 4:11; Phlm 24; 1 Pet 5:13). It is possible he is found in the narrative of Mark as the young man who fled naked in the Garden of Gethsemane (Mark 14:52). Traditionally, Mark's Gospel is connected to Roman Christianity where it is likely Mark wrote the material near Peter's death. This was a time when Nero was emperor, and Christians were severely persecuted with Nero blaming them for the fire of Rome (Tacitus, *Nero*, 15.44). While many dispute that the writer is this particular Mark and the link to Peter on the basis that the evidence is flimsy, the early church was in no doubt and there seems no good reason to dispute it from this distance.

Mark's Gospel is a fast-moving account of Jesus indicated by the continual use of immediately (*euthys*, forty–two times). He entitles it a Gospel (*euangelion*), a declaration of the good news of God's salvation. Without a doubt, the central theme is Jesus the Messiah, the Son of God (Mark 1:1). There is no infancy narrative, but it begins with John in the wilderness crying out from Isaiah and Malachi that he is the long-awaited herald of the Messiah. Jesus appears abruptly, is baptized as Servant King, tempted by Satan, and launches his ministry as the Messiah.

The central theme of Jesus' ministry is the Kingdom of God. In the backdrop are two sets of presuppositions. First, there are the Jewish expectations of a military Messiah who will cleanse the land of evil, i.e. the Gentiles. If Jesus is this Messiah, it would be expected that he will raise an army and with God's power, do just that. He is named Jesus, Greek for the Hebrew name Joshua, which of course provokes memories of the OT Joshua.

The second point of background is the things happening in the Roman world during Nero's despotic rule in the mid-60s. It was written before or after the Neronian persecution. This is a time of persecution for Christians who are "taking up their crosses" and the story of Jesus stands in vivid contrast to Roman imperialism based on dynastic rule, opulence, military force, and political machinations.

This Jesus gathers twelve disciples, recalling the tribes of Israel—a renewed Israel is being launched. Rather than military conquest, he sets about his ministry of healing, deliverance, feeding, preaching the good news of the Kingdom, summoning disciples, and inviting people into it through repentance and faith. These show what the Kingdom is really about. This Kingdom will grow like a mustard seed and become huge so that the nations enter it. The first half of the Gospel is the revelation of this Jesus.

Through the Gospel, there is great secrecy demanded

when anyone recognises Jesus as the Messiah, whether a demon or a person. This is called the Messianic Secret and is likely because Jesus did not want to excite ideas of revolution, which were associated with Messianic hopes. Hence, he urged quietness from all who recognised him.

The central point of Mark is the confession in Mark 8:29, where Peter states: "you are the Messiah." In the rest of the Gospel, Mark's Jesus unpacks what this Messiah and his Kingdom is about—it is not military power but the power of service, love, prayer, holiness, sexual fidelity, and mercy that will change the world. So, we see Jesus hanging with all the wrong people like children and blind beggars, repudiating the political systems of the world, challenging the rich and powerful alike, calling for the disciples to be servants and like children, and predicting the destruction of the Temple and Jerusalem. This marks the end of Judaism as it is known, and its continuation in Jesus and his people.

The climax of his demonstration of what it means to be the Messiah is his death for the world as a ransom for many. He is Isaiah's Servant, Messiah, Son of Man, and Son of God, all tied up in one, and his modus operandi is servanthood. He dies on the cross deserted by almost all with the only confessor of his Messiahship a Roman soldier. Rather than destroy the Roman world, he is inviting them into his Kingdom, to be his disciples prepared to count the cost of following Jesus.

The earliest texts of the Gospel end abruptly in Mark 16:8 after Jesus' resurrection is announced by the angel. The longer endings are important historically but are not part of the original Gospel. The questions the reader is left with are, "who is this man?" "What are we to do?" The answer the Gospel has given is that he is the Messiah, the Son of God, and that they should repent, believe, and follow him with crosses strapped over the shoulder. Mark speaks powerfully to Romans at the time who are indeed doing this; the call of the gospel is well expressed by German theologian (and martyr) Dietrich Bonhoeffer (*The Cost of Discipleship*, [2001], 44): "When Christ calls a man, he bids him come and die.").

Matthew

Matthew's Gospel includes almost all of Mark and continues the same narrative but with some really distinct emphases. While it is disputed, Matthew is likely a former tax-collector and disciple of Jesus, also called Levi (Matt 9:9; 10:3). Papias is again helpful, telling us that Matthew wrote down his *logia* (words) in the Hebrew language. This is a highly disputed reference which could mean that he wrote a Hebrew Gospel, that he drew on Hebrew sources, or that his Gospel is Hebrew in flavour. Anyway, as with Markan authorship of Mark, there seems no reason to dispute the general agreement of the early church that Matthew is the author. It is believed he wrote in the area of Syrian Antioch after Mark, sometime in the 70s and 80s. This is the area where the church flourished (Acts 11–13).

Like Luke, Matthew draws on Q and his own material, likely drawn from his own experience of Jesus and that of his disciple colleagues.

Whereas the feel of Mark and Luke's Gospels is more Greco-Roman, the emphasis of his Gospel is decidedly Jewish. He writes an apologetic for Jesus as truly being the Messiah of Israel, something Mark clearly implies but does not draw out as much as Matthew. He writes at a time when Jewish and Christian relationships are very strained as Christianity is emerging from the chrysalis of Judaism after Jerusalem's destruction in ad 70. His Gospel is an ideal tool for training disciples, especially to read Jesus against the OT Scriptures, and to defend Jesus against Jewish opposition.

His Gospel is a passionate defense of Jesus messiahship, full of OT quotations demonstrating that Jesus is the fulfilment of the hopes of Israel. Indeed, Matthew is a repository of OT texts pointing to Jesus. Often, he mentions the text using a fulfilment formula, e.g., "in order to fulfil" (Matt 1:22; 2:15; 3:15; 8:17; 12:17; 13:35; 21:5, cf. 5:17). His Gospel functions both to strengthen Jewish Christians being persecuted for their belief in Jesus and through its evangelistic and apologetic power, to draw Jews to Jesus as they read the story. It equips those who engage in mission among Jews for the task.

Matthew fills out Mark's story, adding an infancy narrative written from the perspective of Joseph, Jesus' earthly father (unlike Luke which seems drawn from Mary) (Matt 1–2). He adds the details of the temptation (Matt 4:1–11). He also includes a number of other parables and fresh incidents from Jesus' life, many of which are unique, while some of which are found in Luke's Gospel (Matt 13:1–50; 18:10–14; 18:21–35; 20:1–16; 21:28–44; 22:1–14; 24:32–25:46).

Matthew emphasises eschatology, pointing forward to the culmination when Jesus returns. Mark includes one chapter on the events surrounding the destruction of the Temple and the return of Christ (Mark 13). Matthew includes this, making it clear that it applies to both the fall of Jerusalem and the return of Christ (Matt 24). Then he adds the parable of the ten virgins, the parable of the talents, and the sheep and goat's judgment scene to summon disciples to be faithful until Jesus' return (Matt 25:1–46).

Mark summons people to take up crosses, but Matthew really stresses discipleship, giving additional challenging material e.g. Matt 8:18–22 (as does Luke, as we will see). He has a strong emphasis on God's judgment against false Christians and those who reject the faith; indeed, many of his parables end with darkness and the gnashing of teeth (Matt 8:12; 13:42, 50; 22:13; 24:51; 25:30).

He also emphasizes mission, giving a whole discourse on mission (Matt 10:5–42) and climaxing his Gospel with the Great Commission whereby the gospel is going global (Matt 28:18–20). In fact, Gentiles feature throughout, e.g. the wise men who worship Jesus (Matt 2:1–12) and the Roman soldier (Matt 8:5–13). He fills out the Markan narrative of the resurrection (Matt 28:11–20), telling readers what came next—the women delivered the news to the apostles, and Jesus appeared to some of them. Matthew's Jesus is also harshly critical of the Jewish leadership (esp. Matt 23:1–36).

Although the Kingdom is central to his Gospel, Matthew tends to prefer to use the Kingdom of Heaven rather than the Kingdom of God. This does not speak of something different but is likely driven by the Jewish desire to avoid using the personal name Yahweh.

His Gospel is traditionally seen as being arranged in five discourses and is not so much a Gospel as a catechism for teaching and training Christians.

1) The Sermon on the Mount (Matt 5–7): a gathering of many of Jesus' sayings, teachings, and pithy parables. Along with the Sermon on the Plain in Luke (Luke 6:17–49), this gives us the best material to understand the ethics of the Kingdom.

2) The Mission Discourse (Matt 10:5–42): a gathering of Jesus' teaching on mission into one chapter built on the sending of the Twelve which focusses on mission.

3) Kingdom Parables (Matt 13:1–52): this includes the parables of Mark 4 with some additional extras ramping up the teaching on the Kingdom.

4) The Church (Matt 18): this focuses on matters of church life, focusing on humility, resisting sin, caring for the lost sheep, discipline, and forgiveness toward others.

5) The Return of Christ (Matt 23–25): The fifth and final discourse includes a sharp critique of the Jewish leadership and being prepared for future return of Jesus.

This is followed by the account of Jesus' death, resurrection, and the Great Commission.

Matthew's Gospel stands in contrast to Luke. Matthew's interest is in Jewish Christians. Luke's interest is in Greeks and Romans and especially those like Theophilus who are from the well-educated citizenry of the Roman world. As such, they both give us ideas of how to contextualize the Jesus story dependent on our audience.

Luke-Acts

There is only one Luke named in the NT; Luke the physician (Col 4:14). It is almost certain that he wrote the third Gospel. It is hard to date, with theories ranging from a time just after the point of the end of Acts (ends in AD 61) to the 80s and even the 90s. My sense is that it is earlier, as there is much not included from the 60s including the deaths of James in AD 62 (recorded in Josephus, *Ant.* 20.197–201) and Paul and Peter under Nero (AD 66–68); the Roman-Jewish war and fall of Jerusalem (AD 66–70). It seems strange that these are not included if in fact the Gospel was written later.

Luke addresses his Gospel to a certain "most excellent Theophilus," which may be a cypher for "friend/lover of God," or, as is most likely, an elite Roman. He is perhaps involved in some way with Paul's situation in prison in Rome. He may also be a patron of Luke. He appears to be a Christian but at the least has a good understanding of Christianity, and Luke writes to strengthen this.

Luke's preface is most helpful as it tells us he consulted other accounts in writing his. He spoke to eyewitnesses and ministers of the word. He himself is not a first-generation Christian and is a Gentile (see Col 4:11–14). That in itself is amazing—a Gentile was one of the four Evangelists. Luke's account is also distinctive because it is a two-part work, he writes an account of both Jesus (Luke) and the early church until Paul is imprisoned in Rome (Acts). Many believe that the two-part narrative is one story only separated due to scroll length. As such, his presentation of the gospel includes the story of Christ from his birth to his present situation.

If Matthew has a Jewish feel, Luke is decidedly Greco-Roman in orientation. He writes to an elite Roman, and the way he presents the story of Jesus, he is seeking to challenge Roman ideas of status (humility); the poor, the marginalised, and patronage; and to challenge Roman Christians to live out of the pattern of Christ rather than being conformed to the patterns of the world.

He likely uses Mark and Q, or perhaps Matthew, and he writes as a historian. Luke was well positioned to gather material. The "we-passages" of Acts (where the writer shifts from the third person "they" to the first person "we") indicate that he was with Paul for long periods of his mission. He joined Paul in Troas in Acts 16:10, travelled to Philippi with him, remained behind (Acts 17:1) and rejoined Paul on his third Antiochian mission in Macedonia (Acts 20:6). He travelled with Paul to Jerusalem and would have had great opportunity to gather material from eyewitnesses for his work. He also travelled with Paul to Rome (Acts 27:1; 28:10). In Rome, he would have had contact with a wide range of people who had travelled with Paul and even with Peter himself and others. He writes a historical biography of Jesus and an account of the early church, focusing on the spread of the gospel through the Roman world.

Luke includes an infancy narrative distinctive because it is written with Greek of a similar style to the lxx, the Greek OT Scriptures. Luke seemed to intentionally set out to continue the Septuagint (lxx). He then takes large portions of Mark, blends it with common material from Matthew (Q), and adds significant other material. He includes his own version of the Sermon on the Mount, the Sermon on the Plain, which is presented as the basis of an ethic for the new covenant.

Luke's material has the same types of things found in Mark and Matthew: calling disciples, healing, casting out demons, teaching, and preaching. Jesus is the Davidic Messiah King who come to gather the lost sheep of God and feed them materially and spiritually.

Many see Luke 4:18–20 as critical to understanding Luke's Jesus. Here, Jesus stands in the Nazareth synagogue and preaches. He draws on Isa 61:1–2 with a clip from Isa 58:6. He is the anointed one Isaiah predicted. He will proclaim good news to the poor—not just preaching but feeding them with physical and spiritual food. He has come to set people free and open their eyes. He has come to inaugurate the ultimate year of Jubilee (cf. Lev 25). This sets the program for Luke's Gospel. Later, he will state even more succinctly his mission: "For, the Son of Man came to seek and to save the lost" (Luke 19:10). This is what Jesus is all about for Luke. Empowered by the Spirit at Pentecost and subsequent experiences, believers are to join in this ministry until the completion of the mission.

The turning point of Luke is Luke 9:51 when Jesus turns to Jerusalem, to die as God's Servant. Through to his entry to the city recorded in 19:28–44, Luke uses mainly original L material and Q material. Also dominant is the theme of money and the poor; the reader is challenged to care for the lost greatly. Central to this section are the three lost parables in Luke 15—the lost sheep, coin, and son stories. There is a range of other parables and encounters all calling believers to be radical disciples.

Discipleship is a core theme. Like Matthew, Luke includes the summons to take up crosses and follow Jesus twice (Luke 9:23–26; 14:27). Other passages call believers to do more than merely believe; we have to live out this gospel. The cost is great, but the reward is greater (see e.g. Luke 9:57–62; 14:25–35).

Luke's story is full of unlikely heroes and heroines. There is the commendable Roman centurion (Luke 7:1–10) and the sinful woman who anoints Jesus' feet (Luke 7:36–50). Startlingly, given the cultural situation, women travelled with Jesus, ministering to him and possibly engaging in mission among other women. These include Mary Magdalene who had been delivered of seven demons, and Herod Antipas' household manager's wife, Joanna, a woman of significant social status (Luke 8:1–3). Although despised, Samaritans and not Jews are heroes in the parable of the Good Samaritan and the healing of the ten lepers (Luke 10:25–37; 17:11–19). Mary is another unlikely heroine as she does not participate in the expected hospitality protocols but sits at Jesus' feet as a disciple (Luke 10:38–42). She paves the way for women to be disciples, something forbidden in Judaism.

Another feature of Luke is meals. In Ch. 7, 11, and 14, Jesus is eating in the homes of Pharisees. He challenges them powerfully in each case—only a brave person invites Jesus for dinner. In chapter 14, he tells the story of the Great Banquet which speaks of God sending out invitations to the Great Eschatological Banquet (cf. Isa 25:6–12). We are invited. We are welcomed. All are welcomed if they accept the invitation. We then are sent to invite others. This is mission.

Luke's interest in mission is strongly signalled with Jesus in mission, then the Twelve (Luke 9), and then the Seventy-two (Luke 10). Only Luke includes these two sending narratives. Later, in Acts, mission will begin with the Twelve especially Peter and John (Acts 3–5), then the seven, especially Stephen and Philip (Acts 6–8), and then the whole church will be thrust out of Jerusalem sharing Christ (Acts 8:4, cf. 11:19–21). Dynamos like Apollos emerge from nowhere (Acts 18:18–19:1). We see that the Spirit is the evangelist, thrusting people out to continue the work of Jesus extending the Kingdom into the world.

Luke includes Jesus' death and resurrection as do Mark and Matthew. He tends to play down the Roman role in his death, perhaps sensitive to Theophilus and Roman readers. He includes different accounts of Jesus' appearances, including his apparition to two travellers on the Emmaus Road and Peter. The Emmaus Road account is filled with accounts of Jesus teaching from the OT that the Son of Man must suffer, die, and rise according to the Scriptures. In particular, Jesus is the Suffering Servant of Isaiah (Luke 24:25–26, 46).

Luke also includes his version of the Great Commission, focused not on making disciples as in Matthew, but preaching repentance and forgiveness of sins through the world. They are to wait in Jerusalem for God to imbue them with power for this (Luke 24:46–49). Then they are to go. It ends with the ascension and worship at the Temple (Luke 24:49–52). These themes are all reframed again in Acts 1:1–11 after which part two of the story is launched.

Luke-Acts is great because we not only have the story of Jesus but an account of how the first Christians lived out his commands. We are also part of the story, as the same Spirit is in us and we continue the great drama of God.

John

John was written by the "beloved disciple" or "the disciple Jesus loved" (John 13:23; 19:26; 20:2; 21:7; 21:20). He is also likely the other disciple in John 1:40; 18:16; 20:2–4, 8. The identity of this disciple is vigorously debated. It is agreed that someone with the name John wrote it, however, which John is unclear. There are two main ideas. John the Apostle or John the Elder, referenced in Papias. With the greater focus on Judea rather than Galilee and the relationship the author has with the High Priest (John 18:16), a good case can be made for a John who was a disciple from Jerusalem (e.g. Bauckham). The traditional view that John the Apostle is the author is also strong. This can be seen by cross-referencing with the Synoptics. Most scholars believe the author is the "other disciple" with Andrew in John 1:35–42. From the Synoptics, this is most likely John the Apostle (see Mark 1:16–20; Luke 5:1–11). The author is also referenced at the Lord's Supper, reclining beside Jesus (John 13:23). The most likely candidates for this person are John's brother James and Peter. However, James was dead at the time of writing. Peter is ruled out as he motions to the beloved disciple at Jesus' side. Hence, knowing James and John sought the places of prominence beside Jesus in the Synoptics, including at the Lord's Supper (Luke 22:24–30, s.a. Matt 20:20–28; Mark 10:35–45), by far the most likely person for this is John the Apostle. Early church tradition also supports John the Apostle. Whichever of the Johns wrote it, it is a masterful eyewitness account to the life of Jesus.

When one reads John after the three Synoptics, it is clear John is not singing from quite the same hymn sheet. It is still about Jesus and many of the same characters are there. He is in the same parts of the world, although in Jerusalem a lot more than Galilee. John the Baptist precedes his ministry. He preaches. He heals. He teaches. He raises the dead. He encounters harsh opposition. He is arrested and tried before the Sanhedrin, condemned to die, and sent to his death by Pilate. He rises from the dead and appears. He sends his disciples into mission. So, it is clearly about the same guy.

Yet, there is much that is different. Scholars explain the differences in varying ways. Some think John had no idea of the other Gospels and wrote from independent sources. Others consider that John knew Mark and probably Luke and that he wrote to tell the story differently. His writings use ideas found in Paul, e.g. faith and love. He recasts the Jesus story, blending his experiences of Jesus with theological ideas in the church, some of which he takes to a new level. He tells us stories of Jesus in Jerusalem, especially at festivals. This material supplements the Synoptic stories and fills out our picture of Jesus.

The call of the disciples in John 1 involves radically different material. In addition, Jesus is in Jerusalem a lot, encountering opponents (the Jews) with whom he is in constant debate. He does not teach in parables, but in long discourses often built around deep "I am" sayings. Yet, while not teaching in parables, he uses a range of parabolic ideas and images: living water, the bread of life, the way, the truth, and the life, the resurrection and the life, the good Shepherd, the vine, and more. The central theme is not the Kingdom of God, although this is mentioned (John 3:3, 5), but eternal life. The right response is not to repent and believe, but faith and belief are required (e.g. John 3:16).

The story begins with a bold declaration that Jesus is God. He is the Word incarnate, made flesh. There is no messianic secret. John declares who Jesus is, and then tells the story to demonstrate it. It is written as an eyewitness account, almost a quasi-legal defense of Jesus, John presenting to those in his world who had different views (e.g. Judaism, and the Gentiles) that Jesus is the Son of God.

One very helpful thing about John is that he tells us his purpose in John 20:30–31:

Now Jesus did many other signs in the presence of the disciples, which are not written in this book; but these are written so that you may believe that Jesus is the Christ, the Son of God and that by believing you may have life in his name.

John then is writing that readers may either come to believe in Jesus or continue in their belief, depending on who is reading. He tells us that believing in Jesus brings eternal life, whereby we will be raised on the last day to live with God forever (John 5:25–29). His message is summed up gloriously in John 3:16 (s.a. John 3:36).

We can note too here the importance of signs to John's story. John's Gospel is arranged around seven signs: 1) turning water to wine (John 2:1–11); 2) the healing of the official's son (John 4:46–54); 3) the healing of the man by the pool (John 5:1–17); 4) the feeding of the 5000 (John 6:1–15); 5) walking on water (John 6:16–21); 6) the healing of the man born blind (John 9:1–42); and 7) the raising of Lazarus (John 11:1–44). Signs are clearly important in authenticating Jesus to his challengers. Knowing that Jews were most interested in signs, this may be to try and convince them Jesus is indeed the one they long for.

There are also seven predicated "I am" sayings, i.e. they have predicates or descriptors (e.g. I am *the life*): 1) I am the bread of life (John 6:35, 48); 2) I am the light of the world (John 8:12; 9:5); 3) I am the gate (or door) (John 10:1, 9); 4) I am the Good Shepherd (John 10:11, 14); 5) I am the way, the truth, and the life (John 14:6); 6) I am the resurrection and the life (John 11:25–26); 7) I am the true vine (John 15:1). Each of these points back to the OT and Jesus as the fulfilment of the hopes of Israel. Each point forward to the hopes of eternal life.

There are also a series of discourses which include debate and Jesus responding with complex teaching which confuses the Jewish hearers: 1) Nicodemus (John 3:1–21); 2) The Samaritan Woman (John 4:1–38); 3) Witnesses (John 5:19–47); 4) The Bread of Life (John 6:26–59); 5) Jesus at the Feast of Booths (John 7:14–39); 6) I am the light of the world (John 8:12–59); 7) I am the Good Shepherd (John 10:1–39); 8) Greeks and Jesus (John 12:20–36).

John's does not have the Sermon on the Mount or Plain but has a substantial section of teaching attached to the

Last Supper. It includes Jesus washing the disciples' feet and teaching of the coming of the Holy Spirit, the Paraclete, or Comforter, Jesus as the vine, and warnings of suffering and Jesus' death (John 13–16). John does not include Jesus in the Garden of Gethsemane but includes the great prayer of Jesus for the perseverance and unity of his people (John 17).

John's account of Jesus' death is similar in outline but has many different details. He does not include the clearing of the Temple in Jesus' final week but places it at the start of Jesus' ministry (John 2). This causes a great deal of debate with some believing there were two clearings of the Temple, that John has the right chronology, or that John placed it first for theological reasons as a prelude to the story of Jesus, for it is this moment that led to his death in ultimate terms. The latter seems best. John recasts the story of Jesus after the other Gospels, which were well known. He places it there for theological purposes. Jesus is the new Temple of God, the locus of God's presence on earth, the living tabernacle in which God lives and reveals himself. We are drawn into this temple by faith.

As in the other Gospels, Jesus appears, but more explicitly to Mary Magdalene (John 20), to Thomas who doubts (John 20:24–28), and to seven on the shore of the Sea of Galilee (John 21).

John's Gospel has a very high Christology, meaning that Jesus is seen as more clearly divine than in the others. He is God from John 1:1. He is God made flesh in John 1:14. He is God, the one and only who exegetes God to the world in John 1:18. He is equal with God in John 5:18, the "I am" who existed before Abraham (John 8:58), one with God in John 10:30, and "my Lord and my God" for Thomas in John 20:28). Yet, he is very human. He gets tired and needs a drink (John 4:6). He dies on a cross. Perhaps John is combatting false ideas of Jesus being only human (later called Arianism) or only divine (later called Docetism and a feature of 2nd-century Gnosticism), by making sure readers know he is God the Son, and also very human. He also uses a whole range of other terms to describe Jesus such as the lamb of God (John 1:29), the light of the world (John 8:12), and many others.

3

Chapter Three: The Kingdom of God-Expectations, Reign, and Eschatology

This chapter begins discussing the Kingdom of God, the central theme of the Synoptic Gospels. The focus is on Israel's expectations, the breaking in of the Kingdom in the person of Jesus, and what is called an inaugurated eschatology.

More Detail

Keown, *Discovering the New Testament*, Vol 1, ch. 11.

Keown, *Discovering the New Testament*, Vol 3, ch. 12.

Suggested Bible Readings

1 Sam 8

Ps 93

Matt 4:12–25

Matt 8:5–13

Matt 11:1–19

Matt 12:22–32

Matt 24–25

The Kingdom in the hopes of Israel

For Israel, God is King. He is enthroned above the world. His Kingdom is Israel. However, Israel has failed him, and he has allowed other nations to rule over her. They were (and remain) convinced that God will at some time in the future deliver them from foreign rule, restore the nation, rebuild the Temple, subjugate the world, and the world will experience the pax-Theos, the Shalom of God. There was a range of diverse expectations including God himself coming sovereignly to establish his reign through a human or semi-divine agent. As mentioned earlier, the most popular were the Davidic Messiah, the Prophet, and a Son of Man. Whoever it was, it would involve God liberating the nation from Roman and Gentile rule.

Another aspect of Israel's worldview was a common idea that the voice of the prophets had gone quiet since Malachi. They longed for and expected God to speak again, perhaps through an Elijah-like figure. This explains why there was so much excitement when John the Baptist turned up, summoning Israel to repent, and baptising people for the forgiveness of sins. He did not go unnoticed and in John's Gospel, Jerusalem's religious leaders came to ask him if he is the expected one. He denies this powerfully, pointing to one coming after him. This man will be the one who will baptise with the Spirit and fire of whom John is not worthy.

Hence, when Jesus turned up, there was again great excitement. Indeed, the hope was far greater because Jesus was full of the power of God to heal. One of the signs of the messianic age was God again doing miracles, as he did with Moses to liberate them from Egypt, through Joshua as he led Israel into the land, and through Elijah to liberate Israel from the Baal prophets. Jesus was clearly full of such power. It was likely that the leaders were waiting for Jesus to do some authenticating miracles as Moses did when he came from Midian to Egypt for the great Exodus.

However, Jesus did nothing of the sort. He began gathering a motley group of disciples. He chose fishermen. He then chose a tax-collector, one of the despised Israelites who had sold out to the Romans and fleeced his own people for the Gentile oppressors. He welcomed Simon the Zealot and others. He chose twelve, a very provocative number considering his name was Joshua.

Jesus, however, at no point sought to convince the general populace of Israel's leaders that he is the Messiah. He quietened down any hopes. He used his power only for the good of others in genuine need—healing, casting out demons, feeding them, and at times walking on water. All these miracles point back to OT moments and hopes, all speak of God's power in the present, and all are windows into the world God is creating in Jesus—a world without hunger, pain, illness, evil spirits, death, and natural disasters. Jesus refused to use his power for his own ends. He refused to arrogate himself before the world openly as King.

Yet, he did announce the coming of the Kingdom of God. Mark 1:14–15 sums up his message:

Now after John was arrested, Jesus came into Galilee, proclaiming the gospel of God, and saying, "The time is fulfilled, and the kingdom of God is at hand. Repent and believe in the gospel."

The Kingdom is the central theme of the Synoptic

Gospels. Jesus is clearly the Messiah, the Son of God, the Son of Man, God's ruler to establish his reign.

As he went about his business, in many ways Jesus disappointed those who were waiting for Israel's redemption. His disciples were a bunch of nobodies. He never used his power as they wanted. He refused to perform signs. He hung out with sinners and people clearly under the curse of God as evidenced by their sicknesses and demon possession. They were so frustrated with him, they accused him of being an emissary of Satan himself. He also said things that offended their religious views. He dared to forgive sin. He healed on the Sabbath, claiming to be the Lord of the Sabbath. He refused to ritually wash his hands at mealtimes and ate with sinners. He even broke bread in Gentile territory as he fed the 4000. His miracles were great, but never enough for those religious leaders who knew that if he really was God's deliverer, he would come knocking at some point. Yet, he openly ridiculed Israel's leadership in debate. They saw him as a threat to God's self-revelation through Moses. He then dared to challenge the Temple system, speaking of its destruction, and clearing it in a breathtakingly daring challenge to the centre of Israel's worship. Believing themselves to be defenders of Judaism akin to Phineas of the OT, they had to kill him.

The final ignominy was his death on a cross—Messiahs kill and are not crucified, hung on a tree, accursed. Even when he was on the cross, they cried out to him to prove himself. Other than assuming the words of David in Ps 22:1, pointing them one final time to his identity, he refused. He died refusing to respond to the challenges to use his power to save himself. Shockingly for a Jew, he died at the hands of Gentiles. To them, this is no Messiah, he is a false-prophet and false-Christ.

Jesus was a failed Messiah from the point of view of their expectations. He held promise but fell well short of their hopes and dreams.

The Kingdom as Reign

Israel's worldview was locked up in their own self-perception as God's chosen. As God's elect, chosen by God through their father, Abraham, they of all the nations of the world, were God's people. As such, the problem with the world was not them, it was the nations full of idolatry and gross violation of the law of God. They were not perfect, but God would move and establish them as he had at the Conquest, and this time for good, to rule the world on his behalf. Their view of God's reign included the world, but it had to be subjugated, and this was to come. Hence, their view of the Kingdom was a classic ancient imperial concept of a geographical kingdom.

The stories of the ancient kingdoms speak of expansion. It begins with the uprising of a warrior-deliverer (e.g. David, Alexander the Great, Julius Caesar). They become king of their locality, be it Israel, Macedonia and Greece, or Rome and Italy. They then extend their reign, claiming territories adjoining them. This involves war as their armies move north, south, east, and west claiming territory. This is done the easy way through surrender, or the hard way, via devastation through armies. As such, the territory expands, and the Kingdom gains more and more wealth and subjects. The Kingdom must establish themselves in these lands, winning the subjects over with benefaction (e.g. citizenship and positions of honour), or, punishment (e.g. crucifixion).

Israel's expectations of the Kingdom of God were locked

in such ideas. God and/or his agent would come. With God on his side, he would gather together the best of the men of Israel and first drive out the Gentiles. He would then extend the territory. This would involve taking Egypt, the Nabateans and others in Africa, overcoming the Parthians to the east, and then confronting Rome. Armies would march through what we call Turkey. Conquest would continue until the world was subjugated. Such events were possible because God was on their side. Insurmountable odds mean nothing. This would continue until the world was God's. Israel would be restored and the world as God wanted.

If we consider the Kingdom from the perspective of the final outcome, it will kind of look like what is described. Evil will be vanquished. The enemies of God, spiritual and otherwise, will be gone. No one will live in this world who is not willingly yielded to this King. The geography of the Kingdom, in one sense, is the world including all nations, the ends of the earth.

Yet, the process of getting there does not involve the taking of geographical territory. The Kingdom is not about taking pockets of land. It is about people entering it by yielding their hearts and lives to God. It is then a reign, not a geographical kingdom (not yet anyway). The good news of the inbreaking of God's kingdom through the King, Jesus, is spread to the world. People hear this and can reject it (or are indifferent, same thing really) and remain alive in the world living their lives. They are not in the Kingdom, but they are in the world and its kingdoms. The other response is to yield and submit to this King, give him our allegiance, repent and believe, and follow him. Those that do are then members of God's Kingdom people, his subjects, part of his purposes, working for the King.

As such, it is better to talk about the Kingdom of God in this period between its beginning and its consummation as the reign of God. The Kingdom is found where God's rule is not only exercised, but also where it is accepted. It is a kingdom then of hearts and minds, a kingdom of people who love this King and God with their whole hearts, minds, souls, bodies, and strength. It becomes a community of people, where two or three come together in the name of the king to worship him and do his will and work. It exercises its influence as these people do their work in the world for the king, and the Kingdom, like salt and light, permeates the world through their actions and words. It spreads, not geographically, but in human hearts.

Yet, there is a geographical dimension as the gospel moves from land to land. It began in Jerusalem with 120 people (Acts 1:15). By the Spirit-power of the King, through his subjects, it spread into the Roman world. It has now penetrated huge swathes of the world. Yet, not everyone in these places is yielded to the king. This is the case in NZ, where there are many Christians and many who are not. The Kingdom is here in NZ, in the sense of God's reign and his subjects who set up colonies of the Kingdom of heaven on earth. Yet, it is not complete. It is now, but not yet.

Recognising that the Kingdom is not a geographical concept is important in ecclesiology (the study of the church). The church is not a building but a people who acknowledge the reign of God and his Son and gather together to worship and serve him, love one another, and engage in mission in the world. We don't go to church on Sunday in the sense of a building; we go to gather and be the people. We are bound together as one when we are separated geographically. Buildings are useful, but they are not the church. We are.

The Kingdom of God: the now and not yet

The Kingdom of God then is the reign of God exercised across the world. Another great area of debate in the history of biblical scholarship is to what extent the Kingdom has arrived. Some emphasise its presence. The Kingdom has come in Jesus and is here. It will expand and come to completion. They play down any future dimension. Others do the opposite. They see what is happening now as a prelude. The Kingdom comes when Jesus returns. So, in what sense has the Kingdom come and to what extent is it here?

God as Reigning King, God as Coming King

Before addressing this question, it is good to take a step back and think of the Kingdom in the biblical story. The day God created the word, he was king. He is king. So, in a sense, the whole world has been, is, and always will be his kingdom. He is reigning king and always has been.

Yet, while this is true and this is confirmed in Israel's Scriptures, he is also the coming king. That is, at the fall of humankind, humanity chose another ruler. Themselves. Unwittingly, they also gave themselves over to the dominion of the evil one and his minions. They became subject to sin. They preferred their own dominion over God. The work of Jesus is to take back what is, and always has been, God's.

Turning to the main question here: to what extent is the Kingdom now and to what extent not yet?

The Kingdom Inaugurated in Christ—the Now

Over time, scholars settled on the concept of an inaugurated eschatology to resolve the dilemma. In this schema, Jesus' birth was the beginning of the Kingdom of God. Or, one can say it was the point of which he became king waiting for his inauguration (below). So, Gabriel tells Mary concerning Jesus: "and he will reign over the house of Jacob forever, and of his kingdom, there will be no end" (Luke 1:33). He is the one Isaiah sang of: the son born and given, on whom the government will rest, the "Wonderful Counselor, Mighty God, Everlasting Father, Prince of Peace" (Isa 9:6, ESV). We also see this in Matthew's birth narrative, where the king of the Jews is born, magi come from the east, Herod the Great is disturbed and challenged, he seeks to kill Jesus (the stuff of ancient kingdoms). He fails, and Jesus the king begins his life. He is raised in the home of the Davidic descendant Joseph (Matt 1:1–18), to be inaugurated officially as the king.

Jesus' inauguration (coronation, crowning, anointing) as king came at his baptism. In Israel's story, the king must be anointed by a prophet. So, Samuel anointed Saul and then his replacement David (1 Sam 10; 16). Nathan anointed Solomon (1 Kgs 1). Even Joshua was anointed by the prophet Moses (Num 27:18–20; Deut 34:9–12). Through the prophet, God gave his choice and approval of the king.

John the Baptist is the last of such prophets. He came from nowhere, God making his move to establish his reign by sending him to prepare the way and to inaugurate his king. This is why the Gospels all begin with John. The Gospel writers recognised that the true Davidic King would be proceeded by a prophet who would authenticate him.

This happened at Jesus' baptism. Unlike the earlier

prophets who poured oil over the king's head, John baptised Jesus. He dunked him in the Jordan. Jesus came up and the heavens opened, and God directly anointed him as Israel's king, the new Joshua, come to deliver his world from corruption. God calls out: "You are my beloved Son; with whom I am well pleased" (Mark 1:11). The language of Sonship speaks of his kingly role. So, in Ps 2:7 God says of the king: "You are my Son; today I have begotten you" (ESV). Here, God authenticates Jesus. This instant also calls to mind Isa 42:1, where God speaks to the Servant of Yahweh, whom we now know to be looking toward Jesus. He says: "Behold my servant, whom I uphold, my chosen, in whom my spirit delights; I have put my Spirit upon him; he will bring forth justice to the nations" (ESV).

Importantly too, the heavens were opened at that moment and the Spirit released. This marks the beginning of the inbreaking of God's rule into the world. The Spirit filled Jesus. He led Jesus in his mission from start to finish. His first job was to find a way for humankind to receive this Spirit and be similarly anointed. That would require dealing with sin and corruption.

So, Jesus' baptism was the moment when the king was inaugurated. The Kingdom began when this king was commissioned by God for his mission. His first move was not to go out to win subjects for the Kingdom. That came later. His first move was to be thrust out by the Spirit to fight his ultimate foe Satan (Matt 4:1–11; Mark 1:12–13; Luke 4:1–13). This recalls Adam and Eve in the garden (Gen 2–3). Jesus succeeds where Adam and Eve failed. He defeats Satan, resisting Satan's attempts to appoint him "king" without conflict (the easy way) (esp. Matt 4:8). This happens in the wilderness. After the Exodus, Israel was tested in the wilderness by God. They failed, constantly succumbing to complaint and contention. Jesus does not. He is the new Israel. He is its rightful king. He will spend his life taking back those under bondage to Satan throughout Israel (Acts 10:38). In him, and by his Spirit, we do so throughout the world

After his first victory, Jesus returned in the power of the Spirit and began to preach, teach, heal, deliver, feed, and raise from the dead (Luke 4:14, s.a. 7:22). He was the new Joshua, coming to deliver the world from the dominion of darkness (Col 1:13), not by might, not by power, but by the Spirit (Zech 4:6).

As noted earlier, he preached that the Kingdom is near. That is, it is here in his person. Its full inbreaking is near as he goes the cross, dies, rises, ascends, and the Spirit is poured out. Israel must repent and believe the good news (Matt 4:2, 17).

Jesus was a man with a plan. His strategy was not to win the world in one fell swoop, but to win people, one by one, beginning in his own nation. He summoned Israel to yield to God's reign through repentance and belief. Some responded. Many were attracted. But most did not yield to him.

The presence of the Kingdom is seen in his ministry. His miracles spoke of the inbreaking of God's reign. His pithy parables taught people what the Kingdom is like. His love drew the lost and broken. His kingdom extended as people yielded to his reign.

Jesus had followers but they were sinners and sin needed to be dealt with. Israel's sacrifice system sets the agenda—the blood of an unblemished animal temporarily dealt with sin. The blood of the unblemished Son of God, the Lamb of God, must be shed. Jesus fulfilled the requirements by living a sinless life, despite being tempted as we are in every way, yet without sin. He died. His broken body and shed blood inaugurated the new covenant dreamed of by Jeremiah.

Jesus looked like an abject failure on the cross. Yet, his death was the victory over sin God required. Hence, death could not restrain him, as sin brings death, and he had no sin. He rose, launching a new creation, a new humanity, the empty tomb a metaphor of the future day when the graves of the dead all over the world will open and God's people will be raised.

In giving his life as a ransom for many, those who repent and believe in him are cleansed of sin and, despite having to die physically, are freed from sin's power and consequences. They are ready receptacles in which the God, who cannot dwell with evil (Ps 5:4), can now reside; temples of the living God. They are also bound together as one Temple in Christ filled with the Spirit.

As such, the Spirit was poured out at Pentecost. By this time, Jesus had ascended and was (and is) seated at the right hand of the Father, King of the Cosmos, Lord and Christ, God the Son. His Father, through Jesus, poured out his Spirit repeatedly on God's people through the book of Acts. This goes on where anyone yields to God as King. In this way the Kingdom is extended.

As Luke emphasises in his Gospel, the Spirit is the key. He fills us and empowers us for this mission, the extension of the Kingdom. After Jesus' death, the gospel exploded out of Jerusalem into Judea, Samaria, and the Roman world. By the deaths of the apostles, the gospel was established in the regions around the Mediterranean. Over time it moved through Europe and now has reached the majority of the world.

The Kingdom Consummated

There is an important future dimension to the Kingdom; the consummation of the Kingdom, when all our hopes and dreams of a world rid of evil and God's reign unopposed will be complete. Jesus must reign until all enemies are subjugated under his feet—the consummation of the Kingdom will be that day (1 Cor 15:24–28). On that day, with a loud angelic cry, the trumpet of God, and with blazing fire, Jesus will return with his angels (1 Thess 4:16). The dead in Christ will rise. With those alive at the time, we will be taken up to meet Jesus in the air, and we will welcome in our King and Lord (1 Thess 4:17). Heaven will come to earth; the new Jerusalem (Rev 21–22:5). God will judge humanity and all those who have not yielded to his lordship, will be swept away in eternal destruction (Matt 25:41–46; Rev 20:11–15). We will be transformed in an instant from perishable mortal beings to immortal and imperishable people, with bodies like that of Jesus, and we will live on with God (1 Cor 15:50–54; Phil 3:20).

This is the not-yet of the Kingdom. God will decide when the time is right. It will be when his mission is completed to his satisfaction, the gospel penetrated into every nation.

The Tension

We live in the tension between the two great moments: in the inauguration of the Kingdom in the first coming of Jesus and the consummation of the Kingdom in the second coming of Jesus. We live out of the pattern of the first coming, emulating Jesus' life patterns—ethics and mission. We live ever prepared for the consummation, even if we do not know the day or hour (Mark 13:32-37). We do so by being faithful servants, finding our place in his mission, and persevering to the end, knowing that our labour in the Lord is not in vain.

We must avoid what is called an over-realised eschatology. This is where we falsely assume that the blessings which we who believe are destined to experience in the consummated kingdom should be fully experienced now. An example is prosperity theology, which claims that if we are obedient, we will be rich in the present. This is not correct for at no point was Jesus rich from the moment his family offered the sacrifice for the poor at his circumcision through to the moment he died naked, deserted, and bereft. Neither did Paul live like a king. Indeed, he mocked the Corinthians who seemed to think that they should (1 Cor 4:8-14). No, he lived in weakness and suffering.

We must not make false claims concerning the present experience of the Kingdom. We should try and live the life of the resurrection now—out of love in particular, and holiness. Yet, we work hard knowing that God is storing up a future inheritance for us. Our call, in the meantime, is to get on with the King's business. That's what good subjects do. They are faithful to their sovereign. Our job is to be available to God so that he can extend his reign through us.

4

Chapter Four: The Kingdom of God-the King, its Power, and its Parables

This chapter continues exploring the Kingdom of God focusing on who its king (Jesus), the power of the Kingdom (miracles), and its teaching (especially the parables of Jesus).

More Detail

Keown, *Discovering the New Testament*, Vol 1, ch. 11–13.

Suggested Bible Readings

Son of Man

Daniel 7

What do you notice about Jesus' use of Son of Man?

Matt 8:20; 9:6; 10:23; 11:19; 12:18, 32, 40, 37, 41; 16:13, 27, 28; 17:9, 12, 22; 19:28; 20:18, 28; 24:27, 30, 37, 39, 44; 25:31; 26:2, 24, 45; 26:64

Son of God

Psalm 2

What do you notice about Jesus as the Son of God?
Matt 4:3, 6; 8:29; 14:33; 26:63; 27:40, 43, 54.

Also, John 1:14, 49; 5:18; 11:27.

Davidic Messiah (Christ)
Isaiah 9:1–7
Jeremiah 23:1–8
Ezekiel 34:1–24
Isaiah 61:1–2
Micah 5:1–6
Note how Christ passage and language is used.
Matt 1:1, 17; 2:3–5; 4:12–17; 9:27; 11:1–6; 15:21–22; 16:13–17:13;
20:29–34; 26:53–68; 27:15–23

Lord
Psalm 110
Isaiah 45
Not how the OT title of God is assumed for Jesus
Matt 7:21–22; 8:2–8; 9:38; 12:8; 14:28–30; 15:21–28;
22:44–45; 24:42; 25:37; Luke 2:11

Servant
Isaiah 42:1–7
Isaiah 49:1–7
Isaiah 50
Isa 52:13–53:12
Note the importance of Jesus as the Servant and what it
means for us.
Matt 12:15–21; 20:20–28; 25:23; John 13:1–15; Acts 3:12–26

The Kingdom of God: The King

Every kingdom needs a king. In our case, God is king, and
he has sent his Son into this world to be its King on his
behalf. He rules through his Son, and his Son willingly rules
on his behalf. There is a range of key terms used of Jesus in

the NT, and in this section, the focus will be on the main ones of these. Then, consideration will be given to Jesus as human and divine.

Christ

The Davidic monarchy came to an end at the Babylonian exile. As predicted by the prophets, because of Judah's sin, led by Nebuchadnezzar, Israel was destroyed. The penultimate Davidic king was Zedekiah, before whom Nebuchadnezzar slaughtered his sons, then blinded him, and then took him to Babylon in chains. When Israel returned from exile, the Davidic monarchy was not re-established. The prophets dreamed of this coming to pass as they dreamed of a new Davidic king, a fresh branch (Ps 89:4–4; 132:11–12, 17–18; Isa 4:2; 9:7; 11:1, 10; 16:5; 55:3; 23:5; 33:15–17; Ezek 34:23–24; 37:24–25; Hos 3:5; Amos 9:11; Zech 3:8; 6:12; 12:7–13:1, s.a. Pss. Sol. 17:4, 32). Unlike some of the other terms (Lord, Son of God, Saviour), and like "Son of Man," *Christos* is very much a Jewish idea, with it never used of the emperor or gods of the wider world. Unlike "Son of Man," it becomes a most important term for the church.

In the NT, Jesus is clearly recognised as this Christ (Heb. Messiah) or Anointed One, the Son of David. In the Synoptic Gospels, the great moment is when Peter confesses that Jesus is the Christ (Mark 8:29, s.a. Matt 16:16; Luke 9:18–20). What Peter is saying is that Jesus is the anointed one, God's Messiah, the longed-for Davidic king, come to save his people.

In both Matthew and Luke, Jesus is born in Bethlehem, the city of David's family, fulfilling the expectations of the Messiah born there (Matt 2:1; Luke 2:1–7). In all the Synoptics, Jesus is not open about this, shutting down anyone who says this out loud, including demons (e.g. Mark 1:25, 34) and Peter himself (Mark 8:30). This is likely because he did not want to excite a revolution. We see this in John 6:14–15 where after the feeding of the 5000, the crowds perceive Jesus is the Prophet (see below) and seek to make him king by force. Jesus slips away. He is not interested.

The story of the Synoptics is that after the confession, Jesus teaches the disciples what sort of Messiah he is. He is not a king who has come to be served, but to serve, and to give his life as a ransom for many (Mark 10:45). He values children, the poor, and the marginalised and acts on their behalf. He has come to take up a cross and die and rise again. Three times he tells them of his death and resurrection (Mark 8:31; 9:31; 10:33–34). He has come to be a crucified Messiah, his body broken for his people, his blood the blood of the new covenant (Luke 22:20; 1 Cor 11:25). He is the ultimate Passover Lamb, given for the sins of the world (1 Cor 5:7; John 1:29).

The claim to be the Christ contributed to his condemnation. The High Priests asks Jesus whether he is the Christ, the Son of the Blessed One? Jesus answers: "I am, and you will see the Son of Man seated at the right hand of the Power, and coming with the clouds of heaven." This causes the High Priest to tear his clothing and condemn him to Pilate (Mark 14:61–63).

At the centre of the sermons in Acts is the claim that Jesus is the Christ (Acts 2:31, 36, 38; 3:18, 20; 4:10; 5:42; 26:23, s.a. 17:3). What had radically shifted in the disciples' thinking is that Jesus would not come to inflict suffering as he claimed back his world, but that he would suffer and die to save the world in a completely different way (Luke 24:26, 46; Acts 3:18; 17:3; 26:23).

After his conversion, Paul the Pharisee who had rejected Jesus' messiahship broke from his own ranks understanding Jesus as the long-awaited-Messiah. In fact, he used the name Christ more than any other term (383 times, cf. Jesus 212 times, Lord 273 times, Saviour thirteen times, Son of God 14 times, Son of Man nil). Jesus is the climax of Israel's story and hope, her king, and Lord of the world.

Paul recognises the problem of a crucified Messiah being a stumbling block to Jews (Gal 3:13; Deut 21:23). Yet, he reframes it, acknowledging that Jesus was accursed on the cross, but for our sakes, taking the curse of sin on himself. He recognises the importance of his suffering and death as the path to redemption.

Lord

Jesus is *kyrios*, the Lord. Unlike Christos, *kyrios* is at home in the Roman and Jewish worlds. *Kyrios* and the feminine *kyria* were used for deities and the emperor. In the Jewish world, *kyrios* translated the Hebrew *Adonai* in the Greek OT and was used some 6,000 times of God. Using *kyrios* of Jesus, from both Greco-Roman and Jewish perspectives, is suggestive of Jesus' divinity.

The use of the term was also dangerous. From a Jewish point of view, Christians took verses from the OT in which *kyrios* clearly referred to God and applied it to Jesus. An example is Phil 2:10–11 where the world bowed to Jesus as Lord whereas in Isa 45:23 in the context, God is in view (s.a. Rom 10:13; 15:11). Hence, to call Jesus Lord crossed the line of monotheism. Similarly, in the Roman world, to say Jesus is Lord was to challenge the supremacy of the Emperor. Christians then would get it from both sides.

Kyrios is used of Jesus through the Gospels, sometimes with the sense that he is a really important person with power to heal (e.g. Luke 5:12), and at other times, especially in Luke, speaking of him as cosmic Lord (e.g. Luke 6:5; 17:6; 24:3, 34). Luke's favourite designation for Jesus in both his Gospel and Acts is Lord. In Acts, Jesus is the cosmic Lord, seated at the right hand of God, sharing his rule (Acts 2:25, 34). This idea is found in Paul and through the remainder of the NT. Lord implies Jesus' complete sovereignty over the world. This builds on Ps 110:1, the verse quoted the most in the NT. Jesus identifies himself as the Lord (*Adonai*) in discussing this verse (Mark 12:36–37). He reigns from heaven as Lord until the completion of the subjugation of God's enemies which will come to pass finally at his return. Other writers in the NT continue to use *kyrios* for Jesus (over 250 times Paul).

Son of Man

Jesus' favourite self-designation was "Son of Man" (14x Mark, 30x Matt, 25x Luke, 13x John). Yet it is only used four times in the rest of the NT (Acts 7:56; Heb 2:6; Rev 1:13; 14:14). The term is ambiguous, often used for a prophet (93x Ezekiel, s.a. Dan 8:17). It is used of humanity in general (Ps 8:4; 144:3; 146:3). It is also used on a figure at the side of Yahweh who is made strong to act to save Israel (Ps 80:17).

The latter idea is also found in Daniel where one like a son of man comes to God and is given authority to rule the world (Dan 7:13–14). This idea is developed in 1 Enoch in a section written between c. 105–64 bc. In this Book of Similitudes (1 En 37–71), this Son of Man is at the same time Messiah and the one who rules, judges, deals with sinners, rewards his people, and so on. He is a mighty transcendent semi-divine figure (see 1 En. 46:2–4; 48:2; 60:10; 62:5–14; 63:11; 69:27–29; 70:1; 71:17).

Jesus used it of himself. He may have done so for its ambiguity, as it would not excite the same messianic expectations that *Christos* (Messiah) did. He used it impersonally, "the Son of Man ..." making it unclear whether he was even talking about himself in some instances. The figure could be a human or all humankind. It could point to a prophet. We know looking back that he clearly meant it in the sense of Dan 7:13–14 and with some of the ideas of 1 Enoch. Yet, listeners would likely be puzzled.

Overall it points to Jesus being a human, but more, the Human, the Son of Man, the one of whom Daniel prophesied, the one who would be given all authority over the nations.

Servant

There are four passages in Isaiah that many scholars call "the Servant Songs of Isaiah." They predict a servant figure whom God would delight in, God will raise him up and anoint him. He will bring justice to the nations and preach God's word. He will be despised, maltreated, and killed. He will be buried with criminals and in some texts is raised. He will be a covenant for the people, a light to the nations, and through him, salvation will go to the ends of the earth. Before him kings will fall (Isa 42:1–9; 49:1–7; 50:4–11; 52:13–53:12).

In Judaism, these passages were not associated with the Messiah; rather the Servant was seen as the prophet or Israel herself. In the Gospels and Acts, Jesus is identified as this figure (esp. Matt 12:18–21, s.a. Matt 20:28; Mark 10:45;

Luke 1:69; 14:17–23; Acts 3:13). Paul also describes Jesus as being in the form of a slave, invoking the same ideas (Phil 2:7).

As we read the Gospels, all other titles given to Jesus are mediated through the figure of this image. He is the Christ but in the form of a Servant. He is the Son of Man but in the form of a Servant. And so on. The writers have an interlaced Christology in which they bring these ideas together.

We need to grasp this very clearly. Jesus came as God and King of the world yet came washing feet (John 13) and serving the needs of the world. We are called to follow in this path and told that greatness comes from service (Matt 20:26–27; 23:11–12; Mark 9:35; 10:43–44; Luke 22:26). His self-humbling is our call. The path to greatness is service.

Son of God

In the OT, angels, people, and the king were all sons of God. For the Greeks and Romans, kings were the sons of God. There were not many Jewish prophecies expecting a Son of God, but for most people it was another way of thinking of the Messiah. However, in the NT, Jesus is more than just a king, he is God the Son. The devil calls him the Son of God (Matt 4:3, 6). He claims God as his Father and the only one who knows him (Matt 11:27, s.a. Matt 24:36). People confess him as the Son of God including the Roman centurion (Mark 15:39, s.a. Matt 14:33; 16:16; 27:54). Jesus' claims to be the Son of God were part of the reason he was killed (Mark 14:61–62). In the Parable of the Tenants, he distinguishes himself from the prophets as the Son, killed, and thrown out of the vineyard—a prophecy of his death (Mark 12:6–8). This is strongest in the writing of John, where right from the start, Jesus is God and the one and only unique Son of

God (John 1:1, 18, 34, 49). Jews seek to kill Jesus for calling himself God's Son (John 5:18; 10:36–39; 19:7; 20:31). God has given him all things (John 3:35) and he is the personal revelation of God. One is saved by believing he is God the Son (John 3:36; 11:27). The Greeks believed in the gods copulating and having children. This is not how Jesus is to be understood. He is God in person and Spirit made flesh without such things as procreation. He is eternal. Jesus' divine sonship is found through the rest of the NT (e.g. Acts 9:20; Rom 1:4; 2 Cor 1:19; Gal 2:20; Heb 1:8; 4:14; Rev 2:18). John writes in 1 John 5:20 that Jesus is the Son of God who is the true God and eternal life.

This is an important doctrine as we become children of God through this Son. We never take his place and become divine, but we are considered sons and daughters of God by faith in him (e.g. Matt 5:9; John 1:12; Rom 8:14–21; Gal 3:26; Phil 2:15; 1 John 3:10; 5:2). We know what it means to be a Son of God for God's Son has shown us. It means to live with total obedience to our Father, emulating his humility, service, and love, and seeking the Kingdom of God and his righteousness above all things.

The Prophet

Another very Jewish idea was the hope of a prophet. This is found in Deut 18:15–19. God will raise up a prophet like Moses and he will be God's spokesperson. Israel must listen to him or die.

This idea is swirling in the NT. John the Baptist is asked by Jerusalem religious leaders whether he is the Prophet, something he denies (John 1:21). The Samaritans were anticipating a Taheb, a figure based on Deuteronomy. In the conversation Jesus has with the Samaritan woman in

John 4, she likely means this when she considers Jesus the Messiah (John 4:25–26). The crowds consider Jesus the Prophet in John 6:14 and wish to enthrone him and start a revolt. In Acts 3:22–23, Deut 18 is cited, with Jesus the fulfilment of the Mosaic prophet figure (s.a. Acts 7:37). Jesus is King and Prophet. In Hebrews, he is also High Priest (e.g. Heb 5:10). He fulfils the three-fold leadership of Israel.

For Jesus as Human and Divine see Keown, *Discovering*, Vol 3, Ch. 9.

The Kingdom of God: its Power, its Miracles

A miracle is something that occurs that appears to violate the natural order of things. Jesus is famous as a miracle worker. In Israel's story, he is not unique in this. Moses performed miracles authenticating his mission, the plagues that enabled Israel to leave Egypt, the destruction of the Egyptians in the Red Sea, and a few others. Joshua also performed miracles like stopping the Jordan River in flood to cross it, the destruction of Jericho, the stopping of the sun, and so on. Elijah and Elisha performed miracles of provision, military defeat, and raised the dead. It was hoped that the age of the Messiah would bring miracles (Isa 29:6; 35:5) and the Servant would open the eyes of the blind (Isa 42:7) and "and by his wounds we are healed" (Isa 53:5, LEB).

Jesus was unique in the huge number of miracles he performed. His miracles included miracles of provision including turning water to wine and feeding enormous crowds (John 2:1–11; Mark 6:30–44; 8:1–10); exorcisms where he casts out demons (e.g. Matt 4:24); a huge range of healings (e.g. Matt 8:16); raising the dead (Mark 5:21–43; Luke 7:1–10; John 11:1–44); miracles over nature including walking on water and calming a storm (Mark 4:35–41; 6:45–52); and prophetic predictions such as the destruction of the Jerusalem Temple (e.g. Mark 13:2). John's Gospel revolves around the seven signs (see on John earlier). All the Gospels indicate that Jesus was a miracle worker. Even the Jewish writer Josephus mentions it (Josephus, Ant. 18:63–64). Other Jewish sources also credit Jesus with miracles.

The miracles have a three-fold impact.

The Past: Fulfilment

First, they point back. I have noted above some of the texts which expected miracles. There is more than this. Jesus' miracles of calming the weather and sea speak of God's creation power and his dominance of chaos, Joshua stopping the sun, and so the restoring of Shalom. The provision miracles recall God through Moses providing manna (see esp. John 6) and Elisha and Elijah providing for the needy (1 Kgs 17:8–16; 2 Kgs 4:4–7, 42–44). The healings fulfil the hopes of Isaiah (Isa 29:6; 35:5; 42:7; 53:6). Raising the dead points to OT hopes of resurrection and Elijah and Elisha raising the dead (1 Kgs 17:17–24; 2 Kgs 4:18–37). The prophetic predictions speak of the hope of God raising a prophet like Moses (see previous section).

The Present: the Breaking in of the Kingdom

The miracles also say something about the present inauguration of the Kingdom and who Jesus is. In Jesus, we see the inbreaking of the power of God making right the world wracked in evil, poverty, sickness, death, and despair. God's power is present in Jesus. He can heal, provide, deliver, raise, and bring hope. In that Christ has given his people the Spirit, and the gifts of miracles and healing are distributed, we should pray and expect God to act in the present. However, we must not overstate this, as we are still all subject to decay and death and miracles are temporary fixes. So, we pray passionately for them hoping God will act. He will, but this will not fix our problem. We need to die and rise for this to happen.

The Future: The Consummation of the Kingdom

The miracles are also enacted parables telling us what the Kingdom is about and what it will be when fully consummated. They are signs of the Kingdom. John rightly recognises this, calling them signs. They point to who Jesus is. They point to God's ideals for us. They tell us what the consummated kingdom will be like. They summon us to join God in bringing this closer.

So, the provision miracles are a window into a world free of famine and poverty, the haves and the have nots. They also summon us to work for this in the interim between Jesus' comings. As Jesus says to the disciples in the feeding of the 5000, "you give them something to eat" (Mark 6:37).

The exorcisms point to the day when Satan will be finally destroyed in the lake of fire. As demons are driven out, his power is reduced (see Luke 10:18). We are to withstand evil in the meantime, not giving Satan a foothold (Eph 4:27, cf. 1 Pet 5:8).

Jesus' healings look to the end of sickness. While personal sickness is not necessarily a result of personal sin (see John 9:1–3), sickness is a symptom of the decay that blights God's world through sin (Rom 5:12; 8:19–23). Jesus' healings show his power to end illness. The world to come will be free of all such things, we will be immortal and imperishable.

The resurrections from the dead performed by Jesus and his resurrection show the power of God to raise the dead. The final enemy to be defeated is death (1 Cor 15:26). People who have given allegiance to God and his Son will live forever, amazingly transformed from bodies of humiliation to bodies of glory like Jesus (1 Cor 15:50–54; Phil 3:21).

Prophecy gives us glimpses of God's future for us, often with warnings for the present. In the age to come, prophecies will end for we will know and be fully known (1 Cor 13:8–9).

Faith and Miracles

Often faith is associated with miracles. For example, "your faith has delivered you" (Matt 9:22; Mark 5:34; 10:52; Luke 7:50, s.a. Matt 15:28). This has led to some Christians thinking that faith is required for miracles to occur and leads to people believing they are not healed for deficient faith. However, while they show that faith can be a factor in healing on occasion, there also situations where faith is not mentioned (e.g. Matt 4:24; 8:16). In John's Gospel, faith is never mentioned as a reason for healing. Rather, miracles produce faith, a faith that is not a saving faith, but must flower into it for salvation (e.g. John 2:23–25). We must remember too that no amount of faith can stop decay and death. It can be hindered if God chooses to intervene. But it cannot be stopped—Jesus' healings and even his resurrection of people from the dead are merely temporary moments. Also, both Jesus and Paul experienced God saying no to their prayers of deliverance (Mark 14:32–42; 2 Cor 12:7–9). God did so as he wills. Our call is to believe in God's capability to answer prayer, pray for those in need, trust God to do what is best, accept his decision, and continue to believe in him.

The Kingdom of God: its Parables

In the Synoptic Gospels, Jesus taught in parables. The word parable comes from *parabolē*, which has at its root "comparison." It is used in Jesus' teaching of a range of sayings and short stories he used to convey the message of the Kingdom. Parables are found in the OT. One of the best examples is that told by Nathan to David after he had Uriah killed and married Bathsheba. The parable exposed David's sin and duplicity (2 Sam 12:1–15). Solomon had 3,000 parables (1 Kgs 4:28 [lxx]; 1 Kgs 4:32, Heb. *maschal*).

Jesus used a whole range of them. His parables were concerned with explaining the Kingdom of God to his listeners. They have two levels of meanings: 1) the obvious surface daily life level; and 2) the Kingdom of God level. They function to summon people to respond to the Kingdom and the point(s) being made.

Parables have been the bone of a lot of contention in biblical studies. Throughout the history of interpretation, they were mainly taken allegorically. The most famous example is Augustine's allegorisation of the Good Samaritan which reframed it into the story of the gospel. In Augustine's interpretation:

the injured man = Adam; Jerusalem = the heavenly city; Jericho = the moon and our mortality; the robbers = devil and demons who take away the man's immortality and beat him by persuading him to sin; the priest and Levite = the corrupt priesthood and OT ministry; the good Samaritan= Christ; the binding of the wounds = the restraint of sin; the oil and wine = the comfort of hope and the encouragement to work; the animal = the Incarnation; the inn = the church; the next day = after Christ's resurrection; the innkeeper = the apostle Paul; the two denarii = the two commandments, or, the promise of this life and that which is to come (Augustine, *Quaest. Evan.* 2.19, see Snodgrass, "Parable," in *DJG* 591).

This meant that it lost its central challenge to love one's neighbour. Rampant and contextually unsound allegorisation led scholars away from this to reading them like Aesop's Fables, in which there is one point being made. As such, discussion was focused on what one interpretation is to be found.

However, since then, others have found a middle ground recognising that a number of parables are allegorical as seen by Jesus explaining them (e.g. Parable of the Sower and Weeds, Matt 13:1–30, 36–43). Others, like the Parable of the Banquet (Luke 14:12–24), the Prodigal Son (Luke 15:11–32), and the Parable of the Talents (Matt 21:33–44) are also allegorical. In these parables, the main characters correlate with God, the prophets, Jesus, Israel, and so on. They are clearly allegorical to an extent. The key is not trying to impose onto the parable later ideas, such as a certain form of the gospel. Rather, we need to think in context what Jesus wants the characters to align with.

Parables cannot also be seen as having one meaning. There may be an overall point, such as "love your enemies," in the Parable of the Good Samaritan. Yet, one must think more carefully in the more complex parables. Even in the Good Samaritan, there are differing points being made. We are not to be like the priest and Levite who ignored the injured man on the side of the road, whatever our reason. We are to be like the Samaritan, despite his being a despised figure in his world.

Each parable is to be carefully considered and the possibilities of interpretation carefully assessed. Here are some core principles of interpretation.

1) How would they have been understood in Israel at the time? We must first interpret it as it would be understood by original readers and then apply it thoughtfully to our situation.

2) What are the cultural, historical, and social ideas that help us understand it? For example, an older man would not run to his son as the Father does in the Parable of the Prodigal. Hence, this enhances his love for his son.

3) What is Jesus trying to teach about the Kingdom of God? This is easier in those that begin, "the Kingdom is like …" Yet, we should ask this about all the parables. What do they teach us about the King? The Kingdom? What does it mean to be a subject of the King?

4) How does its material align with his other teaching? We should look through the wider Gospel and its content and see how it connects. So, for example, the Good Samaritan parable enacts Jesus' command to "love your enemies" (Luke 10:25–48, cf. 6:27, 35).

5) How do they connect with the wider biblical story, particularly the OT? Sometimes there are links to the OT. So, the Mustard Seed parable can be read with the tree of Ezekiel 17 in mind.

6) Who do the characters potentially align with in his situation? In the Prodigal: the father aligns with God. The older son with Israel. The younger son with the sinful marginalised Jews and Gentiles. In the Banquet: the banquet master aligns with God. The servant with Jesus,

and later missionaries. Those invited, the poor and disabled. Those further distant with the Gentiles.

7) How do they end? This often points to meaning. So, in the Parable of the Tenants in Mark 12, Ps 118 is quoted, and they seek to kill Jesus. They recognise that they are tenants Jesus is challenging; the prophets are the servants and Jesus the loved son.

8) How does the preceding and following material help in interpretation? We must always read bible passages in context. How does the parable fit into the whole Gospel? What section is it in, e.g. the Travel Narrative of Luke? What is before and after?

Theology

Drawing theology from Parables requires a bit of thought. Parables are stories and we cannot assume that the image given is exact theology. So, for example, in the Parable of the Rich Man and Lazarus, Abraham and Lazarus are in Paradise while the rich man is in Hades. Does this mean that in the final state we will see those in Hell from Heaven? This needs careful thought. As the remainder of Luke's Gospel and the wider NT does not give any indication of this, we should not instantly make this a theological point. We must form theology from a wider range of texts as parables are stories first and theology drawn should be paralleled in Jesus' other teaching.

Why did Jesus Teach in Parables?

Mark 4:11–12 suggests Jesus may have taught in parables to intentionally blind people to who he is. Yet, this is a misunderstanding of this passage. There is a little "so that" which starts v. 12. This is a *hina* in Greek. *Hina* usually indicates purpose or result. If the *hina* here is purposive, then Jesus did intend to blind people with his esoteric teaching. However, this is almost certainly a result *hina*—Jesus did not intend to blind them, it resulted in them not understanding. They were genuinely invited to believe in him through the parables. He knew they would not and would ultimately kill him.

It is likely Jesus taught in parables because of their genius. Parables draw on real life situations and are easily understandable even for a child and people without higher education (as were the majority at the time). Parables draw us to basic ideas from life (coins, seeds, fishing, banquets, priests, fathers, sons, and so on). They have a deeper layer than we can perceive if our hearts are open. Jesus was using stories to give people a vision of a different world. We are invited into them and challenged to accept or reject the vision.

Stories are critical to cultures, especially oral cultures like that of Jesus. Stories bring laughter (e.g. logs hanging out of eyes). They bring shock (e.g. a Samaritan hero). They bring surprise (e.g. a super-large harvest as in the Parable of the Sower). They make us think about meaning (e.g. Christians as the salt of the earth, the light of the world). They grip us in a way that propositional teaching does not.

We should think deeply about the meaning of the parables and also how we might use stories when we preach.

5

Chapter Five: The Kingdom of God-Ethics, Culture, and Leadership

This chapter continues the discussion of the Kingdom of God focussing on its ethics (especially the Sermons on the Mount and Plain), how culture and cultures are understood under God's reign, and patterns of leadership.

More Detail

Keown, "The Ethics of the Kingdom," Accessible on Academia: https://www.academia.edu/41159580/THE_ETHICS_OF_THE_KINGDOM.

Suggested Bible Readings

Ethics

Leviticus 19:18, 34

Isa 58

Micah 6:6–8

Take note of the ethics Jesus is calling us toward in the Sermons

Matthew 5–7
Luke 6:17–49
Matthew 22:34–40
Luke 12:32–34
John 13:34–35
Gal 3:28
Culture
Matt 15:22–28
Luke 7:1–10
Galatians 3:28
Rev 7:9–17
Leadership
Mark 10:35–45

The Kingdom of God: Ethics

Ethics is about moral principles for life. Ethics are very important in the OT, found in Israel's complex legal code. The emphasis in OT ethics is holiness, being ritually clean. The concern was contamination, which could come through a range of things such as a dead body, a menstruating woman, the wrong food, a person with a skin disease, impure hands, and so on. Personal holiness was very important, and although Deuteronomy called for the circumcision of the heart (Deut 10:16; 30:6), Israel tended to be overly concerned with external holiness. However, Israel's law was also concerned for people and was full of injunctions to care for the poor and socially marginalised (e.g. Exod 22:22; 23:3, 6, 11; Lev 14:21; 19:10, 15; 23:22; 24:17, 19, 20; Deut 15:4–11; 24:14; 27:29). The second great commandment, to love your neighbour as yourself, is also found in Lev 19:18. In context, it applies to love for one's fellow Jew. However, in Lev 19:34, this includes love for the immigrant.

The prophets of Israel were heavily critical of Israel's leadership and people for their failure to care for the poor and needy (e.g. Isa 1:23; 3:14–15; 10:2; Jer 2:34; 5:28; Ezek 16:49; 18:12; Amos 2:7; 4:1). They called Israel to show the mercy and love of God to the marginalised (e.g. Isa 1:17; 58:6–7; Jer 22:3; Zech 7:10). Their God "executes justice for the fatherless and the widow, and loves the sojourner, giving him [or her] food and clothing" (Deut 10:18, ESV). Jeremiah called people to be concerned about circumcised hearts (Jer 4:4). The Messiah would preach good news to the poor (Isa 61:1).

The summons to yield allegiance to Jesus the King includes a call to a certain lifestyle. It stands in continuity with, and fulfilment of, the OT law, not its abolition. Yet, its focus is a holiness of heart and mind expressed especially in love (Matt 5:17–20). It is not merely faith, and then do what we want (see Rom 6). We are called to live by the value system of our King and kingdom. The supreme virtue is love which is drawn from Lev 19:18 and 34 (cited above). For Jesus, one's neighbour is anyone one meets on the journey of life, including one's enemy (Matt 5:43–48; Luke 6:27–36; 10:25–37). Paul and John in particular emphasise love for one's neighbour (e.g. Rom 13:8–10; 1 Cor 12:31–13:13; Gal 5:14; John 13:34–35). This is not mere sentiment, but action on behalf of the other (1 John 3:16–18). For James, living by the royal law which means to care for orphans, widows, and the poor (Jas 1:27–2:26). For Matthew, love is expressed in the golden rule: doing for others what we would want them to do for us (Matt 7:11).

Another great ethical principle is humility and service, seen in Jesus' summons to take up one's cross and follow him. This means to be devoted not only to our own good but also to the good of others (Mark 8:34, s.a. Matt 10:38, 39; 16:24; Luke 9:23; 14:27).

It is in the Sermons on the Mount and Plain in Matthew and Luke that we find the biggest collections of Jesus' ethical teaching (Matt 5–7; Luke 6:20–49). These summon people to purity of heart and living lives showing mercy, seeking reconciliation, caring for the poor, the grieving, and others in need. We are to renounce fits of anger, retaliation, sexual immorality, be faithful in marriage, and keep our word (Matt 5:21–42). We are to give lavishly to the needs of others, not for public recognition, but quietly, and God will reward us (Matt 6:1–4; Luke 6:38). We are to be utterly devoted to God, his Kingdom, and his righteousness, and not money and possession, trusting God to provide for our needs (Matt 6:19–34). We are also to hold ourselves accountable, not focussing on the failings of others (Matt 7:1–5; Luke 6:37, 39–42).

This is not merely an ethic to be lived when we are together as Kingdom-people. It is to be lived 24/7 in the world. As the salt of the earth, we are to bring flavour, preservation, and healing to wider society. We are, similarly, the light of the world who are to shine brilliantly before the world through good works (Matt 5:13–16). This is an ethical life bathed in prayer, fasting, and forgiveness of the other (Matt 6:5–18; 7:7–11; Luke 6:37). It is to be based on a strong relationship with God (Matt 7:21–23). It is living by the teaching of Jesus (Matt 7:24–27; Luke 6:46–49).

There is a huge range of other ethical things across the NT. Paul, especially, recognises that it is the Spirit that is the key. We receive the Spirit at conversion, and by the Spirit, God transforms us if we are willing. We are to be people of personal holiness in every aspect of our lives.

Socially, we are to be governed by love for everyone we meet. We are to be non-discriminatory, full of grace, merciful, compassionate, kind, gentle, humble, servant-hearted, constructive of speech, sexually pure, and give witness to the world of the patterns of God's Kingdom. Where these are lived well, great societies form, and the world is transformed.

The Kingdom of God: Culture

The coming of Jesus inaugurates a cultural revolution. The world that Jesus came into was extremely ethnocentric. The Jewish worldview divided the world between Jews and Gentiles. Jews were God's people. While there was the hope of the Gentiles eventually submitting to God's rule, until that happened, the Gentiles were idolatrous sinners. They needed to become Jews to be God's people. This is called Judaising, whereby a person who is not born into Judaism converts from paganism to God. This involved circumcision for men, ritual cleansing (a kind of baptism), and submission to the laws of Moses, especially the boundary markers: Sabbath, ritual purity, eating protocols, the Jewish calendar, and so on. Being a member of God's people involved conforming to Jewish culture.

The rest of the world was extremely ethnocentric. Romans loved Greek culture and absorbed it. They saw themselves as Greeks and saw the rest of the world as uncivilised barbarians. The term Barbarian is derogatory, formed by onomatopoeia to imitate the babbling of other languages. While there were some Gentiles who respected Judaism and Jewish culture, there was a widespread anti-Semitism toward Judaism. Their belief in circumcision and refusal to eat pork were especially ridiculed. Indeed, for some, "Jewish religious rites such as circumcision seemed barbaric, the dietary laws appeared ridiculous, and the refusal to acknowledge other gods was impious atheism" (Richard Berchman, "Pagan Philosophers on Judaism in Ancient Times," in *The Encyclopedia of Judaism*, ed. Jacob Neusner, Alan J. Avery-Peck, and William Scott Green [Leiden; Boston; Köln: Brill, 2000], 3:1041).

In the ancient world, religions were tied to culture. Judaism is associated with Israel and Jews; Hinduism with Indian culture; Buddhism with SE Asian cultures; and so on. Christianity marks something new.

Jesus could be critiqued for being focused on Israel. So, in Matt 15:24 he says to the Canaanite woman: "I was not sent except to the lost sheep of the house of Israel" (NET). He also told the Twelve to limit their apostolic mission to "the lost sheep of Israel" (Matt 10:6).

Yet, this neglects Jesus' radical relationship with Gentiles. The first worshipers of Jesus in Matthew are Gentile magi from the east (Matt 2:1–12). When a Roman centurion approached Jesus to heal his servant, Jesus is prepared to break cultural rules and go into his home. This is only prevented by the Roman who did not want Jesus to do so, trusting him to heal his servant from a distance. Jesus commends his faith as superior to that of the people of Israel (Matt 8:3–13; Luke 7:1–10).

Although Jesus' statement concerning the dogs is puzzling, he commends the faith of the Syro-Phoenician woman and heals her daughter (Matt 15:21–28). He willingly healed people from the Gentile region of the Decapolis (Matt 4:25; Mark 3:8; 5:1–20). He entered Gentile territory including Tyre, Sidon, and the Decapolis (Matt 15:21; 7:24–31). While he was in Gentile territory, he fed the 4000, breaking bread with Gentiles without concern for uncleanness (Mark 8:1–10). In Luke, he challenged the ethnocentricism of his own people in Nazareth with stories of the widow of Zarephath and Naaman from the OT—both Gentiles (Luke 4:26–27, cf. 1 Kgs 17:9; 2 Kgs 5:1–14).

John also mentions Greeks approaching Philip wanting to see Jesus at Passover. Philip and Andrew came to see Jesus. Jesus then predicts his death through which he will draw *all* people to himself (meaning every nation, not every individual). He encourages them to believe and receive eternal life (John 12:20–36).

As has been noted, Samaritans were hated by Jews. Yet, Jesus is prepared to stay in a Samaritan town, only to be rejected. This leads James and John to seek to destroy the town with fire. Jesus rejects this and rebukes them (Luke 9:51–56). Twice Samaritans are the heroes—the Good Samaritan who is commended and the priest and Levite tacitly rebuked (Luke 10:25–37), and the only grateful leper who returned to thank Jesus after he healed the ten (Luke 17:11–19).

Then there is the stunning story of the Samaritan woman in John 4. She is also an adulterer and perhaps a prostitute. Yet, Jesus willingly asks her for a drink, prepared to drink what her supposedly unclean hands offered him. Later, he accepts an invitation to stay in Sychar and many come to faith in him. In the first-century Jewish context, this is stunning.

Throughout his ministry, Jesus was unafraid to hang out with tax-collectors, despised for being traitors to Rome (e.g. Matt 9:10–11). Indeed, one of his disciples was Levi a tax-collector who is almost certainly the Matthew who wrote one of the Gospels (compare Mark 2:14 and Matt 9:9; 10:3). Then there is the great story of Zacchaeus who accepts Jesus into his home and finds salvation demonstrated in his radical generosity to the poor and defrauded (Luke 19:1–10).

Jesus also spoke of people from every nation becoming disciples who are taught and baptised (Matt 28:19). The gospel, then, would be preached throughout the world (Matt 24:14; Mark 13:10). The disciples were to preach repentance and faith throughout the world and make disciples of all nations (Matt 28:19; Luke 24:46). Jesus is the saviour of the world (John 4:42).

In Acts, the gospel began among Jews in Jerusalem. The Spirit fell, and they spoke in the tongues of the nations. God was beginning the reversal of the scattering of the world and confusion of languages at Babel (Gen 11:1–9). Eventually, after Paul's persecution, the gospel spread, and they began to preach to non-Jews in Syrian Antioch (Acts 8:4; 11:19–21). The church had to work through whether a new Gentile convert had to Judaise as well as believe in Jesus. This was roundly rejected; all that is required is a sincere faith (Acts 15).

So, Paul could sum up the Christian attitude to culture in Gal 3:28: "for in Christ Jesus there is neither Jew nor Greek." We are one in Christ. We are bound together by faith and the Spirit. Our fundamental culture is the fruit of the Spirit with which we love one another and the world.

The Kingdom story ends with people from all the nations gathered around the throne of God worshiping God and his Son, the lamb who was slain (Rev 5:1–14; 7:9–17). The city of God descends to earth, and in the new heavens and earth is the tree of life, and its leaves are the healing of the nations (Rev 22:2).

The gospel brings a cultural revolution. No longer is there Jew and Gentile, Roman and Barbarian, Pakeha and Maori. Our cultures are still in many ways unique and wonderful. Culture is to be celebrated. Yet, we are not to be divided culturally. All are welcome to come to Christ as they are. We are bound together as one by faith. No culture can be allowed to dominate another.

This needs to be thought about. Any church has a dominant culture, whether it be a particular ethnicity (e.g. Korean), or a particular way of doing church. Our challenge is to break open our churches so that no culture dominates. We need to be open to the different, the other, and embrace them as they come. All they need is to come and belong. To be a member of God's people, they simply need a sincere faith. Cliquey groups, dominant cultures, "the way things are done around here," rules that divide us, are all to be challenged. The vision of God is not a whole lot of people like us all together hanging out feeling cool. It is the wide variety of humankind all together as one, despite our differences. This is way more challenging than just hanging out with our mates and people like us. But this is the challenge of the gospel and we must take it up.

The Kingdom of God: leadership

The undisputed leader of the Kingdom of God is God the Father. It is his kingdom. He has appointed his Son king, anointing him through his prophet John, by the Spirit. Jesus leads his kingdom as Christ, Lord, Son of God, and King of kings.

Jesus appoints leaders. In his life, he appointed the Twelve. These were designated apostles, a Greek political term, speaking of an emissary who travels on behalf of a ruler. The task of the apostle was to establish faith-communities of God throughout the world. There were also others who were commissioned with leadership roles in Luke's Gospel, the seventy-two sent into mission (Luke 10).

The appointment of the Twelve in Luke's Gospel (Luke 6:12–16) is followed by the Sermon on the Plain (Luke 16:17–49). The implication here is that the ethics espoused in the Sermon, are integral to the life of the Apostle and Christian leader. They are to be utterly devoted to embodying the Kingdom ethic and being an example to others.

The fundamental call of the Christian leader is to lead as did Jesus. After Jesus is recognised as Messiah, the following verses teach what it means to be a Christian leader. Fundamentally, leaders are to deny themselves, take up their cross, follow Jesus, be prepared to lose their lives for his sake, and never be ashamed of Jesus and his words (Mark 8:34–38). They are to listen to Jesus (Mark 9:7). They are to lead by example in their worship lives, in the way they treat others, and in their missional desire.

They are to renounce selfish ambition and concerns for greatness in the eyes of others. They are to be as humble as children, servants, leading through servanthood (Mark 9:33–35). Unlike John who was threatened by others in ministry, they are to be permission-giving leadership, releasing people into their ministries (Mark 9:38–41). They are to be holy, but not holier-than-thou people; determined to please God but not self-righteous and judgmental (Mark 9:42–50; Matt 7:1–5). They are to seek sexual purity, faithfully celibate or married (Mark 10:1–12). They are not to get in the way of people coming to Jesus, whether old or young, but open the pathway to the Lord (Mark 10:13–16). They are not to be covetous of wealth, they are to serve God and not money (Mark 10:17–31, cf. 1 Tim 6:3–10, 17–19).

The most important teaching on leadership in the NT

is arguably Mark 10:35–45. James and John come to Jesus telling Jesus that they want him to do something for them. Herein we see their basic problem—although they know Jesus is Messiah, they have not grasped what that means. They want their way, when all that matters is the way of Jesus! They think that they can tell Jesus what to do. It is the other way around for a Christian leader.

Jesus goes along with them. He asks them what they want. They arrogantly ask for the premier positions of power either side of him when he enters his glory. Jesus challenges whether they can go through the suffering he is about to. They likely think Jesus is referring to war with the Gentiles, and as the "sons of thunder" are over-confident of their ability. Of course, Jesus is not talking about killing others, but crucifixion. Jesus, however, does not grant their wish, telling them that this is up to God. This is important for us too. We may aspire to leadership or a particular role. God decides who does what. Our job is to do what he tells us, not what we want from him.

Understandably, the other ten disciples are annoyed at the arrogance of James and John. They likely felt miffed—why them? Why not me?

Jesus then takes the opportunity to teach them about leadership. He points them to what they know—that the rulers of the Gentiles, the likes of the Caesars and the Herods rule autocratically. They are despots, ruling arrogantly, with masses of attendants and servants, who rule by might and power. We have the likes in the world today, ruling North Korea and other totalitarian contexts. Some western leaders behave more like them than Jesus.

However, the Christian leader is not to be like this. Greatness is found in the service of all others. Even Jesus came as a servant to serve others and give his life for them, not to be served by others.

The challenge of Christian leadership is having the courage to lead, yet to lead through service. This means not simply demanding people do what we want, when we want, how we want. It is about building teams, and together, working to build community. This is a slower process than dominating autocracy. Yet, it is God's way.

God could have sent Jesus as a Gentile leader, with armies, demanding the world submit. However, he would not have had our willing allegiance. It would be the exercise of rule by fear. God's way is rule by service and love.

Through Acts and the rest of the NT, we see first the apostles leading with courageous example, prepared to be punished for God. When the work of feeding the poor widows in the community became too much for the apostles, a new leadership group was formed. This is the Seven, two of which became great evangelists: Philip and Stephen. Stephen is the first martyr of the church.

God chose Paul. He plucked him from persecuting Christians to be the leader of his mission to the world. Paul chose a range of men and women co-workers to work with him. He summoned them to "imitate me" (e.g. 1 Cor 4:16, Phil 3:17) recognising that authentic Christian leadership is more caught than taught. He called them to live cruciformly, led by the Spirit, leading out of love, leading by example, worshiping men and women, holy, faithful, filled with the Spirit.

6

Chapter Six: The Kingdom of God-Jesus' Death, Resurrection, and Mission

This chapter brings the discussion of the Kingdom to an end focussing on the death of Jesus (his Passion), his resurrection, and the mission he summons us to.

More Detail

Keown, "The Passion and Resurrection of the King," Vol 3 Ch. 10–11.

Keown, "The Mission of the Kingdom," Notes on Moodle: https://www.academia.edu/41159857/ THE_MISSION_OF_GODS_PEOPLE_THE_GOSPELS.

Suggested Bible Readings

Jesus' Death

Matt 26–27

John 18–19

Romans 6:1–4

1 Peter 2:18–25

Jesus' Resurrection
Matt 28
Mark 16:1–8
Luke 24
Acts 1:1–11
1 Cor 15
Mission
Matt 28:18–20
Mark 13:10; 14:9
Luke 24:46–49
Acts 1:6–11
Matt 9:36–10:42
Luke 10:1–24

The Kingdom of God: Jesus' Death

The most important moment in the ministry of Jesus is undoubtedly his death. All four Gospels lead to this moment. In the Synoptics, Jesus directly told the disciples three times that he would die. He would be rejected by the Jewish leadership and be killed by the Gentiles (Mark 8:31; 9:31; 10:33–34). He had come as God's Servant "to give his life as a ransom for many" (Mark 10:45). He knew his ultimate purpose. He is the beloved son the tenants would kill and throw from the vineyard (Mark 12:6). He is the shepherd who was struck, and the sheep scattered (Mark 14:27). At the Last Supper, Jesus explained the reason for his death. His body was broken, and his blood poured out for the forgiveness of sin and to inaugurate a new covenant (Mark 14:22–25; Matt 26:28; Luke 22:14–23).

In John's Gospel, Jesus knows he will die. For John, he is the lamb of God who takes away the sin of the world (John 1:29). In John 3:14, Jesus tells hearers that just as Moses lifted up the snake on a pole in the wilderness so that Israel would be delivered from the serpents attacking them (Num 21:9), Jesus, the Son of Man, would be lifted up. In so doing, Jesus is the means by which they can be delivered from the eternal consequences of sin through faith (s.a. John 8:28; 12:32, 34). He referred to his going away. He is going to prepare a place for his people. Some cannot come (resistant Jews), but his people will join him for he is the way. And, when he goes, he will send the Spirit (John 8:21; 14:3–7, 28; 16:7). When Philip and Andrew brought Greeks to Jesus at the Passover, Jesus predicts his death as his glorification. He is like a grain of wheat falls into the dirt, dies, and becomes a plant bearing much grain. Troubled of heart, he refers to his hour to come when he is to be lifted up. Through his death, he will draw all people to himself (John 12:20–34).

The story of Jesus' betrayal, arrest, trial, denial, and death is like a brilliant horrific Netflix *Game of Thrones*-like drama in which the forces of evil and fallen humanity collude to kill him off. Satan is involved, inducing Judas to betray Jesus (Luke 22:3; John 13:2). Jesus is betrayed by Judas for money (Matt 26:15) and with a kiss (Luke 22:47–48). Jesus knew this was coming, yet still broke bread with him (Matt 26:21). He still washed his feet (John 13:5). We see the unconditional love of Jesus.

We see Jesus in the Garden of Gethsemane, deeply anguished, pleading with his Father to release him from the horrors of what is to come. God refuses; rather, he strengthens Jesus for the death that would change the world (Mark 14:32–42).

The Jewish leadership, normally divided over matters of theology and law, come together to collude to destroy him by stealth (Mark 14:2). They harness false witnesses to create a pretext to have him killed. The best they have is that Jesus would destroy the Temple. Just how was one man with a small group of disciples going to do this? At the meeting of the whole council were two members who would later turn and bury Jesus: Joseph of Arimathea and Nicodemus, shafts of light in the darkness of this meeting (Mark 14:53–65).

Despite his bravado, Jesus' leading disciple, Peter, also denies him. He is the bravest of the men, following Jesus at a distance. Yet, he fails the challenge of denying himself, taking up his cross, and following Jesus (Mark 14:29–31, 54, 66–72). James and John are nowhere to be seen. They have failed to drink from Jesus' cup and to be baptised with him at this right and left hand (Mark 10:37–39). The only ones who do not completely desert Jesus in the Synoptics are the women who watch from a distance (Mark 14:40–41). In John's account, the women are much closer to the beloved disciple (John 19:25–27). Whichever is closest to the truth, the women put the men to shame.

The Romans are involved. The Sanhedrin had no power to kill Jesus lawfully (John 18:31). Hence, they handed him over to Pilate—Jews and Gentiles colluding! In Jewish law, the alliance of the clean and the unclean is questionable. Pilate interrogates Jesus asking if he is king of the Jews. Jesus is, as usual, ambiguous responding, "you say so" (Mark 15:2). Pilate is intrigued and ambivalent about Jesus, who he realises is no threat. He looks for a way out.

Consistent with the practice of the governor releasing a prisoner he offers them a choice between Jesus and a revolutionary, Barabbas. Barabbas means "son of the Father." In some ancient witnesses, in Matt 27:15–17, his full name is Jesus Barabbas. So, the choice the crowd is given is between Jesus Christ Son of God, or Jesus Son of the Father. Incited by the Jewish leaders, they opt for the revolutionary. Jesus will go to his death between two of his revolutionary partners. The real Son of God is crucified, the real revolutionary goes free.

Pilate then has Jesus crucified for political expediency, to placate the Jews and end any question of a revolt.

Jesus' death is horrific. He is flogged and beaten. He is mocked as a king with a crown of thorns and a purple robe. He then carries his cross to his death. Some unknown in the crowd (who we know from Mark to be Simon of Cyrene) is conscripted to carry it for him when Jesus is too tired. We see the humanity of Christ. We also see the first person who carries a cross for him. He is a Gentile. His sons are named, suggesting they became a part of the church (Mark 15:21; Rom 16:13). It is a Gentile who helps Jesus carry his cross; the disciples are again nowhere to be seen.

Jesus is crucified meaning he is nailed by his hands (or wrists) and feet to the cross. He is lifted up, as he predicted in John. Soldiers gamble over his robe. The crowds mock Jesus, challenging him to come down from the cross and save himself. Jesus speaks only seven statements from the cross. He cries out the words of abandonment from Ps 22:1. This is Israel's last chance to recognise that he is the one predicted by David in this Psalm. They misunderstand him (Matt 27:46; Mark 15:34). In Luke 23:34, in a disputed text but which is likely authentic, Jesus prays for his killers asking God to forgive them in their ignorance. Again, in Luke, one of Barabbas' revolutionaries recognises Jesus as a crucified King, pleading that he remember him when he comes into his reign (the first to recognise a crucified Messiah). Jesus promises him salvation on that very day (Luke 23:43). In John's account, Jesus gives his mother over to the beloved disciple for his care (John 19:26–27). He cries out his thirst (John 19:28). His final words in Luke are to commit his spirit to his Father (Luke 23:46). In John, it is *tetelesthai*, "it is completed"—Jesus has finished the work he has come to do (John 19:30).

There is then a three-hour period of darkness (Mark 15:33); evil seems to have won! Yet, the curtain hiding the Holy of Holies in the Temple is ripped asunder (Matt 27:51; Mark 15:38; Luke 23:45). Access to God is now open for all humanity through Jesus. In Hebrews, he himself is the curtain (Heb 10:20). Some tombs are cracked open, and dead saints are seen in the city (Matt 27:52–53).

And after his death, the Roman centurion confesses: "surely this man was the Son of God" (Matt 27:54). He is the first Christian of the new era, recognising in Jesus' amazing death that the true saviour of the world is not Caesar, but Jesus Christ, despite his crucifixion. He is a foretaste of a Roman world that would in 300 or so years, adopt faith in this crucified Messiah as its state religion.

What does the death of Christ mean? This is not fully developed in the Synoptic Gospels where the writers focus on telling the story. It is John in his Gospel, Paul especially in Romans and Galatians, and other NT writers (e.g. Hebrews; 1 Peter) who draw out the theological and ethical implications of the death of Christ. Four things stand out.

Our Forgiveness and Salvation

The death of Christ is the willing sacrifice of an unblemished human to deal with sin once and for all. He is the completion of Israel's sacrificial system (and any other such system in the world). No more animals need to be killed. Jesus' death is the solution to sin. Jesus was sinless.

He died for us. If we believe, his death brings complete forgiveness for sin for all humankind.

It brings our justification before God. We are declared righteous by God if we believe because Jesus is our substitute, our representative, and the one who conquered sin and death.

It opens the way for the Spirit to be poured into us. When we believe we are cleansed of sin and declared holy so that the Spirit can be given to us, as the Spirit can only dwell in the holy. This holiness comes through Jesus' holiness, imparted to us. We receive his anointing, we are sealed for redemption, and the Spirit is deposited as a guarantee.

We are then redeemed, ransomed, and our life purchased. We are no longer slaves of sin, law, death, and eternal destruction.

God's wrath is propitiated, dealt with where there is faith. He will act to cleanse the world of evil, removing its every vestige when the time is right. But this will not include those who believe in him, for the cross dealt with our evil.

The cross also reconciles us to God. It deals with the problem of sin which separates us from an intimate relationship with God. Now sin is dealt with. We have peace with God through our Lord Jesus Christ.

Our Death

As such, the death of Christ becomes our death. Paul develops the idea of being "in Christ," in which we are participants in Jesus' death, burial, and resurrection life. As we are "in Christ," we can say with Paul: "I have been crucified with Christ" (Gal 2:19 [Greek text]). We have crucified our old natures (Gal 5:24) and when we die physically, this will merely be a transition to our eternal life. Hence, in a sense, while we live on, we are dead in Christ and alive to God in Christ Jesus (Rom 6:11).

A New Covenant Inaugurated

At the Last Supper, Jesus speaks of his blood as the blood of the new covenant (Luke 22:20). The writer of Hebrews states the premise that every covenant is established with blood including the Mosaic covenant (Heb 9:18–22). Christ's death is the blood inaugurating the new covenant. He has been offered once for all to bear the sins of many (Heb 9:28). His blood is "the blood of the eternal covenant" (Heb 13:20). This covenant is the fulfilment of Jeremiah's vision of a new covenant in which God would inscribe his law on the hearts of his people and forgive their sins permanently enabling people to walk in close relationship with him (Jer 31:31–34). It speaks of an agreement between God and all humankind whereby he will be king and people who yield to his reign will have their sins forgiven. Then they will receive eternal life in his everlasting Kingdom.

Our Life-Pattern

Most of us know that "Christ died for our sins" (1 Cor 15:3) and we are saved through his death. Yet, the NT says something more about the death of Christ that we must grasp deep in our beings so that we can be the people God calls us to be. It is this: Christ's death is the pattern by which we should live. The term used for this is cruciformity—to be conformed to the pattern of the *crucis* (cross) of Jesus. We are to live *via crucis*, by the way of the cross.

The cross is the summit of Jesus' life and sacrifice. Despite being king of the cosmos, his life was one of humble service in which he used his immense divine power only in the service of others—healing, feeding, comforting, raising the dead, liberating, giving sight and hearing—spiritual and physical—and seeking and saving the lost. He never used his power for his own ends. He was totally devoted to the good of others.

As Paul puts it, "he emptied himself ... taking the form of a slave ... he humbled himself and became obedient to death, even death on the cross" (Phil 2:7). He poured himself out for the world.

Our call as God's people is to take up our crosses and follow him—a summons to walk in the way of the cross. Wherever we are, among the people we are placed, we are there to live out of Christ's humility, serving them, in whatever station God has placed us. This applies to dads at home, kids at school, women at work, when in church, at play—anywhere we are. We ask God to show us how to see the world and people as he does and live cruciformly.

We are to do what Jesus did and spend ourselves for his Kingdom, his people, and the world. It will be hard. Suffering is essential to the journey, for the path to glory is to participate in Christ's sufferings (Rom 8:17). Yet, the reward is great. We already have it: eternal life. We are to press on to win this prize, working out the salvation we already have (Phil 2:12–13; 3:12–14). Put another way, we are to take up our towels and follow Jesus, washing the feet of the world (John 13:1–15).

We each walk in relationship with God. We are to spend time with him, allowing him to guide us and shape our life directions. We live out of his direction, not our desires, which are always flawed. As we go about living in this way, whatever the challenges are, we do so cruciformly. This is the pattern of the cross: humility, service, sacrifice, suffering, love, seeking justice, and a million other virtuous attitudes. We renounce the patterns of this age but are transformed with renewed minds. The key is the Spirit who is in us transforming us to be more and more like Jesus. We are to yield to the gentle nudging of the Spirit which is the impulse toward cruciformity.

The world will respond again to Christ when it sees Christ's patterns lived. This is what Jesus was driving at in John 13:35: "By this all people will know that you are my disciples: if you have love for one another."

The importance of the death of Christ makes communion as celebrated in the church a most important ritual. When we celebrate communion, we proclaim Christ's death until he comes (1 Cor 11:26). We remind ourselves of the central event that shapes us—our salvation and life pattern. Alongside the proclamation of the word, communion is the centre of worship.

The Kingdom of God: Jesus' resurrection

If the death of Jesus is the most important moment in Jesus' life, then its climax, the resurrection is arguably the greatest moment in history. All the Gospels tell essentially the same story with some detailed variations.

The Burial

First, Jesus is buried late on the day before the Sabbath

begins at sunset (Friday of Passover) in the tomb of Joseph of Arimathea. A group of women sees the burial (Matt 27:61; Mark 15:47; Luke 24:55). Matthew records that a guard is set to ensure the body is not stolen and that the tomb's entry is covered with a stone (Matt 27:62–66).

The Women at the Tomb

Second, the women go to the tomb early on the following Sunday, the third day from Friday (inclusive), and find the stone rolled away from the tomb. In Matthew, Mark, and Luke they are met by an angel (or two) in white who tells them Jesus has risen.

Tell the Others

Third, in all the Gospels, the women are the first evangelists of the resurrection taking the message to the others. They are the apostles to the apostles. There are different details in each Gospel at this point. In Matthew and Mark, they are instructed by the angel to tell the other disciples to meet Jesus in Galilee. Mark ends at this point. Yet, we know that the women told the others because Mark's Gospel exists, and Christianity had spread into Rome at this point. Matthew's Gospel tells us that they went and met him and were commissioned to take the gospel to the world. In Luke, they remember Jesus referring to his resurrection, and go to tell the men who come and see. In John, Mary Magdalene tells Peter and John, and they run to the tomb to see.

Appearances

Fourth, there are other appearances.

Mark

The authentic early ending of Mark has no appearances. However, his second century longer ending supports that the early church accepted that Jesus appeared to two on the Emmaus Road (Mark 16:12, cf. Luke 24:13–32). It also includes Jesus appearing at a meal (s.a. Luke 24:36–49) and commissioning them to preach to the world and its fulfilment. It is a retelling of Luke's commission and summary of Acts (Mark 16:14–20).

Matthew

Matthew adds an appearance to the two Marys (Matt 28:9–10) and the Great Commission appearance in Galilee (Matt 28:11–20).

Luke

Luke has the Emmaus appearance and names one of them as Cleopas, an appearance to Peter (Luke 24:35), and a meal appearance with the disciples where he commissions them to preach to the world (Luke 24:36–49).

John

John includes an appearance to Mary Magdalene (John 20:11–18); the disciples minus Thomas where they receive the Spirit (John 20:19–23); the disciples with Thomas (John

20:26-28); and seven disciples (Peter, Thomas Didymus, Nathanael, James and John, and two others) meeting Jesus at the Sea of Galilee.

Acts

Acts includes Jesus appearing over forty days convincingly proving his resurrection and commissions them to be his witnesses, a retelling of Luke 24:36–49). Luke tells the story of Paul's experience of the resurrected Christ three times (Acts 9:1–18; 22:1–21; 26:12–23).

Paul

Paul has a neat summary of some of the appearances in 1 Cor 15:5–8: 1) Peter; 2) the 12 apostles (actually, the 11, as Judas was gone); 3) an appearance to a great crowd of 500; 4) James; 5) to all the apostles; 6) Paul (s.a. Gal 1:16).

Synthesis

Overall, with moderate harmonisation, we get something like this list of appearances:

1) An appearance to Mary (and possibly another Mary) (Matt 28:9–10; John 20:11–18).

2) The Great Commission appearance in Galilee (Matt 28:11–20).

3) The Emmaus appearance including Cleopas (Luke 24:13–32, s.a. Mark 16:12).

4) Peter (Luke 24:35; 1 Cor 15:5).

5) A meal appearance with the disciples where he commissions them to preach to the world (Luke 24:36–49, s.a. Acts 1:4–8; Mark 16:14–20; Matt 28:11–20).

6) The apostles minus Thomas (John 20:19–23; poss. 1 Cor 15:5).

7) The disciples with Thomas (John 20:26-28; poss. 1 Cor 15:7).

8) Paul (Acts 9:1–18; 22:1–21; 26:12–23; 1 Cor 15:5–8; Gal 1:16).

9) An appearance to a great crowd of 500 (1 Cor 15:6).

10) James (1 Cor 15:7)

Mission

Fifth, the disciples are commissioned to engage in mission throughout the world on Christ's behalf (Matt 28:18–20; Luke 24:46–49; John 20:21, s.a. Matt 24:14; 26:13; Mark 13:10; 14:9; 16:14–20). In Luke's second account of the resurrection period, he again emphasises mission to the world (Acts 1:8). Paul's includes his own commission to the nations (Acts 9:15; 22:21; 26:16–18). (See further on mission in this chapter).

Importance

The resurrection is vital theologically. Jesus' resurrection begins God's fulfilment of the hopes of resurrection in the OT (e.g. Job 19:25–27; Ps 16:10; 49:15; 73:24; Isa 25:8; 26:19; Ezek 37:1–14; Hos 13:14; Dan 12:1–3). It fulfils the hope of the resurrection of the Servant (Isa 53:9–10) and in Judaism (e.g. 2 Macc 7:10–11; 14:46; 1 En. 22:13; 46:6; 51:1–2; Pss. Sol. 3:11–16; 13:9–11; 14:4–10; 15:12–15; Sib. Or. 4:176–82). At the time of Jesus, although the Sadducees rejected an afterlife, (Acts 23:8; 26:8; Josephus, *Ant.* 18.14; b. Sanh. 90b), the Pharisees expected resurrection and eternal reward for the righteous (Acts 23:6–8; *b. Sanh.* 90b; *b. Ketub.* 111b).

Jesus' resurrection is a victory over sin and its consequences (1 Cor 15:55). Being in Christ, we have died in him and are raised (Eph 2:5). Presently, this resurrection is spiritual, Christ's Spirit regenerating our inner beings while our bodies decline. It will be our complete restoration at his coming. His resurrection is the firstfruits of a harvest of people to be raised (1 Cor 15:20). His resurrection guarantees our resurrection (1 Cor 14:22). He is the first of a new humanity and renewed creation (cf. 2 Cor 5:17; Gal 6:15). His resurrection body is a prototype of ours (Phil 3:21). He ate after being raised (Luke 24:42). He remains human. However, as flesh and blood cannot inherit the Kingdom of God (1 Cor 15:50), he is no longer flesh and blood but flesh and bones (1 Cor 15:50; Luke 24:39). He bears the scars of his suffering (John 20:25–27). His body is a spiritual body (1 Cor 15:44); still a body but empowered by the Spirit. We will receive the same body of glory he has, but our bodies of humiliation will be set free from bondage to sin and death (Phil 3:20). We will be transformed in an instant, the perishable will become imperishable, the mortal immortal (1 Cor 15:50–54). Unlike those raised from the dead in Israel's story, Jesus' ministry, and the wider NT, ours will be final and eternal as is Christ's.

Did it happen?

Did the resurrection happen? Something happened, for the world has never been the same. While there are differences in detail, the early church saw no reason to remove these as they formed the canon. They let the variations stand, demonstrating that there was no collusion to come up with a neat tidy story. Rather, they let the witnesses give their voice. There are also other things that add to an argument for historicity. The testimony of women is included, even though in the ancient world it carried no weight. There is the multiplicity of witnesses, which is astonishing. There is the determination of these disciples to tell the world, even though they would be persecuted and martyred. People might die for a lie to protect their reputations and families, to gain wealth for them, or something similar. There was no reason for the early Christians to die for this one. There is the amazing story of monotheistic Jews converted to believers in God; the Father, Son, and Spirit, and this must be explained. Similarly, how was it that this story could not be stopped among Romans who rejected the concept of resurrection and yet it ultimately became its governing story? This is because there is power in it that defies explanation.

Then there is the problem of a decent alternative. Jesus was clearly dead, speared through the side. His tomb was guarded by a Roman *custodia* and a huge rock; he could hardly have got out. Nor could others get in. The idea that the women had the wrong tomb is dumb, as they were witnesses to his burial. Further, the body would be produced to dispel the myth if it lay in a tomb in Jerusalem. No one produced it. The idea that their experiences of Jesus were hallucinations is hardly likely when one considers the number of people involved and the geographical spread of the appearances. Without a doubt, the best explanation is that Jesus did indeed rise.

Response

The resurrection does not prove Jesus' divinity, but it

strongly suggests it. The right response is that of the women who worshiped him (Matt 28:8, 17). It is with burning hearts empowered by the Spirit to go and tell the world (Luke 24:32, 46–49; John 20:21; Acts 1:8). We cry out with the angel, "he has been raised" (Matt 28:6, 7; Mark 16:6; Luke 24:6). With Thomas we declare: "My Lord and my God" (John 20:28). Just as the eucharist is important to recall the death of Jesus, so baptism is vital as a marker of new life in Christ (Rom 6:3–4). We must celebrate each new conversion to Christ with it.

The Kingdom of God: Its Mission

The Kingdom of God is God's great mission project. Jesus comes as God's king and heralds the Kingdom. The right response is to repent and believe the good news (Mark 1:15). Moved by compassion (e.g. Matt 9:36; 14:14), Jesus moved through the nation of Israel, preaching, calling people to join him, feeding the poor, healing, driving out demons, and raising the dead. He is God's anointed king, his sent one (e.g. John 3:34), preaching good news to the poor and releasing people from bondage (Luke 4:18–20). His mission is to seek and save the lost (Luke 19:10). He sought out the lost sheep and brought them home (Matt 9:36; Luke 15:3–7). He invited people to the banquet of God (Luke 14:16–24).

He was not satisfied to do this himself. Twelve apostles were selected. An apostle is a "sent one," and they are sent into mission. The Synoptics all record this initial sending. The disciples are to take nothing much with them, relying on God's provision and the hospitality of people—a short term training exercise. Mark's account is brief, focused on their casting out of demons (Mark 6:7–13). Luke's account involves the deliverance of demons, healing, and preaching the Kingdom (Luke 9:1–6). Matthew's account also includes exorcism, healing, preaching the nearness of the Kingdom, and even raising the dead (Matt 10:1, 8). Matthew adds a full discourse on mission, equipping readers for their own participation in the mission of God (including us).

The mission does not stop with Jesus and the apostles. In Luke 10 there is a second short-term mission assignment with the Seventy-Two (or in some texts, the Seventy) sent out. This may involve the Twelve gathering their own teams of five and leading them in mission, as Jesus has led them to this point. These people are told that "the harvest is great, but the labourers are few" (Luke 10:2). They are urged to pray for Christ (the Lord of the harvest) to send out labourers, for the mission begins in prayer (Luke 10:3, s.a. Matt 9:38; Acts 4:29–31; Eph 6:18–20; Col 4:3). They are sent again to rely on hospitality, heal, and proclaim the Kingdom (Luke 10:9). When they return, Jesus sees Satan fall from heaven; mission is the progressive defeat of Satan (Luke 10:18).

Each of the Synoptics ends with mission commissions. The original ending of Mark has the women sent to tell the men that Jesus is risen (Mark 16:6). Earlier in the Gospel, the good news will be preached to the whole world before the end (Mark 13:10, s.a. 14:9). Matthew's Gospel ends with Jesus sending the disciples to make disciples of all nations, teaching and baptising them (Matt 28:18–20). Luke also includes a Great Commission narrative; the disciples sent, empowered by the Spirit, to preach repentance and forgiveness of sins to the entire world (Luke 24:46–49). John's Great Commission involves Jesus sending the disciples as he was sent. He breathes the Spirit on them. He sends them to grant forgiveness of sins on God's behalf

(John 20:21–23). In Acts 1:8, Luke's retelling of Luke 24 includes the disciples receiving power by the Spirit to be Christ's witnesses to the ends of the earth. The story of Acts is the story of this mission. It ends in Rome, which is not the ends of the earth but will be the locus from which the mission will be completed.

Like the restoration of Europe after WW2, the mission of the Kingdom is a wholesale restoration of the world. It began with the seed of Jesus' incarnation, God the Son becoming flesh and beginning the work. It will end with the world transformed into what it was always created to ultimately be—a world free of evil, sin, decay, death, and pain (Rev 21:1–4).

Jesus preached. At its heart is the salvation of people. The central work of mission is that they come into God's salvation. They hear the good news of the Kingdom. They repent and believe. They follow Jesus. They are his. So, at its core mission must include the proclamation of the gospel in an understandable and clear way, people submitting to its God, and receiving eternal life. This is commonly called evangelism.

Yet mission is also more than verbalising the message, important though this is. Jesus trained his disciples. Mission involves training new disciples, caring for them, ensuring they grow in the faith. Mission includes discipleship.

Jesus fed the poor. In the feeding of the 5000, Jesus said to his disciples, "you give them something to eat" (e.g. Mark 6:37). Many other texts support that we are to do the same (e.g. Matt 19:21; Luke 14:13, 21; 16:19–31; 19:8). The early church in Acts took this seriously as they ministered to the poor among them (Acts 4:32–37). So, must we. Preaching good news to the poor (Luke 4:18) is not purely verbal, it includes acting as did Jesus.

Jesus healed the sick and cast out demons. By the same Spirit, we are to lay hands on the ill and demonised and ask God to heal them. He will act as he wills. Where someone is healed and set free, we praise God. Where God in his wisdom chooses to leave a person in a state of unwellness (as in the case of Paul, 2 Cor 12:7), we are to continue to minister to them. We are to care for those in need. The nations will be judged on how they cared for Jesus' people (Matt 25:37–40). It is obvious we are to do this. The marginalised are invited to the banquet, and whether healed and set free or not, they are invited to dine, and we are to care for one another (Luke 14:12–24). Mission involves social justice.

Jesus built a community. He called people to him, and aside from the demoniac sent home to tell his testimony to his people in the Decapolis (Mark 5:1–20), all who wanted to join Jesus were welcome. A good example is Bartimaeus, who followed Jesus along the way (Mark 10:52). The ethics of the Kingdom (see Ch. 5), are to be lived out in community. We gather to love God (worship). We gather to love one another (koinōnia). We disperse into the world week by week to be the salt of the earth and the light of the world (Matt 5:13–16). Mission is building authentic Christian communities in every context which are filled with love. By this love, they will know that we are Christ's disciples (John 13:34–35).

Jesus went. When a group of people truly imbibe the principles of the Kingdom, the church can become great. This can be amazingly missional, people attracted to the faith—what missiologists call centripetal mission (mission to the centre, mission by attraction). This is what God wants. Yet, centripetal mission is not enough. There must also be centrifugal mission (like a centrifuge, mission from the centre, mobilised mission, going). The Great Commissions do not tell people to sit and wait for the world to come. We are sent people. We are to go. Like Jesus, we are to have sinners as our friends. We are to participate in families, workplaces, sports and social contexts, and wider society, flavouring, leavening and lighting the world. We are to share Jesus as we go with the attitudes Christ, good works of justice and kindness, and with winsome wise salty conversation. Western Christianity has lost its sense of going. We must regain it. Going into our own nation with the good news. And reclaiming our place as the world's leading sender of missionaries.

We must also remember our call to mission in terms of the big picture of what God is doing on planet earth. We are created in God's image to rule over and care for the world. This involves building human society across the world, using God's resources wisely, and ensuring the preservation of the ecology of the world. I call this the Great Cosmission of God—his mission to build a cosmos, a world.

Sadly, sin has seen this dream marred deeply. The world is built and being built, but it is flawed, rife with corruption and sin, broken and hurting, subject to decay and death, full of brokenness.

Even in the garden, God the Missionary began the work of restoration, clothing Adam and Eve and allowing them to produce children. He called Abraham from whom he would save the world. Abraham became a nation, and God blessed them and foretold his future intervention to transform the world into what it should and could be. Jesus is his intervention. He has come, and the new creation and humanity are launched.

We are his people, filled with his Spirit. Each of us is to take up our role in the Great Cosmission—to build God's world. Hence, work is important. Not all of us are sent to be fulltime missionaries or ministers. We are to go out and do work that builds God's world. This involves all sorts of work from digital work to the very pragmatic trades; from IT to accounting to education to science, to art to politics to you name it. We are to be creative, designing, creating, and renewing with all that God has given us. We are to do so in a way that nurtures God's world and humankind.

We also carry with us the Great Commissions referred to above. We are about evangelism, discipleship, feeding the poor, social justice, social transformation, love, exorcism, healing, and more. We build churches. We build schools. We build hospitals. We do whatever God summons us to do.

Our prayer lives are most important, in order that we hear his personal call for our part in the mission. We find out what our gifts are. We are always led by the Spirit.

And we always do mission cruciformly. We are here to serve the world. We are to be humble. We are to take up crosses. We are to be God's people emulating the Master Jesus and taking our part in his mission.

The mission will end when God, Father, Son, and Spirit, are satisfied that the good news has penetrated the nations to God's satisfaction (Matt 24:14; Mark 13:10). Then, Jesus will return, and the final work of restoration will be completed. We will be as we are created to be, and the world will be liberated from its bondage to decay (Rom 8:21). Heaven and earth will merge, evil vanquished, and we will live forever in the new heavens and earth (Rev 21–22).

Perhaps then our mission will be complete. Or will it? What does the God of universes have in store for us? Only time will tell. In the meantime, "go and make disciples from all nations" (Matt 28:19).

7

Chapter Seven: The Jerusalem Church

This chapter digs into the amazing church of Jerusalem drawing lessons particularly from Acts 1 to 8 for us on how we might reimagine doing church today.

More Detail

Keown, *Discovering the New Testament*, Vol 1, ch. 10.

Suggested Bible Readings

Acts 1–8

Introduction

As has been noted, Acts is the second part of Luke's narrative. This is the wonderful thing about Luke's writings—we not only have a brilliant narrative of Jesus' life, but we get to see how those who were with him lived it out. We learn so much from their lives.

It begins with Jesus telling the disciples that "you will

receive power when the Holy Spirit has come upon you, and you will be my witnesses in Jerusalem, and in all Judea and Samaria, and to the end of the earth" (Acts 1:8). This sets the agenda for Acts. Roughly speaking, part one of Acts occurs in Jerusalem (Acts 1:1–8:4). Part two is based in Judea and Samaria (Acts 8–11). Part three is to the ends of the earth (Acts 12–28). It ends in ad 61, not with part three complete, but with Paul in the centre of the Roman world, Rome, preaching and teaching the Kingdom (Acts 28:31). The implication is that part three will go on as the gospel continues to work its way beyond the Mediterranean rim where it is planted. When the mission is complete, Jesus will return as he left (Acts 1:11). In the meantime, we continue the work.

This chapter will focus on the Jerusalem Church as described in Acts 1–8 in three parts: worship, inner life, and mission. The account of the Jerusalem Church seems intentionally given not only to tell the story of the spread of the gospel but to inspire us to see what church can be if we live as obediently as they did.

The Jerusalem Church: Its Worship

The first Christians were utterly dedicated to living obediently. They had no idea of an unchurched faith. To believe in Jesus meant to belong to the local Christian community. Hence, they gathered together daily and in unity (e.g. Acts 1:12–13; 2:1, 42; 3:1; 4:23–31). They met daily at the Temple, participating in Israel's prayer life and worship without engaging in sacrifices (Jesus had come!) (Acts 2:46).

As they met, they were filled with awe toward God (Acts 2:43). They praised God together (Acts 2:46). They prayed together a lot (esp. Acts 1:14; 2:42)! These prayers saw amazing results including the right people being moved into leadership such as Judas' replacement Matthias, and the appointment of the Seven (Acts 1:15–26; 6:1–6). There were many signs and wonders performed including people seeking healing by Peter's shadow (esp. Acts 2:43; 5:12–16). There were huge numbers of people converted. We also see the inner life of the church strengthened, with people sharing their possessions in a radical way. For Luke, there is a definite link between prayer and God's resultant action—renewal begins in prayer (esp. Acts 4:23–5:16).

They did not just meet together at the Temple. They broke bread together, which likely including having meals in each other's homes during which they celebrated the Lord's Supper and remembered Christ's death (Acts 2:42, 46).

They focused on God's word and learning from the apostles (Acts 2:42). They were determined to be obedient to Christ's teaching and example, even if they were persecuted (e.g. Acts 4:19–20; 5:29).

A huge emphasis was to live by the Spirit, promised by Jesus before his ascension, and given bountifully across the narrative of Acts (Acts 2:1–4). They also baptised new converts (e.g. Acts 2:38, 41).

The first Christians sought to take seriously the greatest of commandments: love the Lord your God with everything you have (Luke 10:27). This worship life began in a very Jewish way, likely patterned on the Synagogue as they met at the Temple. This would mean that they sang the Psalms and prayed many of the prayers of Judaism, like the Shema. They would have created their own liturgical elements to go with their worship. We see potential hymns embedded in the NT which may have been written in this time (e.g. Phil

2:6–11; Eph 5:14). Their desire was to convert their people to Christ in these contexts. Over time they were driven out of the Jewish settings and worshiped in homes.

The Jerusalem Church: Its Inner life

Not only was the early Jerusalem church a worshiping community, but they were very dedicated to one another in a way that few churches today can match. We are deeply challenged to seek to be more like them in this.

Mentioned above is their commitment to gather daily at the Temple and to meet together in one another's homes. They ate together, worshiped together, prayed together, celebrated communion together, and grew as a community. They were very committed to one another. They made decisions together in prayer and meetings (e.g. Acts 1:12–26).

Acts 2:42–47 is a rich summary of this shared life devoted to fellowship/*koinōnia* (Acts 2:42). The term is used widely in Greek writings of a range of partnerships, whether marriage, business, and in other shared life contexts. It becomes an important term across the NT to refer to partnership and fellowship.

Aside from the shared worship activities already referenced, it is important to take careful note of their fellowship over meals (Acts 2:42, 46). In ancient cultures and many today, to eat together is a highly symbolic act of unity. It connotes welcome into the family, the whanau. Indeed, it is at meals that real fellowship is experienced.

Another amazing aspect of this first church was their sharing of all they had. They had "everything in common" (Acts 2:44). They sold possessions and belongings and distributed what was made to those as they were in need

(Acts 2:45–46). This is sometimes called "economic *koinōnia*" by biblical scholars. These Christians clearly took seriously Jesus' teaching in Luke 12:33: "Sell your possessions and give alms." They were dissatisfied with the rich getting richer and the poor poorer. They sought to resolve the discrepancy between the haves and have nots.

More detail is given on this in Acts 4:32–5:11. The church was "one hearted and one souled, and no one said that any of their possessions belonged to him [or her] own, but they had everything in common" (Acts 4:32). There was no needy person in the church (Acts 4:34). People sold land or homes to finance the care of those in material need (Acts 4:35). The prime example is Joseph a Levite from Cyprus who was renamed Barnabas (Son of Encouragement) for his acts of generosity. The church took this all with deadly seriousness as seen in the story of Ananias and Sapphira who made false claims of giving but kept back money for themselves (Acts 5:1–11). We can note too that this outpouring of radical generosity of the rich for the poor flowed from the prayer of Acts 4:29–31 asking for God to move in signs and wonders. What more wonder is there than the rich are prepared to sacrifice their wants for the poor? We are profoundly challenged in a material and consumptive age.

Their commitment to continue their economic *koinōnia* is seen in Acts 6:1–7. By this time, there was a daily distribution of food to the widows attached to the church. Some were Hebrew-speaking Jewish Christians (Hebrews); others were Greek-speaking Jewish Christians (Hellenists). Inadvertently, the Hellenists were being neglected. In a church committed to egalitarian care, the Twelve were understandably unhappy with this. They gathered all the disciples together to resolve the issues—a brilliant example of church decision making (s.a. Acts 15). They took personal responsibility for the failure, identifying the problem as their inability to maintain their core business: preaching and prayer (an important lesson to those summoned to preach and lead). They agreed with the community to pick seven new well regarded, Spirit-filled, wise leaders to ensure the distribution of food (another important lesson on the right kinds of people who we are looking for toward leadership). This would enable the Apostles to focus on prayer and preaching and teaching the word. They chose seven men all with Greek names suggesting that they were Hellenists. One was a convert to Judaism, Nicolaus the proselyte (Acts 8:5). One would become the only person called an evangelist in the NT, Philip, who evangelised Samaria and had a large home with four prophetess daughters in Caesarea Maritima (Acts 8:5–40; 21:8–10). Another would also be a brilliant evangelist who would be Christianity's first martyr, Stephen (Acts 6:8–7:60).

Some sceptical biblical scholars have been critical of the concern for the poor seen in the church. They see it as communism. However, this is not communism. Communism is a state-sponsored non-voluntaristic system whereby the state forces people to pay tax and imposes artificial wage schemes on them. The system of giving at Qumran was much more like communism than Acts. To join the Qumran community, one had to relinquish all personal property and put it in a shared purse. Acts does not demand such a sacrifice. Rather, it speaks of voluntaristic giving, where people gave as they desired. It was heart-giving not forced giving.

Some scholars also criticise the Jerusalem church because later Paul had to twice collect money for them from other churches to relieve their poverty (Acts 11:26–30; 1 Cor 16:2–4; Rom 15:26–31; 2 Cor 8–9). Yet, it is surely unfair to critique Christians for giving to each other when times are good yet later facing struggles because of their generosity. These things come and go. When this happens, other Christians should move in and support them as Paul does here. In fact, Paul's collections prove the point already made—the early Christians were highly committed to giving to each other in need. So, churches in Turkey and Greece gave to the needy in Jerusalem. This is a glorious example of international economic *koinōnia*. Such things are possible today as richer Christian communities help those that are poorer across the world.

We see here not only the importance of care for the poor but the openness to different cultures. The appointment of the Seven is one of the most important steps in the movement from a monocultural church to an intercultural one. One didn't have to be an apostle or a native Jewish male to be a leader. Leaders could come from Gentile converts or Greek-speaking Jews. Over time, this would broaden further as women are involved in leadership in Acts in keeping with Luke's citation of Joel's prophecy that daughters and female servants shall prophesy (Acts 2:17–18; Joel 2:28–29). This includes Lydia who is the only real candidate for the first leader of the Philippians church (see Acts 16:14–15, 40). Then, there is Priscilla, who is usually named before her husband Aquila in Acts (Acts 18:18, 26 but see Acts 18:2), and who with her husband (and named before him), taught Apollos a better understanding of the faith—a woman teaching a man (Acts 18). We can also note the importance of women in Luke's story of Jesus (esp. Luke 8:1–3; 10:38–42). Later we will discuss the women of Paul's churches reinforcing this.

We must not forget, either, that the writer of Luke-Acts is not a Jew, but a Gentile. This is evidenced in Col 4 where

Paul carefully lists his Jewish co-workers, and Luke is not one. Yet this Luke penned 27% of the NT!

The Jerusalem church shows the way in terms of community care. They cared for each other spiritually and materially. We live in an abundant part of the world. Yet, there is a growing gap between rich and poor (e.g. this Stuff article on inequality in NZ). With the costs of living as they are and the generally frozen wages of Kiwis, those at the bottom are suffering more and more. If we name Jesus as Lord, we cannot merely pray for one another and care for one another in word, we must go further. The wealthy among us need to consider how best we can use our wealth to better the situation of the poor. The answer is in part state-sponsored care, but that is not voluntaristic and accompanied by the love and compassion of Christ. We must work alongside national and local governments and the many Christian organisations that are already doing great work and build stronger church communities in which the rich care for the poor. This is a profound challenge and only likely to become greater.

The Jerusalem Church (Acts 1–8): Mission

Luke gives us glimpses into the quality of the worship and inner life of the Jerusalem Church. In keeping with him telling the story of the spread of the gospel, he gives us even greater insight into their extraordinary commitment to mission.

The two aspects already mentioned, their worship and koinōnia, are no doubt contributing factors to the astonishing growth of the church from 120 (Acts 1:15) to 3000 (Acts 2:41) to 5000 (Acts 4:4) and more. People were likely really attracted by what they saw in the passionate worship of the church and the genuine care they had for their needy (centripetal mission). Yet, as with Jesus, Luke does not present a static view of mission as merely attracting people to the church, he tells a story of a church zealous to continue Jesus' centrifugal mission to the world.

As mentioned earlier, Acts 1:8 sets the agenda for Acts. It speaks of the disciples receiving the Spirit and power to be Jesus' witnesses throughout the world beginning in Jerusalem. We see this in the account of Jerusalem, the first part of Acts.

The Spirit falls at Pentecost (Acts 2:1–4). All receive the Spirit, men and women, young and old. The impact is that they speak in tongues. This is not tongues as a private prayer language to edify oneself (1 Cor 14:2, 4). This is missional tongues, the beginning of the reversal of the confusion of human language at Babel. God brought about this confusion in the OT to limit the spread of evil. Now that Christ and the Spirit have come, he will begin its reversal for the spread of good. The impact of Pentecost is missional – while some write it off as alcoholic rantings, residents and pilgrims from across the whole Roman world are intrigued as they hear their language being spoken spontaneously (Acts 2:4–13).

This is then the launching pad for Peter to evangelise in response to their inquiry, "What does this mean?" (Acts 2:13). Peter then gives a sermon, the first of a number of sermons included in Acts including Peter (Acts 2:14–41; 3:11–26; 4:8–12; 5:29–32; 10:32–43), Stephen (Acts 7:1–60), and Paul (Acts 13:13–52; 14:15–17; 17:22–31; 22:1–21; 23:1–6; 24:10–21; 26:1–29). These are all generated by moments of opportunity. They all focus on God and Jesus yet are quite diverse in content depending on the context. Some are very Jewish (esp. Peter [Acts 2–4. 10], Stephen [Acts 7], and Paul's sermon in Acts 13). Others in Gentile situations are very different, focusing in a different way on God's work in the world (Acts 14; 17). A number of them include snippets of testimony, and Paul's messages in Acts 22–26 are all effectively testimonies. We get an extraordinary insight into the proclamation of the early church in these messages.

The disciples were utterly devoted to evangelism. They were indeed powerful witnesses, by the Spirit. This began in the Temple in Solomon's Colonnade as they met every day, speaking in public that people could hear the gospel (Acts 2:46; 3:1–26; 5:12–14).

A great example of their courage and commitment is Peter and John who refuse to be silenced by the Sanhedrin, even when flogged and imprisoned. Their response is that they must obey God and speak of what they have seen and heard (Acts 4:20; 5:29). When the Christians are driven out of Jerusalem by Paul's persecution, they preached the gospel wherever they went (Acts 8:4).

The key to their mission was the Spirit who leads the mission. Pentecost directly leads to the first great missionary encounter (Acts 2). The healing of the disabled man at the Temple leads to the second (Acts 3). Imprisonment leads to the messages of Acts 4 and 5 and trials lead to the messages of Acts 7 and chs. 22–26. There is an amazing period of evangelistic success that follows their prayer to God in Acts 4:29 for the Lord to "look upon their threats and grant to your slaves to speak your word with great boldness, while you stretch out your hand to heal, and signs and wonders are performed through the name of your holy servant Jesus." This is followed by them evangelising boldly (Acts 4:31), signs and wonders performed (Acts 5:12), and multitudes coming for healing, even as a result of Peter's shadow falling on them (Acts 5:15).

Persecution plays an important role, consistent with the view across the NT that bad situations and opposition are allowed by God and used for his purposes (e.g. Rom 8:28). In the first phase of the church, the focus was on the conversion of Jews. One may even be critical of the church for failing to look beyond itself to the Gentile world in this period. Whether this is fair or not, the persecution of Saul is the catalyst for the evangelisation of the world beyond Judea. Infuriated with Stephen and the Christians, the young Pharisee launched an assault on the church. He drove out of Jerusalem all except the apostles (Acts 8:1–3). However, this only caused the mission to gain momentum as all those who went shared Christ (Acts 8:4). This included Philip who took the gospel to the "loathed" Samaritans (Acts 8:5–40) and others who took the gospel to Greeks in Syrian Antioch (Acts 11:19–20). Eventually, God would call the one and the same Saul, renamed Paul, to lead his mission to the world (Acts 13:1–3).

Our mission is not just evangelism, although that is very much included. Signs and wonders were very important. No doubt after the radical healing of the disabled beggar, more and more came for healing (Acts 3:1–9). This is also seen when the crowds come to be healed by the apostles and Peter's shadow (Acts 5:12–16).

While there is no evidence that they took their economic *koinōnia* directly to the world to try and solve its poverty issues, there is no doubt that where contact was made, they were extremely generous. As noted, this would also have been a great attraction point. Indeed, in the first phase, the church enjoyed the favour of all the people (Acts 2:47). Some no doubt came to experience healing and provision (Acts 2:43–45).

Those of us who are in ministry should spend a great deal of time considering the life of the Jerusalem community. We see how those on the ground with Jesus sought to live out his teaching. We are inspired afresh to worship God with all we have, to form communities that truly reflect the ideals of God's reign and engage in mission in our communities to the ends of the earth. The story goes on and we must continue it.

8

Chapter Eight: Paul's Life and Mission

In this chapter, the focus is Paul, the named author of thirteen NT letters and the dominant figure in the second half of Acts. Understanding Paul is crucial to grasping the message of the New Testament.

More Detail

Keown, *Discovering the New Testament*, Vol 2, Ch. 1, 15.

Suggested Bible Readings

Acts 7:54–8:4

Acts 9:1–31

Acts 13–28

Gal 1:11–2:14

Paul's Life and Mission: A Summary of his life and mission journeys

Paul is a huge figure in the NT. His writings make up 23% of the NT, and his life dominates a quarter of Luke's writings. So, all in all, around 40% of the NT story is concerned with Paul in one way or another. As such, it is extremely important to get a good basic feel for the life of Paul. This is done by piecing together material from his letters and Luke's account of his life.

Paul was likely born in the first decade of the first century, not long after Jesus. Tradition has it that his family was from Gischala in Galilee and had been taken as prisoners of war to Tarsus. He was raised in Tarsus, an important city in Cilicia (SE Turkey), which was famous for Stoic philosophy. He was then raised in the Diaspora and knew the Greco-Roman culture well. He learned Greek. However, he is clear that he was raised as a passionate Hebrew (Phil 3:4–5), a brilliant young man advanced in Judaism from an early age (Gal 1:14). This means he knew Israel's story through and through. He also had open access to Synagogues and the freedom to teach. This becomes important in his mission.

He was also a Roman citizen. A Jew became a Roman citizen as a gift from the Roman authorities, through purchasing it, or through being born from a family which already has Roman citizenship. Unlike the Roman Tribune who had paid for his citizenship, Paul was in the latter category—he was born a citizen (Acts 22:28). This means his parents or others before them in his family had purchased or had received citizenship after being set free from slavery. This gave Paul some important rights, most especially the ability to move freely, avoid floggings (most of the time, e.g. Acts 16:22–23), freedom from crucifixion, and the capacity to appeal to Caesar (Acts 25:11).

Paul was a tentmaker (e.g. Acts 18:3). We are not sure where it started. Cilicia was famous for cilicium (goat's hair) with which people made a range of items. He may have learned the trade from his father. He may have developed his skill as a Pharisee, for it was not uncommon for Pharisees to have a trade. In the wider contexts, he likely worked with leather. This became a point of controversy in Paul's life. First, his stained hands meant that he was easily identified as someone beneath the upper classes where no Roman would do such a thing. Secondly, and more importantly, Paul used his tentmaking to support himself in his ministry to avoid being manipulated by donors (esp. in Corinth), being a burden (e.g. 1 Thess 2:9) and being seen as a peddler of the gospel (2 Cor 2:17).

Paul may have been married in his pre-Christian life but if so, he was no longer so in his ministry. There are two reasons for this. First, as a young Pharisees he would have been expected to marry. Second, the word he uses in 1 Cor 7:8 concerning his state is *agamos*, which means widower. It is balanced in this text with the term "widow" and some scholars read it this way. Whether he was married prior, all evidence suggests that he was single in his life of Christian ministry. If he was previously married, his wife has either left him after his conversion (cf. 1 Cor 7:15–16) or died.

As a young man he was taken to Jerusalem where he studied to become a Pharisee under the Great Gamaliel. Gamaliel was a great Pharisee, some of whose sayings are still around today, and who was a moderate where Christians were concerned, arguing against using violence against them (Acts 5:33–40). Paul then became a Pharisee. This meant he was one of Israel's leaders, brilliantly skilled in OT interpretation, passionate for Judaism and its traditions. Unlike Gamaliel, he was no moderate. He was enraged by the Christians and sought to destroy the movement. He was prepared to drag them into prison and vote for their deaths if need be (Acts 7:58–8:4; 26:10). With the support of the High Priest, Paul travelled to Damascus to destroy the church (Acts 9, 22, 26). He was a passionate worshiper of God but rejected Jesus.

En route to Damascus, Jesus appeared to him. Paul was blinded and came to believe in Jesus along with his love for Yahweh. His worldview was turned upside down. Jesus was the Messiah, the Son of God, and Lord, even though he had been crucified! He had been wrong about the Christians. He became one of them. The same zeal he had had for God was now applied to God and his Son.

He was also commissioned by God to lead his mission to the non-Jewish world, the apostle to the Gentiles (Rom 11:13). Acts 13–28 is mainly focused on his missions to the Gentiles. These are also referenced through his letters. Some people put together the life of Paul purely from the letters, arguing that Acts is unreliable. However, a number of scholars have powerfully argued that Luke was a careful ancient historian and his chronology can be trusted. As such, we can create a harmony of Paul's letters and Acts and piece together the main threads.

Arabia

It is traditional to talk about the three great missionary journeys of Paul and his final trip to Rome. Some also mentioned a fourth journey after Rome. Yet, this neglects the earlier phases of Paul's life in which he engaged in mission before his first mission from Antioch.

In Galatians 1:17, we are told Paul's first mission was to Arabia. This is the Kingdom extending south into the Arabian Peninsula from Damascus. It is likely that there were two emphases on this journey. First, Paul would have spent a lot of time in prayer and study working out the theology that flowed from his experience of Christ's self-revelation to him. He may have visited ancient Mt Sinai during this period of time. Second, Paul would have preached in the cities and synagogues of Damascus (see Acts 9:19–22) and Arabia beginning his mission to the Gentiles.

This phase of mission is not mentioned in Acts, but that is not a big issue, as Luke does not include everything Paul did in his account of his life.

Jerusalem Visit 1: Meeting Barnabas, Peter, and James

In Gal 1:18–19, Paul went to Jerusalem for fifteen days, a period in which he met with Peter and also met Jesus' brother James. According to Acts, he also met Barnabas and engaged in evangelism but was then driven from the city (Acts 9:26–31). This is a critical time of learning, first-hand, the accounts of Jesus' life and ministry.

Syria and Cilicia

In Gal 1:21, Paul mentions his mission work in Syria and Cilicia. This includes mission work in Antioch and his home city of Tarsus which was in Cilicia. Luke in Acts 9:30 agrees that Paul went to Tarsus. Syria is important in Acts as the base of Paul's operations as he goes on the three great Antiochian mission journeys.

Jerusalem Visit 2: The Famine Visit

Some scholars consider Gal 2:1–10 an account of Paul's visit to Jerusalem to discuss circumcision in Acts 15. Others argue that the Galatians account aligns better with Acts 11:30 where Paul travelled to Jerusalem to deliver a monetarymoney as a result of famines. It is difficult to decide between the two as circumcision and a concern for the poor are both mentioned in Gal 2 (vv. 3, 10). However, there is no mention of the later Jerusalem Collection in Galatians, Barnabas fits an earlier date, and aligning Gal 2 with Acts 11 fits better with Luke's chronology and so is to be preferred. Hence, there were two motivations for his visit in around ad 46—to bring money to the struggling Jerusalem Christians and to ensure that Paul's gospel was consistent with the apostolic gospel of Peter and the Twelve. This is important before Paul and Barnabas set off on their great Antiochian missions.

Paul's First Antiochian Mission

Acts 13–14 include an account of Paul's first Antiochian mission. As the NET Bible map below shows, Paul and Barnabas travelled from Antioch, by sea to Cyprus, through the island, landed in Asia (mod. Turkey) in Pamphylia, travelled north to Pisidia and east to Lycaonia, evangelising in the main centres.

The map of this trip can be accessed here: http://classic.net.bible.org/map.php?map=jp1.

During the trip, Mark abandoned Paul and Barnabas for Jerusalem, an event that led to a schism between Paul and Barnabas before the second Antiochian mission.

Jerusalem Visit 3: The Jerusalem Council

After Paul's return from his first mission west of his home region, other Judaising gospel preachers attacked his new churches and the church in Syrian Antioch, demanding that new converts Judaise by being circumcised, and obey the law of Moses, for salvation and inclusion in God's people (Acts 15:1; Galatians). Paul wrote Galatians to his churches, warning them that if they go down that path, they will be cut off from justification before God. He also travelled with Barnabas to Jerusalem to discuss with the Jerusalem leaders who had it right—a law-free gospel (Paul) or the Judaising gospel. After much debate, Paul, Barnabas, Peter, and James, supported by those there, agreed that Paul had it right—new converts were justified by faith alone and did not need to yield to the requirements of Jewish Torah including its boundary markers. A letter was drafted asking Gentiles to be considerate of Jewish cultural customs to ensure unity and ongoing Jewish mission (Acts 15). Silas and Judas Barsabbas were chosen to take the letter to Antioch.

Paul's Second Antiochian Mission: Macedonia and Achaia

After returning to Antioch, Paul set out again to visit the churches he had planted and to push the gospel further west. As noted above, Barnabas and Paul's conflict led to Barnabas and Mark going to Cyprus and Paul taking Silas with him. Paul no doubt wanted to carry the letter from the Jerusalem Council to the Galatian churches to add support to his earlier letter to ensure that they did not succumb to the Judaisers (Acts 16:4). This map shows his route: http://classic.net.bible.org/map.php?map=jp2.

While in Lystra, Timothy was added to Paul's team (Acts 16:1–3). Paul had him circumcised, not to Judaise him, but because he was a Jew already and this would enable Timothy to enter synagogues and Temple to share Christ with Paul.

Paul also planned to push further west planting churches. He wanted to go into Asia Minor where Ephesus was the capital or Bithynia in northern Asia Minor near the Black Sea. However, the Spirit had other ideas and through a vision guided him and his team to Macedonia (Acts 16:6–10). Luke joined Paul for this portion of the trip (the we-passage begins Acts 16:10).

Paul then moved through Macedonia planting churches in Philippi, Thessalonica, and Berea (Acts 16:11–17:15) and was persecuted in each city. He then went alone to Athens where he gave his famous Areopagus message, and established a small church (Acts 17:16–34). He then ministered in Corinth for eighteen months, establishing a church there (Acts 18:1–17). He travelled back by ship stopping at Ephesus where he left Priscilla and Aquila behind.

Jerusalem Visit 4: Passing Through

Luke records that Paul landed in Caesarea (Acts 18:22). He may have gone to Jerusalem again, although we cannot be sure.

Paul's Third Antiochian Mission: The Jerusalem Collection (ad 55–57)

Paul then returned to Antioch (Acts 18:22) and then returned again through the regions of the first churches he had planted on his first Antiochian mission (Acts 18:23).

This link takes you to a map that shows the path he took: http://classic.net.bible.org/map.php?map=jp3.

We know from the letters that his purpose was not merely to strengthen his churches but to gather money for the second Jerusalem Collection. Luke does not mention this until Acts 24:17. This has puzzled scholars who think it may be because when he returned to Jerusalem after the trip, his prayers that the collection will be well-received in Rom 15:26–31 were not answered, and they were not. However, Acts 21:17–20 indicates the converse. Aside from the reference to the collection in Romans, the Corinthian letters confirm that collecting gifts for Jerusalem was the core reason for the journey (1 Cor 16:1–4; 2 Cor 8–9). Aside from Timothy, Titus, and Luke who all travelled with Paul at some point or another or were sent on errands, he also gathered representatives from the churches to join his team and support the collection (Acts 20:4).

Aside from strengthening believers and churches and gathering the collection, Paul also stopped for three years in Ephesus. There he established the church and there was an extraordinary time of mission success. He led a period of intense training of disciples in the lecture hall of Tyrannus from which Ephesus experienced a spiritual revival and the whole region of Asia Minor was evangelised (Acts 19:9–20). No doubt the churches Peter addresses in 1 Pet 1:1 and the seven churches of Revelation (Rev 2–3) were planted in this time. The churches of Colossae and Laodicea were also established through the work of Epaphras who was probably one of Paul's key co-workers in Ephesus (Col 1:7; 2:1; 4:12).

Paul also experienced terrible persecution when the gospel's penetration began to affect the sales of idols. A riot occurred and Paul was brought before the authorities (Acts 19:21–40).

Paul wrote the Corinthian letters in this time in Ephesus. There is an earlier lost letter to Corinth which was to some extent misunderstood by the Corinthians and part of the reason for 1 Corinthians is to clarify its meaning (1 Cor 5:9–13). 1 Corinthians confirms he faced some serious suffering in Ephesus (1 Cor 15:32). 2 Corinthians also confirms that Paul experienced terrible persecution in Ephesus (2 Cor 1:8–11). It also tells us at some point he travelled from Ephesus to Corinth, a very painful visit (as evidenced in 2 Corinthians 2:1; 13:1). Some consider that the letters of Colossians, Philemon, Ephesians (if a general letter), and Philippians were written in this period from Ephesus. However, there is no concrete evidence Paul was in prison in Ephesus and tradition consistently places these in his Roman incarceration.

He returned to Ephesus and then travelled through Macedonia collecting money for the collection. Again, he suffered greatly (2 Cor 7:5–6). He then travelled to Corinth for three months (Acts 20:3). During this time, he wrote Romans. He planned then to travel for Syria, but, due to a death threat, travelled to Macedonia again and, with the collection and retinue, struck out for Jerusalem. The most memorable events of this trip were the resurrection of Eutychus in Troas (Acts 20:7–10), and the meeting with the elders of the Ephesus' church in Miletus where Paul delivered his great pastoral sermon (Acts 20:17–38).

Jerusalem Visit 5: Prison

As noted above, Paul was welcomed first in Caesarea at the home of Philip the evangelist and then by the Jerusalem church which was expanding greatly. He was encouraged to fulfil a vow of purity at the Temple, which Paul duly did. However, he was recognised and accused of bringing an unclean Gentile into the Temple (Acts 21:1–36). He was seized by the crowd who tried to kill him, only to be rescued at the last minute by a Roman tribune and soldiers, who arrested and bound him. Paul was then permitted to speak to the crowds, which he did, only for his message to end in chaos as he spoke of his mission to the Gentiles (Acts 21:37–22:31). He was saved from the crowd and the next day appeared before the Sanhedrin (Acts 22:22–23:11). A plot against his life was uncovered by his relatives, and he was sent to Caesarea (Acts 23:12–35).

Prison in Caesarea (ad 58–59)

Paul spent two years in a Caesarean prison (Acts 24–26). Some think he wrote the letter to the Philippians in this period. However, few agree. Paul faced a series of trials in this time before the governors Felix and Festus, and Herod Agrippa II. With Jews still seeking his life, Paul ultimately exercised his citizen's right to appeal to Caesar. This was accepted and Paul was sent to Rome.

Prison in Rome (ad 60–61)

Acts 27 is the amazing account of the journey of Paul from Caesarea Maritima to Rome including a shipwreck on

Malta, evangelism on the island, and then transport to Rome.

The path of this journey can be viewed here: http://classic.net.bible.org/map.php?map=jp4.

Acts ends in Ch. 28 with Paul in Rome preaching the gospel from his own rented accommodation. This level of liberty shows that his incarceration was initially pretty loose, and that Paul was at this point seen as little threat. In this period if lighter incarceration, Paul likely wrote Colossians, Ephesians, and Philemon, which were delivered by Tychicus.

Harsher Imprisonment in Rome (c. ad 62–63)

Philippians 1, where Paul's life is very much under threat, indicates that Paul's situation worsened sometime after the end of Acts. This fits with Christianity becoming more of a threat to the empire as it spread. In this period, Nero was married to a God-worshiping Gentile woman (see Josephus. *Ant.* 20.195), Poppaea Sabina. She may also have made Nero more aware of the threat of Paul. Anyway, while some consider Paul died in this period, indications are that he gained release as he expected (Phil 1:25–26).

A Final Mission Journey? (c. ad 64–66)

If Paul did gain release, he might have travelled to Spain, a desire he had expressed to the Romans (Rom 15:24, 28). However, the evidence he got there is very weak. More likely, he went east again, visiting Colossae (Phlm 22), Miletus (2 Tim 4:21), possibly Ephesus (1 Tim 1:3), Troas

(2 Tim 4:14), Crete (Tit 1:5), Macedonia (1 Tim 1:3), and Nicopolis (Epirus, western Balkans) (Tit 3:12).

Such a journey could have looked like the map viewed at this link: https://www.bible-history.com/maps/images/acts-pauls-final-visits.gif.

However, this is all suppositional.

Death in Rome (c. ad 66–67)

Tradition supports that Paul and Peter died under Nero sometime after the Neronian persecution and before the emperor's suicide 9 June ad 68. It is held that Peter was crucified upside down whereas as a citizen, Paul could not be crucified and so was beheaded.

Paul's Life and Mission: Core Principles of his Mission Strategy

Just as Acts 1–8 lays down core principles of what it means to do church, we gain tremendous insight into the basics of mission from Paul's missionary strategy. In fact, it is fair to say that contemporary mission is shaped more by Paul than any other figure, aside from Jesus himself. Here, I will assume that Paul did have a strategy, which it seems obvious he did, and outline its main points.

Led by the Spirit

Paul's mission was Spirit-guided. His first Antiochian mission was sparked in worship as the Spirit spoke: "Now, set apart for me Barnabas and Saul for the work I have called them to do" (Acts 13:2); they were "sent out by the

Holy Spirit" (Acts 13:4). He was guided through the mission as well. The decision of the Jerusalem Council was "great to the Holy Spirit" (Acts 15:28). A clear example is Acts 16:6–10 when he wanted first to go to Asia Minor and then to Bithynia, but the Spirit forbade him. He was guided to Macedonia by a vision. Paul had other spiritual experiences that guided his mission. God spoke to him in Corinth, telling him to keep speaking out for he was with him and he would not be harmed (Acts 18:9–10). In Ephesus, he "resolved in the Spirit" to travel to Jerusalem via Macedonia and Achaia and then Rome (Acts 19:21). He went to Jerusalem "constrained by the Spirit" (Acts 20:22). The Spirit testifies to him that he would face imprisonment and persecution in every city ahead (Acts 20:23). Agabus by the Spirit warned him that the Jews of Jerusalem would bind him and hand him over to the Gentiles (Acts 21:11). In Acts 23:10, the Lord spoke to him telling him to have courage for as he has given witness in Jerusalem, he would also in Rome. On the ship heading for Rome, an angel spoke to him telling him not to fear, for he would stand before Caesar and that God had granted him all those sailing on the ship (Acts 27:23–25). In the letters, Paul speaks of "gospel doors" opened by God which caused him to remain in situations (1 Cor 16:9; 2 Cor 2:12; Col 4:3). While Paul had a strategy, it was subject to change on the leading of God by the Spirit, as well as by angels, direct revelation, visions, opportunity, or prophecy.

Moving west toward Rome and Beyond

Overall, Paul moved west in his mission journeys. His vision was first to plant churches from Jerusalem to Illyricum, a city on the very west of Greece, just across the

Adriatic from Rome. When he writes Romans, he has completed that work (Rom 15:19). His plan was then to travel to Rome, use it as a base, and then take the gospel to Spain, where it was not yet established (Rom 15:24, 28). Acts ends with him in Rome, the gospel thoroughly established through Pentecost pilgrims (Acts 2:10) and reinforced by his own ministry (Acts 28:30–31).

Main Urban Centres

One of the real differences between the missions of Jesus and Paul is that aside from Jerusalem for festivals, Jesus rarely ministered in the major cities (Sepphoris, Tiberias), focusing on the smaller towns and rural areas. Conversely, Paul focused on the cities. His strategy was to plant churches in the main centres in each region. From there the gospel could radiate out into the city and region. A great example is the Thessalonians who heard the gospel, and then the word of the Lord sounded forth from them into their region Macedonia, south into Achaia, and elsewhere (1 Thess 1:5–8). Paul was confident the Spirit would continue the work begun in each church and expand its influence.

Gentiles

Paul's specific call was to the Gentiles. He is an example of someone God directs to a specific people-group. This began at his conversion where Ananias tells him he is Christ's instrument to carry God's name before the Gentiles (Acts 9:14). He is the apostle to the Gentiles (Rom 11:13). This call is recognised by the Jerusalem leadership alongside Peter's call to lead the mission to Jews (Gal 2:7–9). It is not uncommon for people with a missionary calling to have a specific call to a people group.

Team Ministry

Neither Jesus nor Paul were lone ranger evangelists. They worked with others. Jesus called the 12 and 72 and sent them out. Paul had a whole raft of co-workers across his career. The key ones were Barnabas (Acts 13–15), Timothy (Acts 16 onwards, and in many letters including 1, 2 Timothy), Titus (esp. 2 Cor 7–8 and Titus), Silas (also Silvanus, esp. Acts 15–18; s.a. 1 Thess 1:1; 2 Thess 1:1), and Priscilla (also Prisca) and Aquila (Acts 18; Rom 16:3–5; 1 Cor 16:19; 2 Tim 4:19). A range of other co-workers are mentioned (e.g. Rom 16; Phil 4:2–3; Col 4; Phlm 1, 24). Paul worked with others and his passion was training them and releasing them into ministry. He believed in partnership in mission (Phil 1:5). He believed in the church as a body, all parts with different gifts, working in harmony like a great sports team. True Christian ministry is team ministry. It is collaborative. It is relational. One person is not enough. On our own, we will be eaten alive by the devil who roams like a roaring lion seeking prey (1 Pet 5:8).

Evangelising the Lost

You don't have to be a rocket scientist to recognise that Paul was an evangelist. It was core to his ministry. He had a strong sense of compulsion and obligation to preach the gospel to the lost (Rom 1:14–15; 1 Cor 9:16). He believed that the preaching of the gospel brought the opportunity for salvation as people heard, believed, and received the seal and deposit of the Spirit (Rom 10:14–17; Eph 1:13–14). Hence, he sought to win people to Christ at every opportunity. His life was governed by a soteriological motivation; namely, that everything he did in the presence of others would bring them to faith or reinforce their faith (cf. 1 Cor 10:31–33).

Synagogues

To achieve his strategy of converting the world, in every city Paul went to, he sought first to convert the people of the synagogues. Synagogues for Diaspora Jews were all over the Roman world. In some cities such as Philippi, there were insufficient Jewish men to form a synagogue (ten men were needed). Yet, he still began there when he could. This made sense for a Jewish Pharisee who commanded great respect among Jews. In each synagogue he also found some God-worshipers there to share Christ with (Acts 16:13). He sought to convince his hearers that Jesus is the Christ they long for (e.g. Acts 17:2–3). He did this because he believed that the gospel should be offered first to the Jews and then to the Gentiles (Rom 1:16). If a Jew was converted, he would have a ready leader, someone who was grounded in the story of God in the Scriptures. As noted previously, there were also Gentiles who had become Jews (Acts 13:43) and those with interest in Judaism who worshiped at the synagogues, people like the devout women of Pisidian Antioch (Acts 13:50), some in Thessalonica and Berea (Acts 17:4, 11), Titius Justus of Corinth (Acts 18:7), or the Asian Lydia in Philippi (Acts 16:14). These too would know God's story and quickly come to grips with Jesus the Christ.

Open-Air Preaching

It is commonly thought Paul preached in the centres of each town like a pagan philosopher. However, this is rightly questioned by many scholars. As a Jew it is unlikely. Further, he had dirty hands from tentmaking, meaning he was of lower status. However, there is some evidence he may have spoken and healed in public in Lystra (Acts 14:9). He shared Christ in the open air outside Philippi, but this was a specifically Jewish gathering, not an open public event (Acts 16:13). He also mingled among philosophers, debating Epicureans and Stoics, at the famous Stoa in Athens (Acts 17:17). Yet, this passage does not say he preached openly. His message at the Areopagus was an invitation to a philosophical guild. If indeed early Christians did preach openly in the cities of the Roman world, they clearly only did so once. They were shut down as Jews and pagans reacted against their subversive message. We see the same pattern earlier in Jerusalem. They began openly teaching in the Temple courts (Solomon's Colonnade). They were persecuted and eventually shut out completely. Rather than open-air preaching, the gospel spread through social networks and preaching occurred in specifically Christian gatherings in homes (see below).

Homes

The home was no doubt the place where the gospel spread the most in the early Christian movement. Paul says in Acts 20:20 that he taught the Ephesians in public (the lecture hall of Tyrannus) and "from house to house." After Lydia's conversion, Paul went to her home (Acts 16:15). When the Philippian jailor came to Christ, Paul and Silas were taken into his home and the household baptised (Acts 16:25–34). Similarly, Crispus' whole household was converted in Acts 18:8. Furthermore, many in Corinth heard the gospel and believed as a result of the churches established in the homes of Titius Justus and Crispus. This speaks of the church founded in family groups, which were more than mum, dad, and the kids, but included slaves and clients. Then, others would come to hear the gospel at Christian gatherings and meals. The gospel was penetrating the city through family and social networks.

A Lecture Hall

In Ephesus, Paul rented a lecture hall in the siesta hours (11 am – 4 pm) and taught disciples—a kind of Bible college (Acts 19:9). From there, disciples like Epaphras took the gospel into Asia Minor (Col 1:7). This indicates that Paul took every opportunity to share Christ.

Court and Prison

Paul was often in front of officials, defending himself and the faith. He also spent years in prisons. This included prison in Philippi (Acts 16:16–34), going before Gallio in Corinth (Acts 18:12–17), and before the Ephesian town clerk in a riot (Acts 19:23–41). Paul was in custody for years in Jerusalem, Caesarea, and Rome (Acts 21:27–28:31). While I am sure Paul would rather have been free to move as he willed, Paul did not see this as anything negative. Rather, he took every opportunity to share his faith. In prison settings, he asked his converts to pray for more effective evangelism (Eph 6:18–20; Col 4:2–3). He was delighted that

the gospel is advancing among soldiers and others in Rome
(Phil 1:12–18a).

The Workplace

As noted in the previous section, Paul was a tentmaker.
Scholars have recognised that the ancient workplace was
also a place of religious discourse. In the ancient Greco-
Roman world, philosophical and religious conversations
were not off-limits. It was not yet completely forbidden
to share Christ. Often a shop adjoined a home, and with
homes used for ancient churches, the line between work,
home, and the church was not as clear as in our cultures
where we live somewhere and go to work and church in
other places. The world was more close-knit without the
kind of transportation we have. As such, it is likely Paul,
Priscilla, and Aquila (Acts 18:2–3) shared Christ with those
who came to buy, or repair tents and other objects made
with cilicium or leather.

Signs and Wonders

Paul not only preached and taught. Like Jesus and other
preachers of the NT (e.g. Peter, Acts 3:1–9; 5:15; Stephen,
Acts 6:8; Philip, Acts 8:6–7), God did signs and wonders
through him among those he evangelised. These are
mentioned at the Jerusalem Council and vindicate that God
is working among the uncircumcised (Acts 15:12). Examples
include the blinding of Elymas on Cyrus (Acts 13:8–11),
miracles in Derbe (Acts 14:3), the healing of the crippled
man in Lystra (Acts 14:8), the exorcism of the young slave
girl in Philippi (Acts 16:18), extraordinary miracles

including healings through Paul's tentmaking cloths in Ephesus (Acts 19:11), Paul's recovery from a snake bite (Acts 28:3–6), and healing of Publius in Malta (Acts 28:7–10). In the letters, miracles are an integral part of his ministry alongside preaching (Rom 15:19). They are evidence that one need not be circumcised to experience the work of the Spirit (Gal 3:5). Prayer for miracles then is an essential aspect of apostolic ministry (2 Cor 12:12).

The ancient world believed strongly in the supernatural, whether the gods, goddesses, demons, angels, fate, and a range of other spiritual forces. As Christianity went to each place, there were often spiritual clashes, and demonstrations of spiritual power were a part of the expectation. They also had nothing like our medical options and were utterly dependent on the supernatural in many instances. They were thus open in a way most moderns are not. Yet, it is undeniable that Christianity is not just about preaching and teaching, but prayer and spiritual power. We need to rediscover this without flashy shows, manipulation, and false claims.

Planting Churches

Paul was not just about saving souls, he wanted to plant self-supporting churches in every locale. The goal of mission was the formation of the church. These churches would then replicate themselves. This is organic growth like the multiplication of cells and church reproduction. His work was done from Jerusalem to Illyricum when churches were planted in all the main centres across the region.

Strengthening Christians and Churches

Paul was as obsessed with strengthening existing Christians as evangelism. When he evangelised and planted churches, he also taught them. We see this in his letters where he reminds readers of aspects of his teaching. This includes teaching on the Lord's Supper (1 Cor 11:23), the resurrection (1 Cor 15:3), sexual holiness (1 Thess 4:1–8), eschatology (1 Thess 5:2), living quietly and working for one's own living (2 Thess 3:6), and more generally (Phil 4:9). No doubt it included much more.

He himself visited churches or wanted to do so with the intention of strengthening them (e.g. Acts 15:36; 18:23; Rom 1:11–13; Phil 1:24–26; 2:24; 1 Thess 2:18; 1 Tim 3:14). He sent co-workers, usually Timothy, in his stead to bolster the churches (e.g. 1 Cor 4:16; 16:10; Phil 2:19; 1 Thess 3:2, 6; 1 Tim 1:3). His desire to build up his churches is seen in the letters, which are all written to deepen the faith and commitment of his converts and churches.

He established local leadership in each church (Acts 14:23; 20:17; 1 Tim 4:14; 5:17). 1 Timothy 3:1–13 and Tit 1:5–9 give good instructions for who is appropriate for eldership and deacons. It is likely then that Paul set up groups of elders (or overseers) and deacons in each church (e.g. Phil 1:1). We are not sure of the distinction between the two groups. One of the terms used to describe elders (*episkopos*, "overseer") suggests they had overall oversight of the church. The term "deacon" is from the Greek for serve and suggests that they had a more subordinate serving role. The masculine *diakonos* (deacon) is used to describe Phoebe in Rom 16:1. This suggests she was a deacon of the church in Cenchreae. The substantial influence of Euodia and Syntyche in Philippi may indicate that they are house church leaders, overseers, or deacons (Phil 1:1; 4:2–3). Anyway, the elders were mature Christians who gave lead to the church. There is no idea of an individual church leader in the NT; this came later. The church began with shared leadership. While all elders had to know the word, some had a special role of teaching for which they were paid double, perhaps indicating that elders were paid and the teaching elders receiving more (1 Tim 5:17).

Ephesians 4:11 refers to the five-fold ministry which is not so much about a formal appointment, but charismatic gifts of leadership. The apostle was likely the founder of churches. Prophets were imbued with the gift of prophecy, bringing God's word that edifies, encourages, and comforts God's people (1 Cor 14:3). Evangelists continue the work of mission begun by the apostles, evangelising others. Pastors (shepherds) care for churches as a shepherd cares for his or her flock. The teacher continued the work of teaching disciples in the faith. Their overall role is to equip the church for ministry so that it will grow in new converts and maturity.

Paul's theology of spiritual gifts also includes gifts of leadership. There is the gift of giving lead (*proistēmi*) in Rom 12:8 and a term used of the person holding the helm on a ship (*kybernēsis*) in 1 Cor 12:28.

Finally, we can note that passages like 1 Cor 8, 10; Rom 14–15 are focussed on the strong Christians caring for the weak and doing nothing that will cause them to stumble. We are to bear one another's burdens (Gal 6:2). The mission of the church is to win people to Christ, yes. But it is equally about growing them and caring for them.

Churches Engaged in Mission

Paul did not just plant churches to exist, he planted them to continue the mission of God. They are bodies of Christ, together, and these bodies are to mature and grow in numbers and strength. They are also to support the mission of others.

Prayer Support

This includes prayer support for missionaries. Paul asks for prayer in many of his letters asking that his mission to Jerusalem will be successful so he can go to Rome and Spain (Rom 15:30–32), that he would have the right words as he preaches boldly as God's ambassador (Eph 6:19–20), that God would open doors for the gospel and that he would preach it clearly (Col 4:3–4), that the word may speed through the world and that he is delivered from evil (2 Thess 3:1). Praying for mission and missionaries is a core task of every church.

Financial Support

He envisaged churches supporting mission financially. Hence, his delight that the Philippians have resumed his financial support in Rome (Phil 4:10–19). He believed that churches should support those called to preach the gospel (e.g. 1 Cor 9:1–14; 1 Gal 6:6; Tim 5:17–18). Yet, his letters also show that there is a freedom from control, misunderstanding, and unnecessarily burdening churches in providing for each other in mission. Each mission situation must be assessed to see which is best. Wealthy Christians also provided patronage and hospitality for Paul and others as they travelled, e.g. Phoebe (Rom 16:2) and Philemon (Phlm 22). It is again basic business for churches to support its workers and the wider mission of God. Hence, the importance of Christian giving.

Community and Ethical Witness

Paul envisaged the church giving witness through the quality of its life—its relationships and ethics. For example, he tells the Philippians not to grumble and argue but shine as lights of the world (or stars in the universe), to be blameless, innocent and unblemished children of God (Phil 2:15). The church for Paul is the body of Christ, the Temple of the Spirit, and the family of God in a given context. It is to be shaped by the fruit of the Spirit and by love (Gal 5:22–24; 1 Cor 13). In this way, people will be attracted to the faith by the quality of church life.

Apologetic and Proactive Witness

The church is to continue the work of mission in its community. Mention has been made of the Thessalonians who took the gospel into their region (1 Thess 1:5–8). The Philippians were to stand firm in one Spirit, "contending for the faith of the gospel" continuing the work the co-workers had done with Paul when he was among them (Phil 1:27; 4:2–3). They were to "hold forth the word of life" to their communities (Phil 2:16).

One of the best passages in Paul on this is Col 4:5–6. Following on from Paul's request that the Colossians pray for his ministry of the word (*logos*), he says to them: "Walk in wisdom those from the outside, making the most of every opportunity. Let your gospel-conversation (*logos*) be always in grace, seasoned with salt, so that you may know how you must answer everyone."

Four principles of evangelism are here. First, we are to be wise in the way we act toward outsiders. This means not just doing the same thing on each occasion but acting with wisdom as each situation demands. Second, our gospel sharing (*logos*) is to be gracious, full of the grace of the gospel toward the lost. Third, it is to be seasoned with salt. That is, sharing Christ with flavoursome, winsome, appropriate, enhancing, and upbuilding speech that draws people to Christ. Finally, doing this will enable us to know how to answer the questions raised by outsiders. Paul seems to be saying that if we do the first three, then we will know how to answer people. This sits with 1 Pet 3:15–16 as an excellent text with which to teach appropriate evangelism.

Paul's Life and Mission: The Jerusalem Council (Salvation and Culture)

Mention has been made of the Jerusalem Council in Acts 15. As the apostle to the Gentiles, we have Paul to thank for working out the implications of Christ's coming, and death, for the formation of a new humanity. Paul was a Pharisee and as such, prior to his conversion, he believed that for a person to become one of God's people, a child of Abraham, that person must come under the law of Moses. This meant that men must be circumcised, and men and women must submit to the law. In particular, those laws that demarcated Israel from the Gentile world: Sabbath observance, the cycle of Israel's festivals, pilgrimage and sacrifices in Jerusalem, eating kosher food, eating only with other Jews, and other practices of ritual purity. To be one of God's covenant people one must Judaise, become a Jew. One must do certain works, consequently, creating a theology of salvation by works.

When he came to Christ, he worked through the gospel and concluded that Christ's coming fulfilled the Torah with all its requirements. Jesus did this literally, by never sinning and living perfectly under the law (e.g. 2 Cor 5:21). More to the point, he is the end or culmination of the law (Rom 10:4).

As such, Paul reasoned that a person who comes to Christ no longer needs to fulfil the requirements of the law. Jesus has done this. We place our faith in Jesus, we are included in him, and we are justified by faith, saved, and included in God's people. This is irrespective of culture, gender, age, and status. So, he can say, in Christ Jesus, "there is neither Jew nor Greek, there is neither slave nor free, there is neither male and female, for you are all one in Christ Jesus" (Gal 3:28). A large part of Paul's life and his letters are devoted to this issue.

While Paul worked this through, other early Jewish Christians did not come to this view easily. They were steeped in the law that required circumcision since the time of Abraham (Gen 17; Lev 12:3). Sabbath observance is rooted in creation and in the Ten Commandments (Gen 2:1–3; Exod 20:8–11). Festivals were prescribed in the Law (Lev 23). Food laws were carefully laid out (Lev 11). They couldn't handle the idea that the coming of Jesus ended centuries of ritual and tradition.

It is likely that the Jerusalem Church, up until the gospel reached Syrian Antioch, continued to expect converts to live as Jews. However, when the gospel came to Cornelius' family and the Gentiles in Antioch, it became clear that God was prepared to pour out his Spirit on the uncircumcised (Acts 10:1–11:26).

The question of whether a Christian had to Judaise came to a head after Paul's mission to the Galatian area (Acts 13–14). On his return to Syrian Antioch, Judaising Christians went to his new churches and to Antioch challenging Paul's theology, demanding new uncircumcised converts needed to be circumcised and obey the Mosaic law to be saved (Acts 15:1). Aside from circumcision, Galatians suggests they were particularly concerned with Jews eating with Gentiles (Gal 2:11–14), and calendric observance (Gal 4:10).

Paul went on the offensive, realising that if Judaisers won the day, the gospel would never really grow beyond Judaism as most Gentiles repudiated circumcision and Jewish culture would have to be given precedence over the multiplicity of cultures around the world.

First, he wrote Galatians, a letter which at times is brutal, telling the Galatians to stop messing around with Judaising ideas or they would be cut off from Christ. One is justified by faith and faith alone. If one chooses Judaising, one must keep the whole law, and no one can do it. One must simply believe in Jesus and continue believing with a faith that is sincere.

As previously discussed, the Jerusalem Council reported in Acts 15 saw the matter resolved. There was a sharp dispute, but Paul, Barnabas, Peter, and James the brother of Jesus all agreed that Paul was in the right. A letter was drafted asking Gentiles to show respect to Jewish cultural issues like eating blood and food sacrificed to idols. Otherwise, they must not be required to be circumcised.

While it appears that this was resolved in Acts 15, the issue went on as evidenced by the letter of Romans which continues to reinforce the gospel of grace through faith (s.a. 2 Cor 10–13; Phil 3:2–11; Col 2:16–23; and 1 Tim 1:3–7). The matter came to an end with the fall of Jerusalem in ad 70 after which the pressure from Jews on the church receded.

This issue is the first great theological dispute in the church. They resolved it brilliantly by meeting and working it through.

It is an important issue because it brings two important theological issues to the fore which we need to think about continually. First, if we are justified by works of the law, we are justified by works. No one can perform the works required perfectly. We are then demanding people earn salvation. This is heresy. As Paul says, "For by grace you have been saved through faith. And this is not from yourself; it is the gift of God, not from works, so that no one may boast" (Eph 2:8–9). We are saved by faith to do good works, not by the works (Eph 2:10). By works we work out the salvation we have received by faith (Phil 2:12–13).

Second, it raises the question of culture. If Judaisers are right, one culture has precedence over another. In Jesus, this is wrong. All cultures are different, all are fallen, and all have their own merits. Jewish culture is fine. Paul has no problem with Jews circumcising their boys; but if they tell others they must do so too to be saved, therein lies the problem. One has to be a Jew to be saved. Similarly, when Pakeha brought the gospel to NZ, in the initial phase, for Māori to convert, they effectively had to become European. This is wrong. One can be Māori and Christian by faith. There will be elements of any culture that need to be stopped, e.g. cannibalism and sexual immorality. On the other hand, the protocols of a culture that are not sinful can be maintained, e.g. music style, language, dress (in most cases), head coverings (e.g. 1 Cor 11:1–16), and other matters of style and food.

This becomes important in our churches. Every church as a dominant church culture including the dominant ethnic group(s) and "the way things are done around here." People usually have to fit in to be part of it. In Christ, the dominant culture must not demand that new people do everything by the rules, unwritten or written. People are welcome as they are. The real culture of the Kingdom is found in Christ, in love, in respect, in kindness, and in the other fruits of the Spirit.

As such, churches should be open and welcoming of diversity, ready to adapt as culture changes. Music styles will evolve. The way people dress will be transformed. If it is not, it will die.

We also need to watch ourselves when we begin to allow a culture to seem more important than another. Some people become ultra-nationalistic thinking their culture (e.g. white supremacy) is more important than another. It is not. All cultures are the same before God. Similarly, many Zionistic Christians can privilege Judaism and Israel over the rest of humanity. It is great people feel a need to pray for Israel and hope for a revival among Jews, and if they feel that they should, to pray for it and support Israel. Yet the Jews are in fact no more important than any other people today. Judaism gave us Jesus and God will deal with Israel. Our job is to be non-discriminatory toward all people, "for God does not show favouritism" (Acts 10:34; Rom 2:11; Gal 2:6). This is why Christians must always be welcome to immigrants and not demand they fit our culture, as if our culture is superior in some way.

9

Chapter Nine: Paul's Thought and Leadership

In this chapter, we continue to look at Paul, this time focussing on the main contours of his thought and his approach to leadership. Paul's theology has had a huge influence on Christian thought and history and understanding at least the main threads of his thinking helps us understand our faith. His approach to leadership is clearly drawn from the example of Christ.

More Detail

Keown, *Discovering the New Testament*, Vol 2, Ch. 14.

Suggested Bible Readings

Romans 1–8

Philippians 2:1–11

Paul's Thought and Leadership

Introduction

In this chapter, we will first look into the main theological ideas of Paul. A Pharisee, Paul had a very well-formed theology as a young Jewish man. Meeting Jesus on the Damascus Road changed his life shifting him from a harsh opponent of the Christian movement to its premier theological thinker. Realising Christ is Messiah, God's Son, Lord, and Saviour caused him to rethink his Pharisaic perspective. Much of what he formerly believed remained intact, but now reorganised around a crucified and raised Messiah who is not merely a human Messiah, but is God the Son. More than any other early Christian, Paul grappled with what it means to be saved through Christ's death and resurrection and to live the Christian life. He develops a range of metaphors and ideas that have shaped Christian thought ever since. Some of these we will now consider.

In Christ

One of his favourite ideas is the idea of being "in Christ" (also "in him," and "in the Lord"). He uses this over 160 times. This has huge theological importance. It speaks of us being in Christ spiritually, participating in his death, burial, and resurrection life. We tend to think about Christianity as asking Jesus into our lives. Yet, for Paul, it is more that God in Christ has asked us into his life.

Prior to belief, we are "in Adam," sinners as was he, subject to the death that entered the cosmos from him and destined for the destruction that all evil will experience unless dealt with (1 Cor 15:22).

When we believe, we are no longer in Adam, but are swept up into Christ; his death is our death, his resurrection is ours (Eph 1:13). We have been crucified in him, the old has gone, the new has come, and we are raised spiritually in him, to be raised fully when he returns (Rom 6:11; 1 Cor 15:22; 2 Cor 5:17). We receive redemption in Christ (Rom 3:24; 1 Cor 1:30; Eph 1:7). We are sanctified (declared holy) in him (1 Cor 1:2, 30) and so are saints (holy ones) in him (Phil 1:1). We receive wisdom in him (1 Cor 1:30) and are declared righteous in him (1 Cor 1:30; 2 Cor 5:21; Gal 2:16–17; Phil 3:19). We are reconciled to God in him (2 Cor 5:19). We are forgiven in him (Eph 1:7). Eternal life is granted in him (Rom 6:23). There is no condemnation for those in him, only freedom (Rom 8:1–2). We are loved in him (Rom 8:39). We receive gifts in him (1 Cor 1:5). We receive the blessings of Abraham in him (Gal 3:14). In Christ, we participate in his anointing sealed with the Spirit (2 Cor 1:21). We suffer in him and for him, this is the path to glory (2 Cor 2:14). We receive encouragement in him (Phil 2:1) and experience peace in him (Phil 4:7). It is an ecclesiological concept; we are one body in him (Rom 12:5). We are bound together in him, part of the Godhead (cf. Col 1:19), in an intimate relationship with God, Father, Son, and Spirit, and fused together as a people in him and through him. We are one in him, God's children, regardless of age, gender, race, or status (Gal 3:26–28; Eph 2:13). Churches exist in him (Gal 1:22), the temple of God's Spirit (Eph 2:21–22). Empowered by the Spirit, we participate in God's mission in him (Rom 16:3; 1 Cor 15:58; 2 Cor 2:17; Eph 6:21). We are to take up the mindset of humility and service in him (Phil 2:5). We are blessed with the riches of God's full range of spiritual blessings in him, having been chosen in him before the creation of the world, recipients of Christ's inheritance—the world (Eph 1:3–4, 11, s.a. Col 1:17). Ultimately all will be reconciled in him (Eph 1:10). Christ is the centre of Paul's theology, and being "in Christ" is the centre of his soteriology (theology of salvation).

Justification

Justification is law-court language. In the ancient world, the king was also chief lawmaker and ultimate judge. God is king and the final lawmaker and judge. He is completely righteous. His action toward humanity is utterly righteous and just (Rom 1:17; 3:8, 20). The question is, how can we stand righteous before God? What justifies us before God the Judge?

For Paul, the answer now that Jesus has come, is Jesus' death and resurrection, which achieves the possibility of salvation. All we have to do is respond to the grace of God with faith: trust, intellectual belief, commitment, allegiance. Then, we are justified by God's grace through faith. As has been discussed, some early Jewish Christians struggled with the idea that faith could be enough, demanding new converts add circumcision and Torah observance to complete justification. This is not needed. One is declared righteous before God the judge by faith. Then, they experience the status of "justified by faith" (Rom 3:28; 5:1; Gal 2:16; 3:24). They are right before God. While they continue to believe in God and his Son, they remain in this status. If on their dying day, or when Jesus returns, they continue to believe in him with a faith that is sincere, that status will be final, and they will pass judgement into eternal life with God and his Son forever.

Reconciliation

Reconciliation is political language, drawn from the world of international affairs, treaties, and the like. It is also used in marriage contexts; a reconciliation of husband and wife (1 Cor 7:11). Paul writes in Romans 5:19: "Therefore, since we have been justified by faith, we have *peace with God* through our Lord Jesus Christ." We are then "reconciled to God" spiritually. The sin of Adam drove a wedge between humankind and God. We were then enemies of God. In Christ, this separation is restored, and we are reconciled to him through, and in Christ (Rom 5:10, 11). This reconciliation extends to all things (Col 1:20) and will come to pass at the consummation when all God's enemies are placed under his Son's feet. Mission is a "ministry of reconciliation"—summoning people with "the message of reconciliation" to yield to God in Christ and experiencing reconciliation with him (2 Cor 5:18–19). In Christ too, Jew and Gentile are reconciled together and to God (Eph 2:16). We are called to live by faith and obedience as we live this reconciled relationship. We are to experience reconciliation with one another through love. We are to take the message of reconciliation to the world that they may know this peace with God.

Redemption

Redemption is an idea used in slavery speaking of manumission; being ransomed from slavery. It especially invokes the Exodus, when God redeemed Israel from being slaves in Egypt to be his people. God's redemption of humanity comes in Christ Jesus (Rom 3:24), who gave himself as a ransom for all (1 Tim 2:6). Hence, he is our redemption (1 Cor 1:30) through his blood (Eph 1:7) meaning we have forgiveness of sins (Col 1:14). Christ redeemed us from the curse of the law by taking our curse on himself (Gal 3:13) and instead of being slaves to law, sin, and death, we are God's children and recipients of the Spirit (Gal 4:5). We are then redeemed from lawlessness, to be his holy people (Tit 2:14). Through him, on the day of redemption (Eph 4:30), our bodies will experience ultimate redemption from their enslavement to death through sin (Rom 8:23).

Sanctification

Sanctification speaks of holiness, and is a cultic metaphor, drawn from religious ideas of consecration, purity, and separateness. It tends to be related to things (e.g. sacrifices), places (e.g. temples), and people (e.g. priests) that are divinely consecrated. Israel was deeply concerned with holiness, and its complex laws were designed to keep its people holy before a holy God.

In Paul, the idea takes on fresh meaning because of the all-sufficient death of Christ, the Holy One of God. When we come to faith in Christ, he is our sanctification (1 Cor 1:30). We are holy in him having received the *Holy* Spirit (Rom 15:16; 2 Thess 2:13). We are declared holy before God (e.g. 1 Cor 1:2; 6:11). We are thus given the status of "saints" or "holy ones." In Roman Catholicism, this is only granted by the Pope to the special Catholics who achieve sainthood. Protestantism quite rightly rejects this—all are saints if they believe in Jesus. Paul uses "saints" around 40 times in this sense.

As God's sanctified people, his saints, we are to seek to be what we are in Christ, living holy lives. We are to present our beings as slaves of righteousness for sanctification (Rom 6:19) and then eternal life (Rom 6:22). God's will for us is sanctification including abstinence from sexual immorality and much much more—a whole life given over to God and his service and goodness (1 Thess 4:3). As such, Paul prays for the Thessalonians that God may sanctify them completely for the day of Christ (1 Thess 5:23).

Paul's Thought and Leadership: Culture and ethics

Enough has already been said concerning Paul's view of culture. As noted, Paul sees in Christ the end of ethnic, cultural, and racial divisions (e.g. Jew/Gentile; Jew/Samaritan; Māori/Pakeha; Israeli/Palestinian). In Christ, there is no notion of racial superiority, a rightfully dominant culture, rampant nationalism, and so on. God does not show favouritism, and neither should we (1 Tim 5:21).

Slavery

Other ancient divisions are also dissolved in Christ. Paul says in Gal 3:28 that there is neither slave nor free. In the world of Paul and indeed in western civilisation up until Wilberforce and the American Revolution, slavery was normal. One was born into Roman citizenship (freed people) or slavery. It was set at birth as was gender and ethnicity. It took the church around seventeen centuries to work through to the idea that in Christ Jesus, slavery is ended.

Galatians 3:28 says it outright. It is also hinted at in Israel's law, whereby slavery was not permitted except in exceptional circumstances and the slave was to be released in the 7th year (Exod 21:2; Deut 15:12). However, the slave may choose to remain in slavery out of love (Exod 21:5).

Ephesians 6:5–9 also hints at the end of slavery. In vv. 5–8, Paul instructs slaves to obey their masters and serve them wholeheartedly as to God. Then, astonishingly, he says to Masters: "do the same to them" (v. 9). Some scholars recognise that fully unwrapped, Paul is effectively speaking of the end of slavery as masters and slaves treat each other in the same way.

As will be discussed in our look at Philemon in the next chapter, Paul in this letter also points toward the end of slavery once the implications of the letter are considered.

Women

Paul is seen as a misogynist by many people, including some Christian thinkers. There are texts that seem to point to the subordination of women. Husbands are the heads of their wives who are to submit to them (1 Cor 11:3; Eph 5:21–24; Col 3:18). There is no mention of women elders (1 Tim 3:1–7; Tit 1:5–9). In 1 Cor 14:32–35, he instructs women to be silent in church and only to ask questions of their husbands at home. In 1 Tim 2:11–15, women are to learn quietly and are not to teach or exercise authority over a man because of the order of creation and the Fall.

Yet, this is only one side of the story. First, there is Gal 3:28, which speaks of utter oneness and equality of opportunity in Christ.

Second, there are no limitations on Paul's spiritual gift lists—they appear to apply to all Christians without any limitation given (Rom 12:4–8; 1 Cor 12:8–10, 28–20; 13:1–3; 14:26; Eph 4:11).

Third, there are no such limitations on ministry in eleven of Paul's letters, which leaves us with a question—do we base our theology on the two limitations? Or, on the thirteen letters without the limitations? Do we assume that these two limitations apply to every church and for all of time?

Third, there are many women who work in ministry alongside Paul. Some of these are most interesting. The use of the masculine of *diakonos* to describe Phoebe suggests she is a deacon of the Cenchreae church (Rom 16:1). She is also a *prostatis*, which means patron and can mean a leader (Rom 16:2). Junia is named in Rom 16:7 as either "well known to the apostles" (ESV) or "esteemed by the apostles" (NRSV). The majority of contemporary scholars adopt the second interpretation meaning Junia and Andronicus were an apostolic couple. Prisca (Priscilla) is always named alongside Aquila and is a church hostess with her husband (Rom 16:3; 1 Cor 16:19; 2 Tim 4:19). Can it be assumed she was not active with Aquila in ministry? Euodia and Syntyche mentioned in Phil 4:2–3 are very important women, labelled co-workers who worked with Paul in the gospel. They may be overseers or deacons. Then there is Nympha who has a church in her home. There are also other women mentioned in Rom 16 who worked for the gospel (Mary, Tryphaena, Tryphosa, Persis, vv. 6, 12).

Fourth, the headship and submission texts may not be as absolute as some assume. The word *kephalē* does not necessarily mean "leader" and can mean "source" speaking of Adam as the source of Eve at creation. While this meaning is not as common as "leader," it cannot be ruled out. Also, the command in Eph 5 is found in v. 21: "submit to one another out of reverence to Christ." Ephesians 5:22 and what follows develops this. First, women are to submit to their husbands. Then, husbands are to love their wives as Christ loves the church and gave himself for it. This speaks of a husband subservient to his wife, giving himself for her.

Many see this as mutual service and submission. Further, the whole section is carefully crafted targeting the husband who was the dominant figure in the ancient family. Each part has the weaker partner submitting or obeying (wives, children, slaves) to the paterfamilias (head male). The emphasis is on the husband who is referenced three times. As a husband, he is to love his wife with the sacrificial love of Christ. He is to bring up the children without provocation (I have never heard a conservative demand this of a man!). As a master, he is to yield to his slaves as they are to him. I would argue this passage targets a new kind of masculinity based on the example of Christ that dissolves any notion of men ruling over women. This is a result of the Fall and to be corrected in Christ (Gen 3:16).

Fourth, these arguments cause us to pause and ask whether the texts prohibiting women in 1 Cor and 1 Tim are universal. Were they commands to particular contexts where women were out of control?

Finally, it took the church over 17 centuries to come to terms with the implications of the gospel for slavery. Some see a parallel with the question of women—it has taken us closer to 20 centuries to see that, in Christ, the days of men ruling over women, exclusively leading churches, and demanding submission are over. All can lead, preach, and serve as God engifts and calls. Of course, women will still give birth and nurture children in the first period of their lives—this is creational. However, roles beyond this are not mentioned in the NT, rather, we live led by the Spirit serving as God calls us to serve.

Divisions

Other divisions are challenged in Paul. The Corinthians

were divided over their preference for one preacher over and another: "I am of Paul, I am of Apollos, I am of Cephas (Peter)" (1 Cor 1:12). Paul repudiates this, answering, "I am of Christ!" The church worldwide is beset by denominational divisions, as some follow Luther, others Knox, some Calvin, some a Pope, and others Wesley, and so on. While there is a time to divide and form denominations, it is dangerous to focus our theology on one figure, no matter how amazing. We follow Christ and while there are denominations and false teaching and heresy that must be rejected, we are to work for unity rather than focus on divisions. The division of Christianity is a major stumbling block to the world when our love for one another should be our distinctive feature.

This applies theologically—people gather around their favourite theologians: Barth, Calvin, Luther, Wright, and whoever one likes at a particular time. Rather, we should listen to them all and learn from them, building a theology that aligns with the Scriptures. This is theological maturity.

Ethics

We have noted the ethics of the Kingdom in the Synoptic Gospels and the importance of love in John. For Paul also, we are held together as God's people by a common ethic. Supreme is love for one another which after the faith that saves us, is the attitude that should shape our lives. Love should govern our lives and is seen in a range of other Spirit-imparted attitudes such as the fruit of the Spirit (Gal 5:22–24; 1 Cor 13:4–7). Spiritual gifts are good, but without love they are worthless (1 Cor 13:1–3). It is the sum of all law, the most excellent way, and the greatest of these things (Rom 13:8–10; Gal 5:14; 1 Cor 13:13). As he says to the

Corinthians, "Let all that you do be done in love" (1 Cor 16:14). What should stand out in our churches is fidelity to the gospel, love, and hope.

Limits

There are two equal and opposite dangers when talking about love and unity. One is that we understate it and Christianity becomes rule orientated, divided over non-essentials, with rivalry and bitterness among Christians. The opposite danger is that we over-emphasise or misunderstand love as if Christians can do what they want, and we should just welcome each other no matter what. Paul shows us the middle way. As he says in Eph 4:2–3, we are to live "with all humility and gentleness, with patience, bearing with one another in love, zealous to keep the unity of the Spirit in the bond of peace." Yet, he also tells his readers to have nothing to do with those who utterly violate the gospel's truth (e.g. Judaisers in Galatians) and ethics (e.g. 1 Cor 5, sexual ethics). Unity has its limits. Love sometimes must be tough—for the good of the church and the person, they are to be shut out of fellowship. This is a final decision after a careful process seeking restoration. So, in Tit 3:10–11, Paul urges that a grossly divisive person is to be warned three times, and if they do not change their behaviour, that person is to be repudiated.

Paul's Thought and Leadership: Cruciform Leadership

We have noted that Jesus' endorsed leadership based on service, whereby Christian leaders find greatness in humble service, in bearing their cross on Christ's behalf, repudiating autocratic dominance, and leading cruciformly with others.

Cruciformity

Paul's view of leadership is consistent with this. He recognises the need for leaders appointing elders and deacons and recognising the leadership ministries of apostles, prophets, evangelists, pastors, and teachers. He instructed his converts to "respect (*oida*, know) those who labour among you and who lead you in the Lord and admonish you, and to esteem (*ēgeomai*, consider) them extremely highly in love because of their work" (1 Thess 5:12–13). Yet, he urged a certain type of leadership.

Emulation of God

At its heart is the emulation of God as revealed in Christ. So, he says to the Ephesians: "Therefore be imitators of God, as beloved children, and walk in love, just as also Christ loved us and gave himself up for us, a sweet-smelling offering and sacrifice to God" (Eph 5:1–2). Christians are to embody the death of Christ in their leadership, the pattern of the cross. This begins in a mental outlook consistent with that of Christ in his earthly life who, although being God, did not exploit his equality with God to dominate the world, but he willingly emptied himself for it, taking on the form of a slave, a human, willingly humbling himself, being obedient to his God unto his horrific and humiliating death on a cross (Phil 2:5–8). This is the path of Christian leadership for Paul.

Emulation of Christ

In his own leadership, Paul tried to embrace this ideal. Despite his awesome credentials as a Jew and Pharisee, he considered them loss and dung, compared with knowing Christ, gaining him, being found in him, with the gift of righteousness that comes through faith. His desire was to know Christ and his power, sharing in his sufferings, becoming like him in his death. Like an athlete, he disciplined himself in this pursuit, pressing on to the end patterning his life by the example of Christ (Phil 3:4–14). He saw suffering as an integral aspect of his life as a leader, for Christian life is participation in the life and ministry of Christ (e.g. Rom 8:17; 2 Cor 4:7–18).

Imitate Me

Seeking to emulate Christ himself, he summoned readers to "imitate me" (e.g. 1 Cor 11:1, s.a. 1 Cor 4:16; Phil 3:17; 4:9) and was delighted when they did so (1 Thess 1:6). He shows us that leadership is first being an example to others. Our most profound challenge is to live out of faith, love, and hope in a way that draws others to follow. Our deep faith must be seen. Love must flow from us. And we are ever hopeful, knowing that because God is with us by his Spirit and Jesus is coming, the things we dream of in our lives can come to fruition.

The Corinthians

In his letters he challenged all Christians, leaders or not, to take on such an attitude. The Corinthians were tearing themselves apart with their arrogant parties formed around their favoured preachers. With complex argumentation, Paul calls them back to the gospel of a crucified Messiah—a king who refused to use his power to win the world, to function arrogantly, to seek his own selfish ambition, to pursue self-glory, but gave himself for the world (1 Cor 1:11–2:5). He tells them that leadership is service, and each will give an account of him or herself before God (1 Cor 3–4). The climax of the letter in many ways is 1 Cor 13—the Corinthians are to turn from division and love is the path to make that happen.

The Philippians

To the Philippians who are in danger of becoming a Corinth, he places in the theological centre of the letter the passage mentioned above giving Christ as the supreme example. Also using his own situation in Rome rhetorically, he speaks of two types of Christians. First, there are those motivated for ministry by love and those by selfish ambition, rivalry, and a desire to demean others to elevate themselves (Phil 1:12–18). Then, he summons the Philippians away from these false attitudes to a unity based on humility, love, and considering others above ourselves, exemplified by Christ, Timothy, and Epaphroditus (Phil 2).

Suffering

Christian leadership in Paul is hard work. There is no easy path. There will be opponents within the church and challenges from the world around. We will have to grapple with our own weaknesses. The life ministry calls for is sacrificial and hard. It will be tough on our families. It will be hard on us as people make continual demands. We will fail more than we succeed in winning people to Christ and filling our churches. Yet, Paul is not daunted. He presses on. He urges us to do the same. We do so through deep consideration of the example of Christ, of Paul, and other great leaders who have given their lives for Christ.

Courage and Perseverance

In the context of suffering, Paul emphasises courage in leadership. We see this in the Acts narrative, as Paul determinedly travels from city to city, courageously entering synagogues knowing full well he will be rejected. He speaks before rulers, governors, pagan philosophers, and violent crowds. His catalogues of suffering in 2 Corinthians speak of amazing challenges from enemies, deprivation, imprisonment, and beatings (2 Cor 6:4–9; 11:16–29). After 2 Corinthians he travelled to Jerusalem with the collection and faced even worse in Israel—another shipwreck, Roman imprisonment (Acts 20–28), then another final period of ministry before being beheaded in Rome. Through it all, Paul showed amazing courage and stamina. Faith, hope, and love sustained him. His attitude is summed up in Phil 1:20: "but with full courage now as always, Christ will be honoured in my body, whether through life or through death." Courage was one of the four Greek virtues. Paul hardly uses the language they use (*andreia*, "manliness, courage"), but he does once in 1 Cor 16:13 which sums up the attitude he wants from all Christians, most especially leaders: "Be alert, stand firm in the faith, be courageous (*andrizomai*, lit. "be men"), be strong. Let all things be done in love."

Team Leadership

It has been noted Paul worked closely with others, emulating Jesus and his disciples. While he was clearly extremely capable, he did not try and do it all himself. He worked with co-workers, especially Timothy, along with others including Priscilla, a woman (see the previous section). We see in Phil 4:2–3 that in Philippi he had quite a team including two women (Euodia, Syntyche), a man (Clement), and he mentions a lot of unnamed others ("the rest of my co-workers"). This shows that as he travelled, he quickly trained people up, and released them into ministry. His vision of elders and deacons was always plural (e.g. Phil 1:1). He mentions other apostles and ministers and, as long as they preach the authentic gospel, is positive toward them. He was not threatened by others. In Corinth, Apollos and Cephas gained support from members of the Corinthian congregation at Paul's expense (1 Cor 1:12). No doubt members of the church preferred their preaching. Yet, Paul is not concerned about their effect and popularity, just the silly way the Corinthians are dividing over them. Paul recognised the value of team ministry. Hence, autocratic individual "my way or the highway" leadership is not appropriate. We are to work collaboratively, collectively, sharing ideas, encouraging one another, working in harmony, as we work together toward our common goal.

10

Chapter Ten: Paul's Letters

We now turn to the letters of Paul considering debates over authorship and some approaches to reading them. Attention is particularly given to Philemon as an example of a letter and how we might approach it in biblical studies. Finally, insights from Philemon are made concerning Paul's leadership, culture, and ethics.

More Detail

Keown, *Discovering the New Testament*, Vol 2, ch. 2, 14.

Suggested Bible Readings

Exodus 21:1–32

Lev 25:35–46

Eph 6:5–9

Philemon

Introduction

Most of the NT is in the form of letters from Christian leaders to converts. These include letters from Paul (13), the writer of Hebrews (whose identity is uncertain), James, Peter (2), John (3), and Jude. Revelation can also be seen as a very long letter (Rev 1:4–5). Hence, understanding how to interpret letters is critical to biblical interpretation. In what follows, the focus is Paul. Some comments on the other letters will come in the next chapter. However, much of what is written in the first section below applies to the other letters.

Paul's Letters: Overview and debates

Thirteen letters are attributed to Paul in the NT. Four are written to individuals—1 & 2 Timothy, Titus, and Philemon. The other nine are written to churches or a set of churches: to the Christians in a given location. Most of these are written to a city: Romans, 1 & 2 Corinthians, Ephesians, Philippians, Colossians, 1 & 2 Thessalonians. Galatians is written to a set of churches in the Galatian region. Of those written to churches, Romans and Colossians are written to churches Paul himself did not plant—the Roman church emerged early in the Christian period through Pentecost pilgrims (Acts 2:10). Colossians was written to two cities, Colossae and Laodicea, in the Lycus Valley in Asia Minor. These churches were planted by Epaphras, one of Paul's co-workers (Col 1:7; 2:1; 4:11).

Letters were used across the Greco-Roman and Jewish worlds to exchange communication. We sense this as we read the NT letters; they are parts of ongoing conversations. For example, in 1 Cor 7:1, Paul writes: "now concerning (*peri de*) the matters about which you wrote ..." We also know from 1 Cor 5:9, that Paul wrote an earlier letter. Hence, we see that each letter is a moment in an ongoing conversation. Letter carriers were always on the move back and forth from Paul to his congregations. They read them out to the churches on Paul's behalf (remembering that many early church members were likely illiterate when they were converted). Hence, a letter in the NT is part of an ongoing conversation. It is a snippet of time. It is like one email in a string of emails, one end of a telephone conversation.

The art of interpreting the letters is to work out what is going on in the backdrop, the story behind the letter. This is a lot of fun, working akin to a detective, reading what is there and possibilities to be gleaned from reading between the lines. This we call "mirror reading," trying to discern the story behind the story from the content of the letter.

This leads to a range of ideas that we must sift through to settle on the best possible understanding. For this, we consider the letter-writers situation whether it be Paul, James, Peter, John, Jude, and the author of Hebrews). Where were they? Date? What was going on for them? We think about the wider culture and how what is written should be interpreted in light of it. We consider the situation of the readers. We try to construct a narrative of the situation being addressed.

The ones we have, are shaped in the usual patterns of the Greek letter form. They usually have the sender's name(s), the recipients, a greeting, a thanksgiving/blessing and prayer, and then the body of the letter. They end with greetings, blessings, and a final farewell.

The contents of the letters vary depending on the points being made. They were carefully written, for ancient letter writing was a slow and expensive process, and they were often dictated to a secretary (amanuensis). For example, Tertius wrote Romans down for Paul (Rom 16:22). Silvanus (Silas) wrote down 1 Peter (1 Pet 5:12). These secretaries had differing degrees of freedom, depending on the situation. For example, when the writer was in prison, they might ask the writer to craft the whole letter on their behalf. Or, they would simply dictate it. This likely explains differing styles across the letters by the same author.

Authorship

The authorship of many of the NT letters is challenged by modern scholars. The authorship of seven of Paul's letters is not seriously questioned. The seven undisputed Pauline letters are Romans, 1 & 2 Corinthians, Galatians, Philippians, 1 Thessalonians, and Philemon. This is because of similarities in style and theology. Six letters are questioned: Ephesians, Colossians, 2 Thessalonians, 1 & 2 Timothy and Titus (the final three are called the Pastoral Epistles). Ephesians and Colossians are similar and have quite a different style and theology to the undisputed letters. Some think one of Paul's co-workers wrote it, perhaps after he died. The Pastorals have a similar style and perspective, which is again different from the undisputed letters. 2 Thessalonians is considered to be too similar to 1 Thessalonians, and so a poor replica by someone other than Paul. Many scholars will interpret these six letters with the assumption Paul did not write them. They still see them as Scripture and recognise that they may come from a Pauline perspective. However, this affects their interpretation.

Other scholars, myself included, accept that the early church knew which letters were from Paul and which weren't. They would not have allowed a non-Pauline letter to bear his name and be honoured. This is especially so when Peter, probably writing in ad 65-66 honours Paul's letters as Scripture (2 Pet 1:5–16). We argue that if Paul's name is there, he wrote it. Also, as no one questioned the authorship of Paul's letters until the eighteenth century, it is more a product of modern rational arrogance than anything concrete. However, the differences across the letters are to some extent real, even if exaggerated by sceptics. These can be explained by Paul using different amanuenses with more freedom as they were written (e.g. the same one for Colossians and Ephesians, and the same person for the Pastorals). It is noted that great authors are quite capable of using differing styles (e.g. C. S. Lewis). Some note that we do not have enough of Paul's (and other NT writers) material to be certain that they did not write them (i.e. insufficient to make a fair comparison). The differences in style and theology may also be due to the context and issues being written about. As such, it is likely that the letters of Paul (and the other NT writers) originate from them, even if they vary in style and theology.

The issue of authorship does complicate the interpretation of letters where authorship is questioned. Commentaries include long sections debating the matter. The interpretation that follows this will be affected by that decision. Students of the NT need to be aware of this and know that when they write on a disputed letter, they too will have to deal with it.

Different Approaches

There is a range of approaches used by scholars to interpret letters. One is to try and find similar letters across the ancient world and compare them. For example, some think Romans is written as an ambassadorial letter (a letter written on behalf of a government from an ambassador, i.e.

Paul, see 2 Cor 5:20; Eph 6:20). Quite a few scholars regard Philippians as a letter of friendship.

Another approach is rhetorical criticism. The art of persuasion through speech was a big thing for the Greeks, with young elite men trained in rhetoric in their youth. Rhetorical handbooks exist and NT letters are considered from this perspective. This makes sense to some degree, because, although they are letters, they were also to be read out by the messengers and so were also speeches.

There are three main rhetorical forms: 1) Epideictic: where writers reaffirm common core values using praise and blame. Some think 1 John; Ephesians; 1 Thess use this form; 2) Deliberative: where writers seek to persuade and convince the audience of what is true and best. Some put Philippians in this category; and 3) Judicial: where writers use legal arguments to establish right and wrong. Some consider Galatians to be judicial. Those that use this approach, break up the letters according to rhetorical categories. The *exordium* is the introduction to the letter (e.g. Phil 1:3–11). The *narratio* is a narrative, an account of what happened over time (e.g. Gal 1:11–2:15). The *partitio* or *propositio* is the proposition, the main proposition of the letter (e.g. Rom 1:16–17; Phil 1:27). The *probatio* is the main body of arguments of the letter expounding the main proposition. The *refutatio* is a refutation of opposing views. The *peroratio* is the conclusion with the final arguments.

This all sounds complex but budding biblical scholars will run into these ideas and terminology. Usually, a NT letter does not fit the form these scholars argue for, as each uses a blend of forms. Each has a range of rhetorical devices used by the NT writer. A good example is a chiasm (using the Greek letter *chi*, X), whereby the elements mirror one another: ABCB'A'. The emphasis comes in the centre. These are found in the NT across whole chapters. For example (1 Cor 12–14):

A   Spiritual Gifts (Ch. 12)
B   Love (Ch. 13)
A'   Spiritual Gifts (Ch. 14)

In fact, 1 Corinthians has a number of these macro-chiasms (e.g. 1 Cor 5–6; 8–10).

They may also come in smaller units. For example, Phil 3:8–10:

A that I may gain Christ and be found in him,
B   not having a righteousness of my own that comes from the law,
C   but that which comes through faith in Christ,
B'   the righteousness from God that depends on faith
A' that I may know him

There is a whole range of other devices used in the letters. These help us grasp more closely the point the author is making. This is why it is important to learn the biblical languages if you have time and capacity. You can begin to identify these things yourself. It is also important to use good material on each letter written by scholars, especially commentaries, when preparing a Bible study or sermon, as these will help deepen understanding. However, it still has to be made understandable to the hearers, so don't try and baffle them with too much complexity.

Paul's Letters: Philemon

To get a feel for how letters work, let's focus in on one of Paul's letters: Philemon. This will give an idea of how we might approach a letter of the NT. Philemon has been chosen as it is a short letter (335 Greek words, 25 verses) which we can briefly examine with some detail. In so doing, a clearer understanding of how to interpret the NT letters can be gleaned.

Scholars enquiring into NT letters take nothing for granted, usually asking a range of questions such as, "who wrote it?" (authorship), "when and where was it written?" (setting and date), "to whom was it written?" (recipients), "what is its structure?" (rhetorical form and structure), and "what is its message?" (purpose and themes). Inquiry into such things helps us understand the story behind the letter. We understand it first in its historical and social setting. Then we can apply what we learn to today's world.

Introductory Matters

Philemon is one of the captivity (prison) letters of Paul and one of four written to an individual. It has the form found in many of Paul's letters: 1) Writer/sender—recipients—greeting; 2) thanksgiving and intercession; 3) letter body; 4) final greetings and blessing.

Authorship

While some scholars have challenged Pauline authorship, this is rare and is recognised as one of the seven undisputed letters of Paul. Careful readers will note that Timothy is also named in v. 1. This is not uncommon as a number of Paul's letters have others named with Paul. Timothy may then be a co-writer, a co-sender, or Paul's amanuensis who penned it on his behalf. Scholars consider which is most likely with most seeing him as co-sender and possibly amanuensis.

Date and Setting

Paul is clearly in prison but does not name the city or date (vv. 1, 9, 10, 13, 23). This gives three possibilities.

1) Caesarea Maritima (c. ad 58–59): Few consider this possibility.

2) Ephesus (c. ad 52–55): Some believe this is the best because it is close to Colossae (160 km/100 mi); Paul's statements of suffering in Ephesus make it likely he spent some time in prison in Ephesus (1 Cor 15:32; 16:8; 2 Cor 1:3–11; 4:7 – 5:10; 6:3–10; 11:16–29, esp. 2 Cor 11:23; also 1 Clem 5:6); the imprisonment of Epaphras add to this hypothesis (Phlm 24, cf. Col 1:7; 4:12); an earthquake destroyed Colossae in the early 60s.

3) Rome (c. 60–61): The traditional view is early in Paul's two-year Roman imprisonment (Acts 28:30) and before the earthquake; there is no concrete evidence Paul was ever in prison in Ephesus; Phlm 9 suggests Paul is an old man; co-workers with Paul fit Rome better than Ephesus.

While I prefer Rome, where Paul was located at the time of writing does not greatly affect interpretation.

Recipients

These are named in vv. 1–2: Philemon, Paul's "beloved co-worker;" "Apphia," who is "our sister;" Archippus, as "our fellow-soldier;" and the church in "your (singular) house."

Apphia may be Philemon's wife (or Archippus'). Her naming and designation "sister" may indicate she is one of the church leaders. "Your house" is likely Philemon's home as he is named first. He is wealthy owning a home with a guest room (vv. 1, 22), has slaves (v. 16), and hosts a church (v. 1). He is also generous in his love and benefaction toward other Christians (vv. 5–6) and Paul (vv. 7, 17–20, 22). Archippus is mentioned in Col 4:17 as a fellow-soldier engaged in mission. There are numerous cross-references to Colossians which indicate that they live in Colossae, a city in the Lycus Valley in Asia Minor, inland from Ephesus near Hierapolis and Laodicea (compare esp. Phlm 1, 24 with Col 4:7–17). It is likely that Colossians, Ephesians, and Philemon were written at the same time and sent with the same courier, Tychicus (Eph 6:21; Col 4:7). Philemon is clearly the main person being addressed, the owner of Onesimus the slave, and the host of the church.

The Occasion

Using mirror reading, the story behind the letters becomes clear. Paul is in prison. The occasion of the letter is found in vv. 8–20. One of Philemon's slaves, Onesimus, has left Philemon and come to Paul in prison and has become a Christian (v. 10). He was formerly not much use to Philemon but is now a changed man, useful to Paul and his owner. (Interestingly, his name means "useful one," v. 11). Paul is sending him back to Philemon. The reason for the letter is to lovingly urge (not command) Philemon to receive him back not as a slave, but as "a beloved brother" just as he would receive Paul if he were to come (vv. 12–17). Paul also offers to pay any costs incurred through Onesimus' flight (v. 18). Paul then expresses confidence

Philemon will do what he asks (v. 21) and also asks him to prepare a room for his visit (v. 22).

There are three main views on why Onesimus came to Paul:

1) **Support for Paul**: Some consider Philemon sent Onesimus to Paul to help him. However, this is ridiculous as Onesimus is described as useless and if Philemon sent him to help Paul, this is more an act of sabotage.

2) **Friend of the Master (Amicus Domini Hypothesis)**: In the Roman world, a slave could leave a master to find a "friend of the master" (*amicus domini*) to resolve a dispute between master and slave. Paul would be ideal for such reconciliation.

3) **A Runaway Slave (Fugitive)**: The traditional view has been that Onesimus ran away from Philemon.He is then a kind of "prodigal slave." He fled to Rome because it was crowded, sought out Paul who he knew of from Philemon, and became a Christian. Paul is sending him back as a Christian and is asking Philemon to have mercy on him.

The most likely of these is the third. This was the view of the early interpreters living in the Greco-Roman world.

The Social Setting

Some background issues, especially regarding slavery, help interpretation. Being a slave was tough in the ancient world. Slaves were owned. They had no freedom. Slaves in the Roman world were considered inferior members of the family and lived within the master's home. Some experienced severe suffering. They did all the work required by the master. Some were educated and did important work like medicine, architecture, teaching, and some were even philosophers. They could buy their freedom or could be manumitted. They often ran away when treated badly, escaping overseas, hiding in big cities and seeking asylum in temples. If they did run away, they could be punished; Philemon was legally allowed to mistreat or kill Onesimus; it was his choice. The types of punishment could include Onesimus being resold, scourged, branded, cut, made to wear an iron collar, crucified, thrown to beasts, forced to become a gladiator, or killed by some other means. Often this was done in public. A warrant for Onesimus' arrest would have been issued.

Paul was also in potential danger if he retained Onesimus, for he would be guilty of harbouring a slave. He was already under light custody in his own rental accommodation, and the last thing he needed was to be charged with such an offense! However, with the owner's consent, he was allowed to assist a slave and to purchase (*peculium*) his or her freedom. This may have been Paul's intent.

The Form and Structure of the Letter

Some scholars treat Philemon as deliberative rhetoric; Paul seeking to persuade readers to his point of view (e.g. Witherington). This has not found widespread support. Most break down the letter in this way:

1) Letter Opening: Phlm 1–7

A. Prescript: Phlm 1–3

    1.   Author/senders: Phlm 1a–b

    2.   Recipients: Phlm 1c–2

    3.   Greeting: Phlm 3

B. Thanksgiving and Prayer: Phlm 4–5

1. Thanksgiving: Phlm 4–5

2. Prayer: Phlm 6

3. Assurance: Phlm

2) Letter Appeal: Receive Onesimus back as a brother: Phlm 8–21 (or v. 20 of v. 22 [there are different views on this])

1. Appeal to receive back Onesimus: Phlm 8–17

2. Promise to pay costs: Phlm 18–20

3. Statement of confidence: Phlm 21

3) Letter Closing: Phlm 22–25

1. Travel plans: Phlm 22

2. Greetings: Phlm 23–24

3. Salutation: Phlm 25

Comments on Each Section

Here, I suggest you have Philemon handy and read through it verse by verse with these ideas in mind. These are short notes and questions.

Letter Opening: Phlm 1–7

Phlm 1–3: Prescript

Verses 1–2

We see the usual pattern: writer/sender; recipient.

Note first in v. 1, that Paul does not describe himself as a Roman prisoner, but a prisoner of Christ Jesus. He may be in prison under the Romans, but his Lord is in control and he is there for him.

Timothy is named: is he co-author? Co-sender? Paul's secretary?

Is Apphia Philemon's wife? Archippus' wife? A leader of the church?

Note too that the church meets in the house. We see the rich acting as patrons to the wider church. We see that the early church was a house movement. This speaks of a group of up to 30 people. The church in Colossae was made up of house churches.

Verse 3

This is Paul's standard greeting used in eight of his letters. A prayer for grace and peace is asking God for his full blessings on their lives in every way: sufficient income to meet needs; good health; unity; perseverance; joy; God's beneficent blessings. Note that the source is God and his Son. The means of the Spirit is implied.

Thanksgiving and Prayer: Phlm 4–5

Verses 4–5

We see the usual thanksgiving of Paul using *eucharisteō*, "I give thanks" (see Rom; 1 Cor; Phil; 1 Thess; 2 Thess). There are also other thanksgivings in Ephesians and the Pastorals.

Note Paul's passionate prayer life, always. Note how he remembers people, this is how we should pray.

Verse 5 gives the reason. Philemon is a great example of living out the two great commandments (Mark 12:29–31): love for God and for people. He is clearly a generous man who loves Jesus.

Verse 6

Paul switches to prayer, as he often does in his

thanksgiving. Prayer begins with gratitude for what God has done, then we pray for more.

"The sharing of your faith" is not about evangelism, as the older NIV translation suggests. It speaks of sharing what he has with others. The word sharing is *koinōnia*, the great word in the NT for defining very close relationship and partnership God's love summons us into. Philemon is generous (v. 5), Paul prays for more so that he will have full knowledge. This is leading toward the request that will come.

Verse 7

Some see this as flattery. It is not, though Paul is seeking to win Philemon to his point of view. We again see how generous Philemon is. For wealthy Christians, he is an exemplar. He provides refreshment, leading to joy and comfort. The word for comfort is *paraklēsis* which can also be translated "encouragement" which fits well here. Philemon is what we all should be—a source of joy and encouragement to others.

Letter Appeal: Receive Onesimus back as a brother: Phlm 8–21

Appeal to receive back Onesimus: Phlm 8–17

Verse 8–9

We can note here Paul's pastoral approach. He has the authority to command Philemon, but he chooses not to. He appeals out of love. This is great pastoral leadership. He wants Philemon's willing response, not something coerced with threat and fear.

"Old man" is *presbytēs* which can also mean ambassador. However, closer study of the term favours the former. An old man back in the day was over 50. If this is in Rome, he is likely in his mid to late 50s and possibly 60. This interpretation is also supportive of Rome over Ephesus as the point of origin.

Again, Paul is a prisoner for Jesus Christ—he does a lot of ministry in jail and is not concerned to be there.

Verse 10

With v. 12, this is the central verse in the body. He appeals for Onesimus. He is Paul's child, Paul his father, indicating he became a Christian under Paul (cf. 1 Cor 4:15; 1 Thess 2:11). Paul also uses the mother metaphor (1 Cor 3:1–2; 1 Thess 2:7).

Verse 11

This is a parenthetical note concerning Onesimus. Paul uses a clever play on words. Onesimus means "useful." Yet, he was, up until his conversion, useless (*achrēstos*). Now he is what his name entails, useful (*euchrēstos*). *Chrēstos* sounds like *Christos* (Christ) and was even used of Christ in some instances, and Paul may also have chosen the words because of their potential double meaning.

Verse 12

Note here how Paul describes Onesimus: "my very heart." The Greek for heart here is *splanchnon*, a term related to the guts, speaking of deep affection and compassion. Paul again uses it in Phil 1:8 where he yearns for the Philippians with "the affection of Christ Jesus." He used it earlier in Phlm 7 (hearts of the saints) and will use it again in v. 20: "refresh my heart." The verb is used in the Synoptic Gospels of Jesus' deep compassion for the despairing crowds of people who came to him for healing and hope (e.g. Matt 9:36; 14:14; 15:32).

Verses 13–14

Paul commends Onesimus as an able co-worker. In Col 4:9 he writes of Onesimus to the whole church: "our faithful and beloved brother, who is one of you." One can imagine their surprise to hear that useless runaway Onesimus is now a Christian engaged in mission with Paul! God can really change a person! Hallelujah!

We can note how Paul was not prepared to "steal" what in the ancient world, is rightfully Philemon's (slaves were property).

Again, we note that Paul is a great pastor, seeking Philemon's willing response, not something coerced.

Verses 15–17

Note how v. 15 calls to mind Rom 8:28—bad stuff has happened. Onesimus fell out with Philemon and fled. Yet, there is a reason this happened in God's purposes.

"Have him back forever" speaks of the eternal relationship Onesimus and Philemon will now have now that they are both Christians.

Verse 16 is explosive and potentially speaks of Paul wanting Philemon to set Onesimus free from slavery. Whether this is correct or not, Paul wants him to treat him as a loved brother, not as a slave. In v. 17, he goes further—welcome him back as you would welcome me. For Philemon, after Jesus, Paul is the most important person in the world, for he led him to Christ (v. 19). He is saying to welcome him back as Christian royalty! Like welcoming the great Apostle to the Gentiles himself! This speaks of the end of slavery, even if it is not explicit. Considering v. 22, he is asking Philemon not to take Onesimus back into the slave's quarters, but to house him in a guest room reserved for dignitaries.

Some consider "in the flesh" to indicate Onesimus is Philemon's brother and Paul is mediating matter of sibling rivalry. Rather, "in the flesh" means brothers in Christ in this world, and "in the Lord" speaks of eternal brotherhood.

Promise to pay costs: Phlm 18–20

Verse 18–19

Paul effectively writes a blank cheque for Philemon. Here, he is like the Good Samaritan who offers to pay the costs for the injured man (Luke 10:35). This also suggests Onesimus has wronged Philemon. As a slave, any time spent away from his master without permission was an act of theft.

With Philemon's wealth and generosity, it is unlikely Paul would have ended up paying anything.

Verse 20

The benefit Paul wants is not something for himself, but that he accepts back Philemon. Isn't it interesting that Paul sees him paying the costs of Onesimus as producing benefit?

"Refresh my heart" is not general but speaks of Paul's being refreshed in his heart through Onesimus being accepted back by Philemon. Paul speaks as a father handing over his son to Philemon, and he is kind of saying "please look after my boy." It also makes me think of God sending his own son to the world.

Statement of confidence: Phlm 21

Verse 21

Paul ends with a statement of his confidence in Philemon. This is a subtle final appeal.

Letter Closing: Phlm 22–25

Travel plans

Verse 22

In asking Philemon to prepare a room for him, Paul shows his confidence of being released. This fits with Phil

1:24–26 where despite facing death, Paul somehow *knows* he will get out of prison in Rome (or Ephesus).

It shows that while Paul was a tentmaker providing for himself, he was willing to accept patronage in certain circumstances.

It also shows that Philemon was a wealthy man, with a large house, including guest rooms.

He also implicitly asks Philemon to pray for him, something he asks of his converts a lot (see Ch. 8).

There is also a subtle nudge—I am coming soon to check out what you have done for me and to pay what I owe you.

Greetings

In vv. 23-24, as he usually does at the end of a letter, he sends greetings from those with him. Those named are some of Paul's key co-workers and it adds to our picture of the early church and its key figures.

Epaphras planted the Colossian church (Col 1:7), was a prayer warrior for them, may have also planted the Hierapolis and Laodicean churches (Col 4:12–13), and was in prison with Paul, as this verse testifies. Note again, he is a prisoner of Christ Jesus, not the Romans. God is in control.

Seeing Mark's name here and in Col 4:10 tells us that Paul and Mark were reconciled after the big schism earlier (Acts 15:36–41). From Jerusalem and a relative of Barnabas (Acts 12:12, 25), Mark is one of Paul's few Jewish co-workers. He is traditionally the writer of Mark's Gospel. He is called Peter's son in 1 Pet 5:12, showing their close relationship. Indeed, as we have seen, he wrote down Peter's Gospel in Mark at the time of Peter's death (see Ch. 2).

We also see Luke's name, he's a doctor (Col 4:14), and

traveling companion of Paul as evidenced by the "we-passages." He wrote Luke-Acts, and so in this verse are named two of the great writers of the NT. He is in Rome with Paul, which indicates that he was in the right place to gather material for his work.

Aristarchus is mentioned as a traveling companion of Paul (Acts 19:29; 20:4) and was on the ship to Rome with Paul (Acts 27:2). He is a Macedonian from Thessalonica, no doubt converted on Paul's visit to the city (Acts 17).

Demas is also mentioned in Col 4:14 and is a Gentile co-worker. He deserted Paul near his death and sadly appears to have fallen from faith being "in love with the present age" (2 Tim 4:10).

Salutation

Verse 25

Paul usually starts with a statement of grace and ends with one. He does so here. He asks that grace of Christ be with your spirit, using the singular to speak of the spirits of the people of the church. This is a prayer that they experience God's gracious spiritual benefits in their inner beings.

Paul's Letters: leadership, culture, and ethics in Philemon

Paul's letter to Philemon is very instructive in terms of leadership, culture, and ethics.

Philemon: Leadership

We see the art of a wise leader in the way Paul handles this situation.

Paul's Leadership

Paul is very tactful in the letter. As the apostle to the Gentiles and Philemon's father in the faith, he has the authority and courage to simply tell Philemon what to do (vv. 8, 14). Yet he doesn't exert that authority or exercise his boldness. Rather, with great love and affection, he seeks to get Philemon to respond to what is right. While his words can be seen as flattery, they are in fact genuine. He calls Philemon a beloved co-worker, showing that he loves Philemon and sees him as one of the team (v. 1). He honours all the hard, good work he has done for himself and for others. Philemon is not only using his house for a church but being lavishly generous which has refreshed the hearts and lives of many Christians (vv. 4–7). Paul's language is full of love and affection, not being afraid to express emotion toward Philemon (v. 12).

He uses family language through the letter drawing Philemon into realising their oneness in the family of God (v. 1, 2, 3, 7, 10, 16, 20). Seeing churches as families is a wonderful way to move toward the intimate unity we aspire to. He uses clever plays on words as he describes the situation (v. 11).

The way he interprets his imprisonment as imprisonment for Christ rather than the Romans and the manner in which he sees the good in such a difficult situation shows that he sees the world through what God is doing rather than what appears to be the case. God is in control even if things seem dire. He is working out his purposes (vv. 1, 9, 15–16, 23).

His preparedness to count the financial cost of Onesimus' flight speaks of Paul's material generosity (vv. 18–19). This is astonishing when we consider Paul is not out working at this time, he is in prison. Ministry can bring with it great financial sacrifice as we give up income to pursue God's call and as we sacrifice wealth in the service of our ministries. Yet, for Paul, this is no issue.

All that matters is the reconciliation of the two parties. Jesus said, "Blessed are the peacemakers" (Matt 5:9). Paul gives a brilliant example of reconciliation, he acting as the mediator between two conflicting Christian parties. He receives Onesimus, counsels him, including leading him to Christ. He then acts as a mediator with the one wronged, another Christian, Philemon. Paul seeks to bring peace where there was conflict. In Christian leadership, conflict resolution is one of the most important skills to develop. Paul shows us how here as he lovingly brings unity between the men.

Paul knows he needs support and refreshment, even if he does provide for himself. He welcomes Philemon's refreshment and accepts his hospitality (Phlm 7, 20–21). To be a successful minister of the gospel means that we have to allow people to care for us and provide for us so that we can be sustained in mission. Paul is unafraid to do this. However, he does not impose himself without gratitude.

Other Lessons About Leadership

Philemon and Onesimus

We can also learn some things about leadership from Philemon and Onesimus. Onesimus shows us that God can take a useless criminal, a runaway slave, and turn him into a Christian minister. In Col 4:9 he has become "our faithful and beloved brother" who is granted, with Tychicus, the honour of reporting to the Colossian church Paul's situation in Rome. He is to be taken back as a brother and apostle (v. 16). This is fantastic!

Philemon and Apphia

Philemon and Apphia are also pictured as great and generous Christian leaders. Philemon and Apphia, like Priscilla and Aquila and Andronicus and Junia (Rom 16:3–7), are likely a couple of wealthy Asian Romans who host the church. They then are preparing to use their wealth and home for God's cause (vv. 1–2). They are full of love, faith, and share their love and wealth refreshing the hearts of other Christians and traveling missionaries like Paul and his team (vv. 3–7, 20, 22). Paul may write the letter to get what he wants done, but he does so confident of the right outcome (v. 21).

The Co-workers—Team Ministry

Mention of the co-workers of Paul in v. 23 reminds us of Paul's team philosophy. Those named are clearly brilliant people. Epaphras planted as many as three churches in the Lycus Valley (Col 1:7; 4:12–13). Mark was also a traveling missionary working with Paul, Barnabas, and became a special friend of Peter (1 Pet 5:13). Luke too was amazing—a doctor who travelled extensively with Paul, and who wrote the epic Luke-Acts saga telling the story of the origins of the Christian movement. The Thessalonian Aristarchus too was a traveling companion of Paul, with him carrying the Jerusalem Collection, and ending up on the ship to Rome with Paul (Acts 19:29; 20:4; 27:2). Seeing these luminaries named together shows how brilliant people can work together without being threatened, needing to outdo one another, or caught up in envy and rivalry. Not that Paul was perfect. His breakup with Barnabas and Mark is legendary (Acts 15:36–41). Yet, they were clearly reconciled by this point in Rome. Mark's links to Peter also show that there was unity across Paul and Peter, something also reflected in Peter's positive view of Paul's letters in 2 Pet 3.

Philemon: Culture

Mention has been made of Galatians 3:28, a text in which Paul succinctly states the social implications of the coming of Christ—in Christ Jesus, the great social divisions between Jews and Gentiles, men and women, and slaves and free find their consummation.

Philemon focuses on the great ancient social division between slaves and freed people. Slavery was normative across the world, until in 1833 it was outlawed in the British Empire, and at the end of the Civil War in the US in 1865. The story of Wilberforce's campaign to see it ended in Great Britain is well-known through the movie *Amazing Grace*.

Paul's letter to Philemon is one of the seeds of Scripture on which the movement formed. In this letter, he asks Philemon to take back his formerly useless slave as a brother, welcoming him as he would welcome Paul the apostle. This is astonishing.

We see here the cultural revolution that Christianity is designed to be. Great divisions are no longer to plague us as they have in the past. At the foot of the cross, all humankind, male and female, adult and child, Jew and Gentile, Pakeha and Māori, slave and free, rich and poor, kneel together as one without prejudice.

Our challenge as leaders is to build this kind of culture in the organisations and churches in which we work. While there will always be status differentiation and leaders, for this is needed to bring order from chaos and to move organisations in the direction of growth and God's goals for them, there is in fact no real status differentiation before God. Slaves can be co-workers and preachers (e.g., Onesimus, Col 4:9; Phlm 16). Women are equally able to do the required work of the gospel as men—it is a matter of gifts, call, and the right character.

Where there are hierarchies, the leaders must work extra hard to ensure that while these exist, the "strong" are deeply concerned for the "weak" and the values of the organisation are those central to the gospel: honouring one another, humility, service, love, selflessness, sacrifice for the other (especially the weaker), gentleness, kindness, partnership, and the like (see further below).

The culture must be one of partnership and collaboration, as between Paul and Philemon; Philemon, Apphia, and Archippus; Paul and the co-workers of Phlm 24; and if Philemon hears Paul, between Paul, Philemon, and Onesimus. In this way, Christianity has the power to explode which is not possible without such unity.

In NZ, we see something of this in the transformation of the All Blacks since Graham Henry took over the team in 2004. The team of leaders put together included three of the best coaches in the world: Graham Henry, Wayne Smith, and Steve Hansen. Yet, they laid egos aside, dropped from the team players whose egos got in the way, and set about rebuilding the culture of the team. They also set up a leadership group among the players, removing the top-down "do what I say" type of leadership, replacing it with a collaborative form of leadership led as much by the players as the coaches, who worked as a collective, along with a range of other coaches and supports staff. They began winning almost everything. They had a terrible setback at the 2007 World Cup. Yet, the NZRFU kept faith in the team. They won almost everything from 2007 on, and in 2011 they won the RWC. Then, Steve Hansen took over, and the collective culture continued. They continued to win and won the 2015 RWC. They remain the world's best team and are one of the favourites to win the 2019 RWC. It will be no surprise if they do, even if other nations are improving by adopting their methods.

To me, these men are simply using the tried and true methods the gospel calls us toward–team leadership. Establishing a culture of participation and collaboration. Laying aside egos for the cause. Forming a family culture. Being real with each other. The group working together as one focused on winning. For us, winning means being absolutely faithful to God's call to worship, loving one another, and sharing God's gospel to the world in unity. This will yield results if we persevere for the gospel is the power of God for salvation.

Philemon: Ethics

A culture is set by common values, our shared ethics, the virtues we aspire to. Philemon is full of them.

Love

This is the supreme virtue which sums up all virtues. There is a lot of love language in Philemon. Philemon is beloved (v. 1) as is Onesimus (v. 16). God is thanked for Philemon's love toward Christ and all the saints (v. 5). Paul directly thanks him for the joy and comfort he has received through him, and for the way he has refreshed the hearts of the holy people of God (v. 7). Philemon embodies the twin commands of God to love him with everything and to love one another (Luke 10:27). Paul too exemplifies love as he appeals to Philemon not from a position of dominance, but for *agapē*'s sake (v. 9). Paul's love for Onesimus is also apparent. He is his very heart! —he loves him deep in his gut! (v. 12).

Grace

Grace means "unmerited favour." In Christian thought, it is God's generous kindness expressed toward humankind, especially in and through Christ. Paul begins and ends his letters with grace (Phlm 3, 25). The source of this lavish grace is God the Father and Jesus.

Joy

Joy is the second of the fruit of the Spirit (Gal 5:22). Joy is happiness, but something deeper, something not affected by a surface situation, but something that wells in the heart despite adverse circumstances. Paul is facing the struggles of a first-century Roman prison but casts his mind back to the joy he has received from Philemon (Phlm 7). Where the freedom of the Spirit is found, despite the responsibility we have as God's people to please God and further his mission, there should be a mutual experience of joy.

Encouragement

As noted earlier, the Greek for "comfort" in Phlm 7 can be translated "encouragement" (*paraklēsis*). Philemon has provided Paul with joy and encouragement. *Paraklēsis* is also a spiritual gift that Philemon no doubt has (s.a.

Timothy, 1 Tim 4:13). God is the God of *paraklēsis* in Rom 15:5 and 2 Cor 1:3 (s.a. 2 Thess 2:16). We receive encouragement in Christ (Phil 2:1). True NT prophecy has the effect of *paraklēsis* (1 Cor 14:3). Whether we have the gift or not, we are to be a source of encouragement and comfort to others (see also 2 Cor 1:3–7).

Non-Compulsion

Absolute authority gives people the power to compel people to bend to their will. A Christian value is that we wish people to respond with goodness, not from compulsion but of their own accord (Phlm 14). This we see in Jesus who "emptied *himself*," and "humbled *himself*," "gave *himself*," willingly for the world (Gal 1:3; 2:20; Eph 5:2; Phil 2:7, 8; 1 Tim 2:6; Tit 2:4). We see it in terms of Christian giving with each one not giving out of reluctance or compulsion, but as decided in the heart, "for God loves a cheerful giver" (2 Cor 9:7). The key to a good Christian culture is one in which people want to be there, want to contribute, and willingly give themselves for the cause. Paul's whole letter is designed to see this in the case of Philemon.

Sacrificial Generous Self-giving

We see the value of self-giving and sacrifice powerfully in Philemon. First, Philemon and Apphia are models of self-giving as they use their home for the church and lavish generosity on Paul and the saints refreshing their hearts (Phlm 2, 5, 7).

Paul demonstrates self-giving in sending Onesimus back, a man he has come to love as a brother and co-worker, who is his very heart. He would have loved to have kept Onesimus with him to continue the gospel mission he and his co-workers were doing in Rome. However, as God was prepared to send his heart and Son Jesus to save the world, Paul willingly sent Onesimus back (Phlm 12–13). He knew to keep Onesimus without Philemon's consent was in itself wrong, even if the ends justified the means (v. 14).

Hope

The language of hope is not explicitly used in Phlm. However, v. 15 calls to mind the hope of Romans 8:28 where Paul expresses his confidence that all things work for the good of God's loved and called people. Paul understood that while suffering is horrendous, it is temporary and that as we are buffeted by pressures and pain, the light of God dwells in us jars of clay by his Spirit. This is powerfully expressed in 2 Cor 4–5. We have the light of the gospel in our beings, though we are frail, broken, and vulnerable (2 Cor 4:1–7). Because of the internal power of God in us, the Spirit, we are afflicted, crushed, persecuted, struck down, yet not defeated. We experience the sufferings that come to all humankind and in Christ, but God's life is in us, the burning cauldron of his presence (2 Cor 4:8–12). Hence, we do not lose heart, even if our outward bodies are failing us, God renews us daily (2 Cor 4:16). Further, we are earning an eternal weight of glory that makes our suffering pale into insignificance, eternal bodies, life with God forever (2 Cor 4:16–5:10). The presence of the Spirit and our certain futures give us hope. An authentic Christian community is founded on faith, expressed in love, and optimistic in hope.

Egalitarianism

The letter is written by the Apostle to the Gentiles to a

group of church leaders about a slave, yet all are one family in Christ. There is no hierarchy of demand. The ancient world and much of the modern world is full of hierarchies and pecking orders. Christianity flattens the world out. This can be frustrating for leaders sometimes who can't get things done as quickly as they like. It can be annoying for others who want leaders to just get on with it. A hierarchical world often feels ordered and safe. Christianity is more daring. It invites all to participate, encouraging the priesthood of all believers. This can be slower as it takes longer to get things done. But when there are synergy and people function from the values of the Kingdom, lead as servants, each doing their God-given part, the church can explode with a power seen nowhere else in the world. This is seen as young and old, rich and poor, slave and free, men and women, across all cultures, coming together with the common cause of the Kingdom. This should excite us in a multicultural city like Auckland where the fields are white for the harvest (John 4:35) and plentiful, but the workers are few (Matt 9:36). Who knows what is possible?

Partnership

Paul uses *koinō–* language in the letter. He describes Philemon's generosity toward others as his "partnership (*koinōnia*) in the faith" (v. 7). He describes himself as Philemon's partner (*koinōnos*) in v. 18. He speaks of Timothy as a brother (Phlm 1).

He uses *syn* (with) language to emphasise partnership. Philemon is his "beloved co-worker (*synergos*)," working together for the gospel (v. 1). Archippus is his "fellow soldier," contending in the spiritual war for the world as a tightly knit army (*systratiōtēs*, cf. Eph 6:10–17). Epaphras is Paul's "fellow prisoner" (*synaichmalōtos*) "in Christ Jesus" speaking of a three-way bond between Paul, Epaphras, and Jesus (Phlm 23). Mark, Aristarchus, Demas, and Luke are Paul's "co-workers" (*synergos*), labouring together for the gospel (Phlm 24).

Father and Son are also dwelling in an intimate partnership, extending grace and peace to the church (Phlm 3). There is partnership in prayer as Paul prays for Philemon (Phlm 4, 6) and through the prayers of Philemon, Apphia, Archippus, and the others in the church, he will be released to come to them (Phlm 22). There are a father and son gospel partnership between Paul and Onesimus in Rome, cut short by Paul's need to send him home (Phlm 10–13). This must come to an end because Onesimus must return to Philemon to continue the master-slave partnership but in a completely reframed way—serving together as brothers in the gospel in Colossae and the Lycus Valley (Phlm 11–16). There is partnership between all the Christians involved as they work "in Christ Jesus" (v. 8, 20), and "in the Lord" (v. 20). There is financial partnership as Philemon has blessed Paul and others lavishly (Phlm 4–7, 20, 22), Paul paying back what is owed by Onesimus (Phlm 19).

Hospitality

Hospitality, whereby we welcome and provide for the care of another, is an essential Christian virtue. God and Christ are the ultimate hosts, inviting us into the Godhead so that we are "in Christ Jesus" (Phlm 8, 16, 20, 23). This is seen through Philemon and Apphia who host a church (Phlm 1). They host other saints and Paul himself (Phlm 4–7, 22).

Despite his humble situation in imprisonment in his rented accommodation, Paul has hosted Onesimus as a father with a son and has led him to Christ (Phlm 10). Philemon is also to host Onesimus, not as a slave, but as a beloved brother and as if he were the apostle Paul himself. He is to house him not in the slave's rooms, but in the guestroom set apart for the likes of Paul (Phlm 22). As the Prodigal Slave comes home, as does the Father in the Prodigal Son, he is to dress him in his best robe, place a ring on his finger and shoes on his feet, kill the fattened calf, and party (Luke 15:22–32). As the angels in heaven rejoice when one sinner is saved, Philemon's whanau and church are to party like it's 1999 for the lost sheep who has come home; for the coin that was lost but now is found (Luke 15:7).

11

Chapter Eleven: Hebrews and the General Epistles

This chapter shifts attention from Paul to the other letters of the New Testament. These are full of wonderful theology and ideas stimulating our praxis as God's people. They can tend to be downplayed when compared with Paul's letters, but a fully orbed theology considers them as intently as the Gospels, Acts, the letters of Paul, and Revelation.

More Detail

Keown, *Discovering the New Testament*, Vol 3, ch. 1–7.

Suggested Bible Readings

James

Jude

Introduction

After Paul's letters come a set of other letters beginning with Hebrews, then James, two letters attributed to Peter, three to John, and finally one by Jude. Then comes Revelation which will be dealt with in the next and final chapter.

The General or Catholic Epistles

"The General Epistles" is a term used to describe the collection of seven letters that appear after the Paulines in the Bible. They are James, 1 & 2 Peter, 1, 2 & 3 John, and Jude. The General Epistles are also called the "catholic" epistles, formed from the term catholic (*katholikē*) meaning "universal" or "worldwide." The term originated in the late second century and was used by a number of third and fourth-century writers to describe these letters. They are called "general" because they are considered to have been written for a wider audience, rather than one specific church or individual.

Hebrews

Authorship and Date

Hebrews was considered one of the Pauline epistles amongst some in the early church. As will be discussed briefly below, it is almost certainly not directly from Paul. It is the longest of the other epistles and a wonderful resource for understanding the OT. The central theme of the letter is that Jesus is the culmination of God's speech to the world and the fulfilment of the hopes of Judaism.

Many in the early church considered the letter to the Hebrews had been written by Paul. However, today, few, if any, scholars hold the view that Paul directly wrote it.

This is because of the differences to the Pauline letters, the lack of an ascription, and Heb 2:3 which clearly states that the author was converted by first-generation preachers of the gospel. There is a lot of debate about who did write it, with options including Apollos, Barnabas, Luke (perhaps on behalf of Paul), Clement of Rome, or Priscilla. Origen said, "God alone knows," and never was a truer word said.

The main clues to setting and date are: 1) Heb 13:24: "Those from Italy send you their greetings;" 2) The reference to Timothy being with the author (Heb 13:23). This suggests that it was written when Timothy was in Rome with Paul, before or after Paul left for Philippi (Phil 2:19) and Ephesus (1 and 2 Tim). The most likely date then is ad 60–62 (cf. Acts 28:30–31; Phil 1:12–13). Alternatively, it may have been written when Timothy returned to Rome with Paul's parchments (2 Tim 4:9, 21), i.e. after ad 64.

Core Issue: People Turning to Judaism

The problem in the letter is identified in Heb 10:32–39 where the author refers to his/her readers' falling away from their initial faith in the face of persecution. They appear to be Jewish Christians abandoning Christianity for some form of the Jewish faith. This could relate to the pressure Christians came under in Rome around the time leading into and during the Neronian persecution. The author seeks to convince them not to fall away by presenting Christ as "better by far" and warning of harsh consequences if they fall away.

The Superiority of Christ

The key theme in Hebrews is the superiority of Christ as

God's final revelation (Heb 1:1–4). It begins with a wonderful hymnic statement of the divine Christ as God's final word to the world who saves and who now reigns (Heb 1:1–4). This is followed by two main threads:

1) The superiority of Christ over Judaism.

2) Warnings not to fall away and encouragements to persevere. These warnings and encouragements include constant references to OT examples of believers who struggled.

A High Christology

Hebrews has a very high Christology as the author constantly seeks to demonstrate Jesus' superiority to all that has come before. Jesus is seen as:

1) Superior to the angels because he is God the Son (Heb 1:5–14).

2) The fulfilment of humanity's role to rule over creation, i.e. he is greater than Adam (Heb 2:5–18).

3) Greater than Moses (Heb 3:1–6).

4) The greatest High Priest in the order of Melchizedek (Heb 4:14–5:10, s.a. Gen 14:17–24; Ps 110:4).

5) The certainty of God's promise because Jesus is the Great High Priest (Heb 6:13–20).

6) A High Priest who is superior to the Levitical priests (Heb 7:1–28).

7) A High Priest of a superior covenant (Heb 8:1–13).

8) A High Priest of the heavenly sanctuary (Heb 9:1–28).

9) The supreme once-for-all sacrifice, and as such superior to the Jewish sacrifices (Heb 10:1–19).

One can see the importance of Jesus as High Priest. The author finds in Psalm 110 not only Jesus' kingship, but his high priesthood. He is both the priest and the sacrifice the priest makes for the sins of the world. He also becomes the entry point to God's heavenly kingdom.

Warnings

Throughout Hebrews there is a series of warnings not to fall away, along with encouragements to persevere. These punctuate the teaching on the superiority of Christ:

1) First warning: do not drift away from the truth (Heb 2:1–4).

2) Second warning and encouragement: against unbelief in the same way Israel drifted into unbelief in the wilderness (Heb 3:7–4:13).

3) Third warning against falling away (Heb 5:11–6:12).

4) Fourth warning against falling away, an encouragement to persevere and a reminder of past commitment (Heb 10:19–39).

5) A fifth and final warning against rejecting God's grace (Heb 12:14–29).

Perseverance

After Heb 11 there is a shift away from a concern for the superiority of Christ to strong encouragements to persevere. These are linked to the warnings above which in many cases lead into the summons to endure. These include:

1) The nature of true faith (Heb 11:1–40).

2) The supreme example of Jesus (Heb 12:1–4).

3) Endure hardship as the discipline of the Lord (Heb 12:5–11).

4) Exhortations to right living (Heb 13:1–19).

5) Benediction, final exhortations, and greetings (Heb 13:20–25).

Can a believer fall away?

Some of the theological controversies around Hebrews relate to whether or not a believer can fall away. The majority of contemporary scholars argue that the author is warning against genuine believers falling away as they return to Judaism or some variant thereof. These warnings should serve as a reminder of the dangers of turning from Christ.

Understanding the OT

Finally, we can say that Hebrews is arguably the best book in the NT to grasp the way that the coming of Christ has transformed the institutions of Israel. Now that Christ, God's final word, has come, everything including the covenant, temple, sacrifice system, and the priesthood is fulfilled and transformed because Christ has come.

James

Authorship and Setting

The authorship of James is highly disputed. However, as with the letters of Peter, Jude, and John, it is extremely unlikely that the early church would have accepted a pseudonymous work only supposedly written by the brother of Jesus who was also a leading apostle. James had been converted after seeing the resurrected Christ (1 Cor

15:7) and became the leader of the Jerusalem Church in the early 40s (Acts 12:17; 15:13; 21:18, cf. Acts 1:13; Gal 2:12). Later church tradition says a huge amount about him as James the Just. The letter of James must be dated before ad 62 when James was stoned to death by the Sanhedrin (see Josephus, *Ant.* 20.200). Some, date it before the Jerusalem Council (mid–40s) and so it represents James' pre-Council view. However, more likely it was written between that time and James' death in ad 62. It probably originated from Jerusalem; James' and the Jerusalem church's base and was written to scattered Jewish Christians throughout the Empire.

Style

It is written in excellent Greek with a huge number of imperatives (fifty–nine) and a lot of analogy (e.g. tongues like ships' rudders or sparks). It reads like a series of sermonettes and has no one clear issue. It is jam-packed with links to the OT and the Synoptic Gospels (e.g. the royal law in 2:8), and especially the Sermon on the Mount (e.g. Jas 5:8, cf. Matt 5:8). There are also many links to 1 John (e.g. Jas 1:17, cf. 1 John 1:5).

Purpose and Content

Its main purpose is to encourage and instruct diaspora Jewish Christians in their faith:

1) Encouragement in the face of trials and persecutions (e.g. Jas 1:2–3, 12; 5:7–12.

2) God, the path to wisdom (see Jas 1:5–8; 3:13–18).

3) Problems concerning a theology of wealth (Jas 1:9–11; 2:1–12; 5:1–6).

4) Believers who are falling into sin and temptation which they must withstand (Jas 1:13–16).

5) Contention, anger, slander, and poor speech (Jas 3:1–6; 4:1–2).

6) Nominalism and antinomianism faith, i.e. a workless faith (Jas 1:22–27; 2:14–26).

(Additional Note: Antinomian is "A term used to characterize believers in the early church who wrongly thought that salvation by faith in Jesus Christ freed them from all moral obligations and that they could sin with impunity (Gk *anti*, "against," + *nomos*, "law"). The problem of antinomianism is addressed in such NT passages as Romans 6:1–11 and 1 John (cf. 1 Jn 1:9–10)." (See A. G. Patzia & A. J. Petrotta, *Pocket Dictionary of Biblical Studies* [Downers Grove, IL: IVP, 2002], 12). It is thus the opposite extreme of legalism and Judaising.

7) Submission to God, repentance and contrition, and renunciation of pride, greed, covetousness and the world (Jas 4:1–12).

8) Reliance on God's will and not human plans (Jas 4:13–17).

9) Vows without swearing (Jas 5:12).

10) Faithful prayer (Jas 5:13–18).

11) Bringing back those who stray (Jas 5:19–20).

Reconciling James and Paul

One issue is the supposed clash between James and Paul concerning works and faith. This cannot be discussed in full here. Luther had little time for James, believing it was an "epistle of straw" that should be removed from the canon. The problem is that Paul appears to preach a gospel of salvation by grace without works (Eph 2:8–9; Rom 3:28; Gal 2:16) with Abraham as the role model of faith (Rom 4:1–3). James, on the other hand, argues for a faith accompanied by works and also gives Abraham as an example (Jas 2:14–26). However, this is not such an issue when we realize that Paul is speaking of faith for entry into salvation and James is speaking of what authentic faith looks like; a faith springing forth in works, something that Paul heartily agrees with (e.g. Eph 2:10; Rom 6:14–23; Phil 2:12–13). Indeed, James affirms faith but emphasises the need for works. The greatest value of James is that it teaches us that authentic faith has content and is not just intellectual assent; it is a life lived in obedience to God particularly in caring for the poor.

The Letters of Peter

There are two letters attributed to Peter in the NT. They are both highly contentious in terms of authorship, especially 2 Peter. We will look briefly at each in turn.

1 Peter

Authorship and Setting

The authorship of 1 Peter is challenged. However, the arguments are not strong and there is little reason to believe that the early church would have accepted a pseudonymous letter from the one who was viewed as "the rock of the church." The letter was, in all likelihood, written in Rome toward the end of Peter's life (mid–60s). It is possible that Silas (also Silvanus) penned it for him, although this is disputed (1 Pet 5:12).

Recipients and Purpose

It was written to churches in the northern part of Asia Minor, the provinces of Pontus, Galatia, Cappadocia, Asia, and Bithynia. These are areas that Paul did not personally evangelise and were either evangelised by Peter or others unknown. It is possible that Peter had travelled through this area in the mid–50s after his visit to Corinth and that he had developed a bond with these churches.

He writes to encourage them under persecution and gives direction as to how to live in this world. He calls believers foreigners and aliens, using the language of exile to describe them. There is a strong emphasis on living in relation to governing authorities. Peter encourages his readers to submit to authorities as much they are able without violating their allegiance to Christ, and to give witness through their lives and words of their renewed life in Christ.

Content

The letter begins with a glorious doxology outlining, in a manner similar to Ephesians 1:3–14, the benefits of salvation, including eternal inheritance (1 Pet 1:3–5). There is a strong emphasis on suffering throughout the letter. Peter exhorts his readers to stand firm in suffering (1 Pet 1:6). Their great salvation is their hope in the face of their opponents (1 Pet 1:6). There is a strong call to holiness and obedience and to refusing to fall prey to the pagan licentious living which dominated their Asian world (1 Pet 1:13–15). There is a reference to believers' redemption through Christ and through the word (1 Pet 1:17–2:3).

Believers are being built into a spiritual house and a

priesthood that offers sacrifices to God through Christ (1 Pet 2:4–8). Believers are the fulfilment of the hope of the OT, a chosen people, a royal priesthood, a holy nation, God's people, whose role is to declare the wonderful deeds of God and his salvation (1 Pet 2:9–10). They are to be different from pagans, living good lives that glorify God (1 Pet 2:11–12).

In 1 Pet 2:13–17, Peter says they are to submit to the governing authorities, including the emperor, living freely but as servants of God. This is followed, in 1 Pet 2:18–3:7, by a household code with a strong emphasis on giving witness. Peter tells household slaves to submit to their masters even when they are harsh. They are to follow the example of Christ who never returned abuse, despite his suffering on the cross. He appeals to wives to submit to their unbelieving husbands who have rejected the word, seeking to win them without preaching at them but by the quality of their lives. Husbands are to care for their wives with gentleness.

In 1 Pet 3:8–13, he urges believers to do good, even when they are treated poorly by others. In 1 Pet 3:14–16, they are to always be ready to answer inquirers with a reason for their faith. In this way, the questioners will be shamed. Peter encourages them to do good rather than evil. He speaks of Christ's death for sins and for the unrighteous (1 Pet 3:18–22). Christ also goes to Hades to preach to the spiritual forces of evil (not human spirits) about the victory of God.

In chapter 4, Peter urges the believers of north Asia not to live as the pagans live, but to leave behind the classic Greco-Roman sins of debauchery, drunkenness, sexual immorality, and idolatry, or face judgment (1 Pet 4:1–6). Instead, they are to pray, show love, offer hospitality, serve with their gifts, and speak graciously (1 Pet 4:7–11). In 1

Pet 4:12–19, he encourages them in their suffering. They should not be surprised but rejoice for they participate in the sufferings of Christ.

In chapter 5, Peter gives guidance to shepherds to willingly watch over the flock without exploitation and await their reward (1 Pet 5:1–4). He urges humility and submission (1 Pet 5:5–6), and resistance of the devil (1 Pet 5:7–11).

2 Peter

Authorship and Setting

The authorship of 2 Peter is hugely challenged; so much so, that most scholars believe it is not the work of the apostle Peter. Although there are significant differences to 1 Peter and similarities to Jude's work, it is improbable that the early church would accept a work in Peter's name that was written by someone else. It is most likely that Jude used Peter, Peter used Jude, or they used a common source (the view I prefer).

The date is hard to ascertain. Those who maintain it is pseudonymous argue that it must be later than Peter's death, so opt for a date in the 70s to 90s. Those who accept Petrine authorship date it before Peter's death (unsurprisingly), so sometime between ad 65 and 67. They also believe it was written from Rome where Peter was incarcerated. That he is approaching death is clear in 2 Pet 1:12–13.

Recipients

It is written to "those who have obtained a faith equal in value to ours through the righteousness of our God and Saviour Jesus Christ" (2 Pet 1:1). In 2 Pet 3:1, he mentions that this is his second letter to his recipients. As such, it is probably written to the same churches as 1 Peter.

False Teaching

This time there is evidence of serious false teaching. The main reason for the letter is to challenge them and call the readers to resist and reject them.

Some of the features of these false teachers and prophets from chapters 2 & 3 include:

1) Denying Christ (2 Pet 2:1).

2) Sexual immorality (2 Pet 2:2, 7, 13).

3) Greed and exploitation (2 Pet 2:3, 14).

4) Slandering celestial beings and angels (2 Pet 2:10–11).

5) Sin and seductiveness (2 Pet 2:14).

6) Boastfulness and empty words (2 Pet 2:18).

7) People who previously believed but have turned to heresy (2 Pet 2:20).

8) Repudiating and mocking the return of Christ and the establishment of the new heavens and earth (2 Pet 3:1–13).

9) Distorting Paul's teaching (2 Pet 3:15–16).

Identifying the exact set of ideas is difficult. It has some aspects of Greco-Roman perspectives (e.g. sexual immorality). The teaching seems to question aspects of eschatology found in the wider NT such as Christ's return.

Peter's Response

Peter's letter encourages his audience to trust in God's promises and add to their faith other character attributes including self-control, perseverance, and love which will cause them to be effective for Christ (2 Pet 1:3–9). Knowing he will die soon (2 Pet 1:12–13), he writes to encourage them, reminding them that he is an eye-witness to Christ at his transfiguration (2 Pet 1:16–17) and that the inspired prophecies have been fulfilled (2 Pet 1:19–21).

Peter's rebuke of the false teachers is powerful. He uses very strong language to describe them and their judgment in 2 Pet 2:4–9. He recalls the judgment on the ungodly when the sons of God copulated with human women (Gen 6:1–4), at the flood (Gen 6:5–8:19), on Sodom and Gomorrah (Gen 18), and on Balaam (cf. Num 22). Just as these sinful people experienced God's wrath in history, these false teachers will also experience terrible suffering for all eternity (2 Pet 2:17).

In chapter 3, he speaks of the coming judgment on the scoffers in the last days. Just as the world was purged with the flood at the time of Noah and no one but Noah saw it coming, Christ will come unheralded, like a thief, and the world will be purged with fire (2 Pet 3:3–13). This recalls Jesus' teaching in Matt 24 and Luke 17 where judgment is likened to the flood. The earth will be superseded by a new heaven and earth. However, God wants all people to be saved from this (2 Pet 3:9).

Believers should live holy and good lives while they await this day (2 Pet 3:11, 14). Peter mentions the letters of his dear brother Paul which some distort, but which are Scriptures. This is a radical statement as it places Paul's letters alongside the Scriptures of Israel. Peter finishes with a warning to not be deceived by the false teachers and fall from grace but rather, grow in grace and knowledge in Christ (2 Pet 3:15–18).

The Letters of John

Authorship and Setting

The authorship of the three letters attributed to John the apostle is highly disputed. Some consider it was written by the elder John, mentioned in Papias. Many scholars see them as productions of a supposed "Johannine school" centred around the apostle John but not necessarily from his pen. As is discussed on the authorship of John, we have to ask why the early church would have attributed them to the Apostle John without good reason.

They were probably written in Ephesus around the late 70s to 80s, and so after John's Gospel. 2 John and 3 John each have their own addressee, while 1 John does not have a specific recipient or recipients.

False Teaching

The letters of John focus on a heretical distortion of the Christian faith. The letters, and 1 John, in particular, suggest these features of the problem:

1) Some have left the community (1 John 2:18–19).

2) They deny Jesus is the Christ, the Messiah (1 John 2:22) and that he is God's Son (1 John 2:23; 4:14–15).

3) They are trying to lead the Christian recipients astray (1 John 2:26; 3:7).

4) They are false prophets (1 John 4:1) who do not acknowledge that Jesus came in the flesh (1 John 4:2, cf. 1

John 4:6; 2 John 7). Hence, they are docetic (Jesus was divine and not human).

5) They deny their sin (1 John 1:6–10).

6) The emphasis on love could imply that they are showing hate.

In summary, there are false teachers/prophets who are teaching that Jesus is not truly the Messiah because he is not truly a man (not of flesh) and they have broken away.

There are different theories of which heresy this is:

1) *Gnosticism*: a movement based around secret knowledge and a duality between matter and Spirit. In Gnostic thought, Jesus only appeared to be human.

2) *Docetism*: where Jesus appears to be a man but was not.

3) The *Heresy of Cerinthus* who severed Jesus from the divine Christ. The Spirit/Christ came on Jesus at his baptism and left him to suffer on the cross.

While John is not addressing Gnosticism itself, it is likely that John is opposing a docetic tendency and the first seeds of the Gnostic movement. Gnosticism flowered as a full-blown heresy half a century later.

1 John

1 John was written by John toward the end of his life (c. ad 90–100). That he is an eyewitness is found in 1 John 1:1–4 where he recalls walking with Christ, the Word of life.

John's Response to the False Teaching

As noted above, 1 John has heresy in the background. The letter starts by emphasising the reality of Jesus' incarnation. John declares that he saw, heard, and touched the human Jesus (1 John 1:1–4). He introduces the theme of light and darkness; true believers walk in the light forgiven by sin. False believers claim to be without sin. They should confess and be forgiven (1 John 1:5–10).

In chapter 2, John continues the theme of sin, urging his readers not to sin, but telling them that Jesus' death deals with sins (1 John 2:1–2). He urges obedience, perhaps challenging the false teachers (1 John 2:3–6). He states that this is not new but is the truth that they originally heard (1 John 2:7–8). In 1 John 2:9–11, he introduces the idea of love, which is essential to the light. 1 John 2:12–14 is a poem urging all in the church to stay faithful to the truth. This love cannot be directed to the world. Lust and boasting must be left behind for the world is passing away (1 John 2:15–17).

1 John 2:18–27 warns against the false teachers who are antichrists (see above). The believers know the truth and must not be deceived by these liars who deny the incarnation of Christ (1 John 2:20–27). As children they must carry on in him, experiencing the love of God and not be led astray (1 John 2:28–3:10). The letter strongly emphasises that believers must love one another as Christ loved the world, and that they must be obedient (1 John 3:11–24). In chapter 4, John again warns of false spirits and prophets. Believers must not listen to them (1 John 4:1–6). He again stresses love – for God is love (1 John 4:7–21).

In the final chapter, he urges faith and love, obedience, and the reality of Christ's incarnation (1 John 5:1–12). He concludes the letter with a statement of confidence in prayer (1 John 5:13–15), the renunciation of sin (1 John 5:16–17), that Satan rules the world (1 John 5:19), that Jesus is the true Son of God who has come and is God, and eternal life (1 John 5:20. Believers must avoid idolatry which was prevalent in the Asia Minor area (1 John 5:21).

2 John

2 John is written by the "elder," who is either the Apostle John or another disciple and elder from the Johannine community (see also on the authorship of John, ch. 2). It is unique in that it is written to a woman and her children. We do not know who these people are. The letter expresses joy at their walking in the truth, reiterates the importance of love and obedience, warns against antichrists and false prophets who deny the reality of Christ's incarnation (above), and warns of the consequences of such denial, i.e. rupture in the relationship with God. John says they should not welcome such false teachers. The letter concludes with John saying he desires to see them face to face rather than write using paper and ink.

3 John

While this short letter is attributed to the same author, the authorship of this letter remains an open question. This letter is also from "the elder," either John the disciple or another John, this time to Gaius, who is not likely to be the Gaius of Macedonia or Corinth (cf. Acts 19:29; 20:4; Rom 16:23; 1 Cor1:14). He is clearly a believer. John prays for blessings. He commends Gaius' faith and his walking in the truth. Gaius is showing hospitality to visitors and he is commended for it. John speaks of Diotrephes who is not commended for he is a gossiper and will not welcome the brothers. John urges Gaius to do good. He commends Demetrius. As in the previous letter, John ends by expressing his desire to see them in person rather than through writing.

Jude

The letter of Jude is one of the shortest letters in the NT, one chapter, twenty-five verses, and 458 words (NA 28)—only Philemon, and 2 and 3 John are shorter. It sounds and feels a lot like 2 Peter, leading to great speculation as to the relationship between the two letters. Other aspects of the letter are also contentious, including its canonicity, authorship, date, and setting. Despite all these questions, it is a power-packed letter urging its recipients to contend for the faith against false teachers who compromise the gospel. Living in a world where the gospel is challenged in multiple ways, whether from within the church or without, we are encouraged to be faithful to God's word.

Authorship

The letter is attributed to *Ioudas*, Jude or Judas, further described as a "brother of James" (Jude 1). Judas is a common name in the NT, used of a number of figures who we can quickly rule out as author of the letter: Judah the son of Jacob from the OT (Matt 1:2, 3; Luke 3:30, 33, cf. Matt 2:6; Heb 7:14; Rev 5:5), Judas Iscariot (e.g. Matt 10:4; Mark 3:19; Luke 6:16; John 6:71), and Judas the rebellious Galilean (Acts 5:37). Of NT figures named Judas (Judah, Jude, Theuddas or Theudas), possible but unlikely candidates for the writing of the letter include Judas of Straight Street in Damascus (Acts 9:11), Judas Barsabbas (Acts 15:22, 27, 32), Judas (sometimes Theudeus, or Labbaeus) the *son* of James (Mark 3:18; Luke 6:16; John 14:22; Acts 1:13), and Judas, the *brother* of Jesus, James, Joseph (Joses), and Simon (Matt 13:55; Mark 6:3).

Of these, some have argued that the writer is Judas

Barsabbas of Acts 15 arguing that "brother of James" in v. 1 means "co-worker of James" (Ellis). Others prefer the Apostle, Judas the son of James who may also have had a brother James which is possible as often a father's name was passed onto the son (Calvin). Later church history has a couple of others with the name James who could be the author. One is Judas the third bishop of Jerusalem as proposed by Streeter (Eusebius, *Hist. eccl.* 3.34.5; Apost. Con. 7.46).

Yet another option is that the writer is not a Jude at all, but someone who wrote pseudonymously using his name. One suggestion here is that the author is Thomas (also called Judas Thomas, Gos. Thom. 1) or his twin brother. Yet, the overwhelming favourite is Judas the brother of Jesus and James.

The traditional position is that Jude, the brother of Jesus and James (Luke 6:16; Acts 1:13) is the author of the letter (see further below). Those who reject this note that the writer describes himself not as Jesus' brother, but his slave (v. 1) and Jesus as his master and Lord (Jude 1, 4), the one who cares for the called (v. 2), the one who saved the people from Egypt (v. 5), the one the apostles belonged to (v. 17), whose mercy that leads to eternal life believers await (v. 21), and the one to whom he attributes praise (v. 25). Rejectors of Jude the brother of Jesus and James also argue that the Greek is very polished which does not fit with the carpenter's brother. They also think the letter was written a long time after the initial spread of the gospel (see esp. Jude 3, 17).

Supporters of the traditional position note that pseudonymous works were rejected by the early church as they constructed the NT. They also argue that the only Jude in the early church we know to have a brother James is Jude the brother of Jesus. The idea that brother indicates "co-worker" is possible, but the phrase "brother of" in the NT usually means literal brother. Decisively, no early church writer considered Judas Barsabbas as the author. The style of the letter cannot be used to determine authorship as amanuenses were often used and the style reflects that of the secretary not the actual author. The claim that Jude 3 and 17 point to a later date is weak as Paul makes similar statements of prior proclamation in 1 Cor 15:1–3; Gal 1:9; Col 1:6–7.

Judas the apostle is unlikely, as while his father is named James, we have no evidence of a brother with that name. By far the most well-known James in the early church is James the brother of Jesus.

Early church tradition also argues in favour of Jude the brother of James and Jesus as the author. The letter may be referenced as early as ad 110 in Ignatius' letter to Smyrna ("love feast," see Jude 12; Ign. *Smyrn.* 9). The inclusion of Jude in the Muratorian Canon (ca. ad 170–200) suggests it was written by a well-known early church figure. Clement of Alexandria (ca. ad 150–215) describes Jude as "canonical Scripture," (Eusebius, *Hist. eccl.* 6.14.1, s.a. 6.13.6). Similarly, Origen (ca. ad 185–254) accepted Jude as "true, filled with healthful words of heavenly grace" (Origen, *Comm. Matt.* 10:17). While some questioned its authenticity, this was due to its use of 1 Enoch.

Davids sums up things nicely,

we clearly have a Judas who had a brother James who was well known in the early Jesus movement, for James the brother of Jesus was the main leader of the Jesus movement in Jerusalem (and probably in all Palestine) from at least ad 44 (the latest date when Peter had to flee Jerusalem, although James was probably the leader long before this) to his martyrdom in a.d. 61 (see Peter H. Davids, *The Letters of 2 Peter and Jude*, PNTC [Grand Rapids, MI: Eerdmans, 2006], 10.)

Who was Jude?

Jude one of Jesus' younger brothers (Mark 6:3; Matt 13:55–56). Like James and the other brothers, he rejected Jesus in his earthly life (John 7:5). Yet, after the resurrection, he is among the people of the first church, likely due to the resurrection appearances, especially through his brother James meeting the risen Lord (Acts 1:14; 1 Cor 15:7). He was likely in the room at Pentecost (Acts 2:1–4). He appears to be a missionary traveling with his wife perhaps as far as Corinth (1 Cor 9:5). Eusebius claims that Julius Africanus wrote that Jesus' relatives spread the gospel through Judea (meaning Palestine) (Eusebius, *Eccl. hist.* 1.7.14).

Eusebius also records Hegesippus' account of his grandchildren (the second cousins of Jesus). After Domitian (ad 81–96) had ordered the killing of any Davidic descendants, Jude's relatives were also brought before Domitian as descendants of David (cf. Matt 1:1–18; Luke 3:23–38). This suggests Jude was dead by the time of Domitian. Eusebius records that they governed churches and lived through the reign of Trajan (ad 98–117). This confirms Jude was married and had a family that clashed with the emperor.

Date

There is little in the letter that helps us know when Jude

was written. Some would date it late in the century along with 2 Peter or even as late as ad 160, which is extremely unlikely. However, assuming the author is Jude the brother of Jesus and that he died before the reign of Domitian, ad 81 is the upper limit for the letter. It must have been written after the resurrection of Christ in ad 30 or 33. There has been time for some extreme false teaching to emerge. Further, Jude 3 and 17 may indicate a date sometime later in the period ad 33 to 81. However, there is nothing in the letter which suggests the apostles are dead. Neither does "the faith" indicate a late date, as it is used by Paul in the undisputed letters (1 Cor 16:13; 2 Cor 13:5; Gal 1:23; Phil 1:25, 27; Phlm 5, s.a. Eph 4:13; Col 1:23; Col 2:7). If Jude used 2 Peter, then a later date would be appropriate. If Peter used Jude, then an earlier date in the 50s to early 60s would be appropriate. However, if Jude and 2 Peter were drawing on independent traditions, this suggests a date anywhere from the 50s to 81. Finally, "brother of James" could suggest James is still alive, which would give a date before ad 62 when he was martyred. As such, a date in the 50s to early 60s would seem appropriate.

Provenance

Again, there are no real signals concerning the provenance. Most of our scant knowledge points to a location in Israel-Palestine, but Syria cannot be ruled out. Some have suggested Alexandria, as the letter appears to have been accepted early in Egypt and has excellent rhetoric. The use of Hebrew and Aramaic sources is suggestive of Palestine as is James' popularity.

Recipients

Who is Jude writing to? Again, there is nothing clear to indicate his recipients. The letter suggests that they are Christians in a context where the gospel is being gravely distorted in the direction of Greco-Roman licentiousness and ethical failure. Yet, on the other hand, Jude draws on Jewish apocalyptic, especially 1 Enoch (v. 14) and the Testament of Moses (v. 9) in his argument. It is likely that the recipients are familiar with Jewish tradition but are at the same time being lured into pagan sin.

This suggests a context where the converts are either Jewish and being lured into licentious sin, or, they are Gentiles who have become familiar with Jewish Greek writings but are syncretizing the gospel to the immorality of their culture. Most scholars opt for the former, on the basis that the Jewish traditions point this way.

Yet, a reader of Jude does not need a great understanding of Jewish traditions outside the LXX to make sense of his appeal. So, either view remains plausible. Alternatively, we look for a situation where there are a significant number of Jews and Gentiles together in the same church, where Jewish traditions are shared and known, but where there is significant social pressure to syncretize the gospel to Greco-Roman licentiousness. Somewhere like Syrian Antioch would make sense. Although further from the likely point of writing, a situation like Corinth might work, especially as it is possible Paul had travelled there (1 Cor 9:5). Then again, if Jude had travelled as far west as Corinth in Greece (Achaia), he had likely visited a wide range of contexts. As such, he could be writing to a portion of Asia Minor or north in Macedonia. The similarity in tone with 2 Peter could suggest the former. Then again, the early reception of Jude in Egypt may suggest somewhere in north Africa such as Alexandria. As such, scholars have suggested a range of recipients from Israel, Syria, Asia Minor, and Egypt. We simply do not know.

Genre

Jude is written in the Hellenistic letter form. It begins with the usual letter opening (sender, recipients, greeting). The body of the letter is signalled by "beloved" in v. 3 and ending in v. 23. The letter's closing lacks any comments on writing, greetings, and travel plans, but adds a doxology.

Some consider the body more of a homily than a letter, and class it as an "epistolary sermon." It includes loose use of the Jewish technique of midrash seen in the use of OT and apocalyptic texts and applying them to the contemporary situation (vv. 5–19).

Another approach taken is to read Jude as macro-chiasm. Osburn takes it this way (Carroll D. Osburn, "Discourse Analysis and Jewish Apocalyptic in the Epistle of Jude." In *Linguistics and New Testament Interpretation: Essays on Discourse Analysis*, ed. David A. Black [Nashville: Broadman, 1992], 287–319 [esp. p. 309]).

A   Greeting: Jude 1–2

B   Introduction: Jude 3–4

C   Literary Warnings: Rebellion = Fate: Jude 5–7

D   Link Rebellion = Fate of Eschatological Enemies of God to Rebellion = Fate of Intruders: Jude 8–16

C' Apostolic Warnings: Jude 17–19

B' Concluding Appeal. Specific of "Contend" in Verse 4: Jude 20–23

A'   Doxology: Jude 24–25

This fails to convince. First, the chiasm breaks down in vv. 17–19. Second, the verb "contend" (*epagōnizomai*) is not found in vv. 20–23. Third, the parallels lack specificity and are general.

Structure

The structure below draws out the core thematic threads that develop through the letter.
1) Letter Opening: Jude 1–2

1. Sender: Jude 1a

2. Recipient: Jude 1b

3. Greeting: Jude 1c

2) Contend for the faith: Jude 3
3) The false teachers introduced: Jude 4
4) God's Judgment in Salvation-History: Jude 5–7

1. Exodus: Jude 5

2. Fallen angels imprisoned: Jude 6

3. Sodom and Gomorrah: Jude 7

5) Description of the False Teachers and Warnings from Jewish History: Jude 8–16

1. Description: Jude 8

2. Michael, the Devil, and Moses: Jude 9

3. Description: Jude 10

4. Woe, Cain, Balaam, Korah: Jude 11

5. Description and fate: Jude 12–13

6. Enoch's prophecy: Jude 14–15

7. Description: Jude 16

6) Appeal to Live the Apostolic Faith: Jude 17–22

1. Remember the Apostles' Warning: Jude 17–18

2. Final Description: Jude 19

3. Maintaining the faith: Jude 20–21

4. Mercy to those who are swayed: Jude 22–23

7) Letter Closing: Doxology: Jude 24–25

Relationship to 2 Peter

A quick read of 2 Peter and Jude shows that there are many similarities between the two documents, especially between 2 Pet 2:1–18/Jude 4–13 and 2 Pet 3:1–3/Jude 16–18.

Four explanations have been made for the similarities:

1) Common authorship of the two letters.

2) Jude is dependent on Peter (e.g. Luther).

3) 2 Peter is dependent on Jude (majority view).

4) A common source or sources.

A good case can be made for 1) to 3). However, while there are many similarities between Jude and 2 Peter, they are not as pronounced as the literary agreements between Matthew and Luke or their use of Mark's Gospel. There are substantial differences between the two letters. As such, the view that accounts for both differences and similarities is that they draw on a common source which gives a list of arguments against false teaching.

Jude utilizes the Exodus, Michael and the Devil, Cain, Korah, and Enoch, none of which are used in 2 Peter. Jude has a much-abbreviated reference to Sodom and Gomorrah. Jude does not cite Prov 26:11. Hence, rather than either 2 Peter drawing on Jude, vice versa, or a common author, the agreements and variances point to a source which could be Jesus, Peter, or another of the disciples.

There was perhaps a document with a catalogue of examples of rebels and false teachers which they drew on. While the original source is intriguing, the two letters should be analysed individually and in their own right (which would include some discussion of sources). Each letter deserves the same level of treatment every NT letter receives without prior assumptions on authorship and sources.

Opponents

The key reason the letter is written is to deal with false teachers. Jude writes to appeal to his readers to "contend for the faith that was delivered once for all to the saints" (v. 3). Certain people have snuck into the community (v. 4). They are ungodly. (vv. 6, 15).They pervert the grace of God in the direction of sensuality, perverting the gospel in the direction of sexual immorality and associated debauchery (v. 4).

As with the opponents in 2 Peter (2 Pet 2:1), they deny the lordship of Jesus Christ (v. 4). In the warning of vv. 5–7, sexual immorality is emphasised concerning Sodom and Gomorrah (v. 7).

In v. 8, they rely on their dreams, suggesting a pneumatic elevated view of spiritual experience as determinative. This means that they value people's spiritual experiences such as visions, dreams, and prophetic words above the message of Jesus received through the apostles. This is a real danger in churches that have a very charismatic or Pentecostal viewpoint.

They defile the flesh, reinforcing that they misuse their bodies and suggesting a Greek view of the body. They reject authority including Christ (cf. v. 4).

As in 2 Pet 2:10, they blaspheme angels—the illustration of Michael's refusal to blaspheme the Devil, suggests demons are in mind (v. 9). They seek material gain (v. 11). They are participating in the Lord's Supper (love feasts), indicating that they consider themselves members of the believing community (v. 12).

The false teachers are described as shepherds, indicating they are leaders or believe themselves to be so (v. 12). They are not only ungodly (v. 15) but are grumblers like Israel in the wilderness. As grumblers and malcontents, they pursue their own sinful desires (vv. 16, 18), they are boastfully arrogant, and discriminate to gain an advantage. They thus are not only sexually immoral, but moaners, full of arrogance, and seek status.

Jude next describes the pseudo-teachers as "scoffers" who follow their own ungodly passions (v. 18). They cause divisions (v. 19). They are *psychikos*, indicating that they are unspiritual and worldly. They are devoid of the Holy Spirit, meaning that they are not Christians but are dead, worldly people (v. 19).

Although the response to the heresy draws on a range of Jewish traditions, the descriptors give no indication of a specifically Jewish or Judaizing heresy (e.g. circumcision, eating protocols, law). Rather, these sound like the issues faced by 2 Peter—people who are syncretizing the gospel to sins prevalent in the non-Jewish and non-Christian Greco-Roman world. They willingly engage in sexual and other impure behaviours. They seek status. They peddle their gospel.

The key is v. 4, where they pervert God's grace—suggesting abusing the grace of God by arguing that being under God's grace, they are free to do what they like (cf. Rom 3:8; 6:1, 15; 1 Cor 6:12; Phil 3:19; 2 Pet 2:2, 10, 12–14, 19). They may distort Paul's teaching (2 Pet 3:15–17).

A range of opponents is proposed in scholarship. Gnosticism was highly favoured until more recent times where it is now generally agreed that Jude predates the development of Gnosticism in the mid-second century.Others consider them hyper-spiritual pneumatics who highlight spiritual experience, ecstatic visionaries who consider themselves spiritually superior.

The best solution is to avoid labelling them too specifically but rather to see them as a combination of those who are libertine morally and pneumatic spiritually. They have a theology that views grace as a basis for doing as they see fit. They are arrogant self-professing Christians who dare to eat at the Lord's Supper yet engage in debauched living. To an extreme level, they have failed to be transformed by the renewing of the mind and instead live by the patterns of their context. For Jude, they are not Christians and face certain destruction.

Jude's Response

After the prologue and launching his appeal (vv. 1–3), Jude names their problem in v. 4. They are ungodly people who are perverting the grace of God toward sensuality and a denial of Christ.

His first response in vv. 5–7 is a reminder of the past acts of God in salvation and judgment.

First, the Exodus is recalled. In v. 5, Jude attributes the Exodus to Jesus. This is not completely dissimilar to Paul who speaks of the rock in the wilderness who accompanied Israel as Christ (1 Cor 10:4). Whichever is the right reading, God, through Christ, saved a people from Egypt while destroying unbelievers. The implication is clear—the faithful of God including those who heed the letter's warning will be saved by Jesus; those who are unrepentant false teachers will be destroyed.

In v. 6, Genesis 6:1–4 is in view—the angels or "sons of God" left eternity to engage in sexual immorality with human women and were confined to destruction (see also on 2 Peter). This draws on Jewish interpretations (e.g. 1 En. 6–9, 86–88; Jub. 4:15, 22; 5:1; CD 2:17–19; T. Reub. 5:6–7).

In v. 7, the destruction of Sodom and Gomorrah is invoked—they were destroyed by fire due to their engagement with "sexual immorality" and pursuing "other flesh" (that of angels—another jibe at the mockery of the false teachers toward "glorious ones"). Sodom and Gomorrah are a symbol of divine judgment and are common in Jewish and Christian writings (cf. Isa 1:9; Jer 23:14; Hos 11:8; Amos 4:11; Zeph 2:9; Matt 10:15; 11:24; Mark 6:11; Luke 10:12; 17:29). Such destruction is an example pointing toward the final punishment of eternal fire that awaits those who do not believe. In context, this speaks particularly of the eternal destruction of the false teachers.

Verse 8 gives more detail of their false ideas—they rely on their dreams, defile the flesh, reject authority, and blaspheme glorious ones.

Verse 9 focuses on the final of their false attitudes, their blasphemy of "glories" (*doxai*). "Glories" is used of angels in Qumran (1QH 10:8) and in apocalyptic and Gnostic literature (2 En. 22:7, 10; Asc. Isa. 9:32). This is because they participated in or embodied God's radiant glory. In context, it is fallen angels that seem in view (see v. 9). As such, they mock the demonic, probably claiming spiritual superiority over them.

Verse 9 draws on Jewish tradition. In the OT, Moses died and was buried (Deut 34:6). However, as his burial was not witnessed, there was speculation in Jewish literature over what happened at his death and burial. This draws on one tradition whereby the archangel Michael, when disputing claims over Moses' body after his death, dared not blasphemously judge the leading fallen angel, the Devil. Michael is one of God's seven archangels (leading angels) in the apocalyptic literature, also mentioned as a prince in Daniel (Dan 10:13, 21). In Revelation, he defeats the dragon and evil angels (Rev 12:7, s.a. 1QM 9:16; 1 En. 9:1; 10:11; 20:5; 24:6). The language is legal, speaking of the Devil seeking to demonstrate his guilt and claim his body. While Michael could have stood in judgment over the Devil, he did not bring a blasphemous judgment against him. Rather, alluding to Zech 3:2, where Satan sought to condemn Joshua, but God vindicated Joshua and rebuked Satan, Michael called the Lord to rebuke him. Here Michael is an example to the believing recipients—rather than emulate the false teachers who dare to blaspheme demons, they must not do so. They are humbly to let the Lord rebuke them.

The origin of this story is unclear. Supposedly, it comes from either the Assumption of Moses or the Testament of Moses. However, as we do not have the original version this is uncertain. What we know is that the devil challenged Moses' claim on an honourable burial because he had killed the Egyptian. Michael then called on God to rebuke the Devil, and the Devil fled, enabling the completion of the burial. Scholars debate the precise nuance of the dispute, but what is clear is that readers should be humble and not overstep the mark where angels and demons are concerned. That is the Lord's business.

In v. 10, the false teachers are not named, they are "these people." They are not worthy of being named. They are slanderous, blaspheming the sacred. While they are people, they are nothing better than "unreasoning animals." They are corrupting themselves.

Verse 11 is a woe oracle—an interjection crying out their impending doom. The reason is that they have emulated three OT characters who symbolize sinful rebellion to God.

First, Jude compares them to Cain, who presented a flawed offering to God and murdered his brother (Gen 4:1–16, s.a. Heb 11:4; 1 John 3:12). These false teachers participate in the Lord's Supper, yet are utterly corrupt, and drink judgment on themselves (cf. 1 Cor 11:29). In seeking to corrupt others, and lead them astray from the gospel, they are effectively committing fratricide as those they corrupt face God's wrath with them.

Second, they have followed Balaam's error. Balaam was a false prophet who was paid by Balak the king of Moab to curse Israel en route to the land. A donkey rebuked him (Num 22 – 24; Deut 23:4–5; Neh 13:2; 2 Pet 2:15; Rev 2:14). These false teachers are false prophets of a false version of the Christian faith who seek material gain.

Third, they are like Korah, the great-grandson of Levi, who led a rebellion of 250 leaders against Moses and Aaron. The leaders and their families were swallowed up by God and taken to Sheol and the rebels were destroyed by fire. After this, the complaint again broke out and 14,700 died in a plague (Num 16:1–50). The false teachers are rebels like

Korah challenging God and his leaders. They will be eternally destroyed by fire and in Sheol. The readers must not join their rebellion.

In vv. 12–13, Jude's description invokes their fallen state and urges the readers to have nothing to do with them. He describes them as "hidden reefs" or "blemishes" at their love feasts. The love feast was the gathering in which the Lord's Supper was taken (cf. 1 Cor 11:17–34; Acts 2:42, 46).

The same idea is found in Ignatius' letter to Smyrna: "It is not permissible either, to baptise or to hold a love (agapē) feast without a bishop" (Holmes, Ign. Smyrn. 8:2). It is a gathering of love between the triune God and his people. These people shipwreck the faith of others at these gatherings; or, they stain them with their impurity. They "feast without fear," arrogantly believing themselves to be right with God when they are a disgrace before him. They are "shepherds who feed themselves," implying that they are leaders but who are self-absorbed. They are like those in Corinth who go ahead of others taking the choicest food and getting drunk, while others go hungry and thirsty (1 Cor 11:17–22). They are waterless clouds—which means they are nothing, for a waterless cloud is not a cloud. They are swept by the winds (cf. Eph 4:14). They are like trees in fall which have shed leaves and bear no fruit (cf. Mark 11:12–14, 20–25, and pars). They are utterly dead (twice dead), and uprooted from the source of life, Jesus Christ. They are not only non-clouds blown by the wind. They are also like the waves of the sea foaming up shame (Isa 57:20). They are wandering stars, which do not hold to their God-ordained movements. Stars were considered deities, and so, this could imply that they are effectively demons. Further, the astral bodies were used for guidance especially at sea—they provide no guidance or better, they lead people away. Their fate is named: "the gloom of utter darkness has been reserved forever." Jude's theology of eternal destruction is essentially eternal darkness. The warning is apparent—those who join them will experience eternal darkness.

Verses 14–15 draws on another non-canonical book, 1 Enoch 1:9 which reads, "Behold, he will arrive with ten million of the holy ones in order to execute judgment upon all. He will destroy the wicked ones and censure all flesh on account of everything that they have done, that which the sinners and the wicked ones committed against him" (Charlesworth). Jude describes him as the seventh from Adam, counting inclusively. Enoch was described as one who "walked with God" and "was not, for God took him" (Gen 5:21–24). Tradition held that he did not die. A number of apocalyptic writings are attributed to him including 1 Enoch. They are clearly pseudonymous. The section 1 Enoch 1–5 was clearly written by the time of Jude, and so the mid-first century. Clearly, Jude knew it, and so did his readers (or it would be redundant). Jude's use of it (along with the Assumption of Moses), shows his respect for it. However, simply citing it does not imply canonicity any more than Paul's citation of Greek poets Epimenides and Aratus (Acts 17:28; Tit 1:9), should be seen as canonical. Neither 1 Enoch nor the Assumption of Moses is canonical to Jews or Christians of any persuasion. Still, it shows the value of the Jewish apocryphal and apocalyptic writings—they state truth even if they are not inspired. The point of the citation is clear: God is coming in judgment on the ungodly. In v. 16, as they fit the bill with their grumbling, discontent, sinfully lustful lives, arrogant boastfulness, and prejudice, they must be repudiated.

Verse 17 is a call to remember, not OT Scriptures of

doom, but the predictions of Christ's apostles. This implies that they have been taught these predictions. In v. 18, they are cited with a saying that is not found in any of the apostolic writings but should be seen as an example of early apostolic teaching (cf. 2 Pet 3:3): "In the end time there will be scoffers, following their own ungodly passions." These false teachers and those in 2 Peter fulfil this prophecy. In v. 19, they are again described as divisive, worldly, and devoid of the Spirit.

As we come to verses 20–23 it is important for students to be aware that there is a range of readings from the various sources. It is not completely clear whether there are three classes of people or two in mind (for more, see Bruce Manning Metzger, United Bible Societies, *A Textual Commentary on the Greek New Testament, Second Edition a Companion Volume to the United Bible Societies' Greek New Testament [4th Rev. Ed.]* [London; New York: United Bible Societies, 1994], 658–61). Thankfully, these variants do not greatly affect the meaning, and so I have gone with the Nestle-Aland 28 in this brief discussion.

In verses 20–23, Jude instructs them concerning how to live in the face of these challenges. They are first to take responsibility for their faith—building themselves up. This is an important verse reminding us to be responsible to ensure that we grow in the faith. Second, they are to pray in the Spirit speaking of being led by God's leading and not that of false teachers. Third, they are to keep themselves in God's love, rather than violate the love of Christ as the false teachers do at the *agapē* feasts. Fourth, they are to await Christ's mercy leading to eternal life, rather than live abusing his grace.

Where others waver or doubt, perhaps due to false teaching, they are to have mercy upon them, as Christ has had mercy on them. Where believers are being deceived and led astray by the likes of the false teachers, they are to "save" them by "snatching them out of the fire" (v. 23). This speaks of doing everything in our power to save them from the eternal destruction that awaits them. The final category of people is unclear. The best solution seems that these are those who are defiled by sin. To them they must show mercy, but with fear (of contamination), despising their "clothing" of sin. This speaks of reaching out to those swept aside into deep sin, seeking to save them, though without being drawn into their sinful lifestyles.

The final doxology speaks of assurance, God "is able to preserve you from stumbling and present you blameless before" him. As is fitting of a brother of Jesus, he ends with the glorification of God through Christ.

Conclusion

Jude is a really interesting little book written by one of Jesus' brothers, who came to Christ after Christ's resurrection, perhaps due to his brother James' experiencing Christ's resurrection. He was at Pentecost and was no doubt a key figure in the early church. His letter reminds us how important it is to preserve the gospel and that as a leader, we sometimes have to deal with false teachers somewhat strongly. For the NT writers, judgement and eternal destruction are real, and we need to take this seriously. Fascinatingly, Jude cites pseudepigraphal works which make us think about canonisation and sacred scripture. We are warned against compromising our faith in the direction of the world. We must not be flippant about spiritual matters. It is possible to fall from faith, and we need to work hard to maintain a strong relationship with God and Christ. We do this especially by building ourselves up in our faith and praying in the Spirit. We are also urged to be missional, showing mercy to doubters, and saving others from the fires of eternal destruction. The final doxology should be read in worship regularly, it is superb.

Leadership, culture, and Ethics

The All-Sufficiency of Christ

Christian leaders in their zeal to bring the best out of people and see their organisation or church grow can sometimes push too hard. They put burdens on people with this and that expectation. People start to die under the oppression of demands. As the letter of Hebrews reminds us, Christ is all-sufficient. To get the best out of our people we take them again and again to God and his Son, to consider him for this angle and that, reminding ourselves of what he has done for us, and our status in him. Then we are spurred on to action, not merely through demand and warning, but through something inside us that lights up and makes us want to. This is the Spirit. The Spirit is experienced when we grasp the depths of Christ and not through direct demand and warning alone (although that has its place, see above).

The prologue of 1 John speaks to the complete sufficiency of Christ. It is on the basis of having heard, seen, and touched Jesus that he proclaims eternal life to his readers (1 John 1:1–4). Great leaders and preachers begin with Jesus and end with him. In his Gospel, the Spirit is the Paraclete who comforts and helps us. In 1 John 1:1 it is Jesus, the

Paraclete with the Father, and the propitiation of sins (1 John 2:1–2).

Following Christ's Example

Paul stresses imitation of Christ (e.g. 1 Cor 11:1; Phil 2:5–8). In his injunctions to the Asian readers of his first letter, Peter gives Christ's life as the supreme example of how we are to live in relation to authorities. We are to do good. We are to see Christ's life as an example, as he suffered without retaliation of any sort and he brought us salvation. We are to live good lives whatever is thrown at us, that they see our good works and perhaps come to faith (1 Pet 2:19–24, s.a. 1 Pet 3:8). Like Jesus, we are not to repay evil with evil but bless our persecutors (1 Pet 3:9, s.a. Rom 12:17).

Abiding in Him

Peter speaks of the abiding word in our hearts, by which we are to live (1 Pet 1:23). More particularly, John absolutely loves the idea of abiding. Similar to Peter, the word of God abides in us and we overcome Satan (1 John 2:14, 24; 3:9, 24; 4:13). Great leaders who last the distance and do not fall are those who abide in God, his Son, the light, the truth, and the Spirit (1 John 2:10, 24, 27, 28; 4:16; 2 John 2). God abides in them as does his love (1 John 3:17; 4:12, 16). Abiding in him means to confess that Christ is God's Son, to remain embedded in Christ's teaching, and to seek to obey God's word (1 John 3:24; 4:15; 2 John 9). Those who do, walk as he did (1 John 2:6) abide forever (1 John 2:17) and desist from sin (1 John 3:6). Conversely, those who don't, abide in eternal death (1 John 3:14–15). This is a wonderful metaphor of residing in God and he in us. This speaks of taking time to cultivate this abiding relationship, for it is those who do so who last the distance in ministry.

Knowing Who We Are

One of the great passages of the General Epistles is 1 Pet 2:9–10 which tells us who we are in God. All believers, from all nations, not just Israel as before Christ, are a chosen race. They are a royal priesthood, conjuring up ideas of Ps 110 where Jesus is both king and high priest (see on Hebrews too), and we now being a royal priesthood in him. We are a holy nation, a people for God's own possession. Our purpose is clear: to proclaim in church, as we praise God, and in the world, as we engage in mission, the excellencies of him who called us out of darkness into his marvellous light. We are God's people who have received his mercy. This should move us to want to serve God every day without delay.

Peter adds two more brilliant ideas in his second letter. First, we have all obtained a faith of equal standing through God and his Son's righteousness (2 Pet 1:1). Second, we are partakers of God's divine nature, participants in God's very being (2 Pet 1:4).

Confronting False Ideas

These letters warn us that one of the core roles of a leader is to confront false ideas with severe warnings. So, in Hebrews, the writer warns strongly that the readers will face judgment if they fall away. Similarly, in 2 Peter and Jude, OT examples of God's wrath at the flood and Sodom and Gomorrah are prototypes of the eternal fate of false teachers and those who follow them. John too has to deal with false ideas and draws readers back to the incarnated and divine Jesus.

Knowing our Story

The letter of Hebrews is an astonishing reframing of the whole OT through the lens of Jesus. All of Israel's institutions find their fulfilment in Jesus whether it is the Temple, the Sabbath, Mosaic covenant and law, the priesthood, the sacrifice system, and more. He has a rightly high view of Christ and that Christ is the zenith of God's revelation. By knowing the story of Israel inside and out and understanding who Christ is, the author reads the OT with brilliant clarity through the lens of Jesus. Such skill is what a Christian leader must aspire to. This is only possible by living in the story day in and day out. Pre-prayer-ation and time in the word are essential (e.g. Heb 4:11–12). Theological training is a "must have" for all who are serious about being a Christian leader.

James too stresses the importance of the word. However, he rightly says it is not good enough to read it, we need to imbibe it, and obey it. As believers read the word, we are to put aside all sin, and receive the word humbly and we will find salvation (Jas 1:19–22).

Peter speaks of the living and abiding word of God as a seed planted in our beings giving us new birth. This should lead to holiness and love. For it to do so, we must dwell in it (1 Pet 1:22–25).

One of the features of the heresy of 2 Peter is their distortion of Paul's theology. They read his letters and twist their teaching to their own destruction (2 Pet 3:16). We are warned that as we do biblical studies and theology, we should not fall into this trap of twisting the teaching of the Scriptures to suit our own theological preferences. We must allow Scripture to shape us, not the other way around.

Reframing the Story

One of the things I love about Hebrews is the way that the writer can take an idea like the Sabbath and entry to the land under Joshua and find in it the story of Jesus and eternal life as a Sabbath rest (Heb 3–4). He finds Ps 110:4 and develops a theology of Jesus as a High Priest after the order of Melchizedek, a hardly- otherwise-mentioned OT man of mystery. This creates a whole theology of Jesus the Priest who saves us, sacrifices himself, is the curtain to the Temple, leads heavenly worship, and so on. The brilliance of this connection brings the story alive. The writer of John similarly ponders love and God and makes the brilliant connection, "God is love!" The writer of James coins the phrase "the royal law" of the law of love for one another. Such brilliant ideas come from living in the story and seeing connections. These bring alive the story that must be retold again and again so that it hits home and transforms us to be the people God wants us to be.

Knowing our Responsibility

The writers of these letters recognise that the work they do has eternal consequences. The warning passages of Hebrews are not hypothetical but real warnings of the dangers facing those who desert Christ for Judaism and law. As Galatians makes clear too, one must choose one or the other. One is a system of salvation by works, one is salvation by grace through faith. Jude and 2 Peter know too that if their converts follow the way of the false teachers, they are lost. The work we do is to be done in deadly earnest. The fate of those in our care is in our hands and we can make or break them. Hence, we must seek to produce work that is our very best.

Keeping Watch over Souls

There is a neat verse for leaders in Heb 13:17. The readers are urged to have confidence (*peithō*) in their leaders and to submit to them. Leaders are those who "are keeping watch over your souls," soul (*psychē*) here meaning their whole lives. Hence, the role of a leader is to keep watch over the lives of those under our care. This job is to be done with joy and not with complaint.

James also ends with an injunction to his readers to seek the lost soul and bring them back, saving his soul from death and covering a mass of sin (Jas 5:2).

The Need to Confront False Teaching

While we are to love people, sometimes love must be tough. These letters show this clearly. In the warning passages, the writer of Hebrews must warn of the consequences of falling away and challenge his readers to run with perseverance the race marked out for them. The writer of James warns that even demons believe in God but shudder out of fear of their judgment (Jas 2:19). It is not enough to love in words, we must love in deeds (Jas 2:17). The writers of 2 Peter and Jude cannot hold back warning of the fate of the false teachers and those who follow them in the path of greed and immorality (esp. 2 Pet 2; Jude 3–16). John urges readers not to believe every spirit but test them against the revelation of Christ to discern error (1 John 4:1–5). In 2 John, he warns of many deceivers and antichrists who do not confess Christ's coming and that they should watch themselves that they do not lose their reward (2 John 7–8).

Christian leadership is the hardest when we need to confront someone or a group for their faulty behaviour. We might term this "carefrontation." This is what is required in some circumstances. Out of love and care, we confront someone under our care. We do so for their good that they may find healing and forgiveness and reach their potential.

Going Deeper

In Hebrews 6:1–3, it speaks of leaving behind elementary doctrines of Christ and going on to maturity. The elementary doctrines mentioned are repentance from dead works, faith in God, baptisms, laying on of hands, the resurrection of the dead, and eternal judgment. We could add other basic things. Christian leaders are to be lifelong learners, always reading, learning by example, and finding ways to go deeper. As we do, we take our people deeper and deeper into the story of God and his world. We need to ensure that there are ways in which the people under our care can do the same.

A verse that is very helpful is Jude 20 where Jude urges his readers to build themselves up on their most holy faith. This speaks of taking personal responsibility to ensure we grow.

Calling Our People to Faith

The hall of fame in Heb 11 is a brilliant chapter to remind us of the importance of faith and faithfulness. The author of Hebrews is on the same page as Paul, saying that what saves us is faith. What will see us make it to that day is faith. Our call is to generate faith in our people by again and again bringing them back to the heart of worship, Jesus. Hebrews 12 is a brilliant chapter, reminding us of the faithful cloud of witnesses that sit in the stadium around us, cheering us on. Jesus is our supreme example, running with such effort that he shed blood. So, must we. James gets this too, but he warns us of an intellectual faith without teeth, a faith that is espoused but not lived out in action. We must add to our faith works that flow from it. John too repeatedly reminds his readers that we must believe in the name of our Lord Jesus (e.g. 1 John 3:23).

Being an Example

In Heb 13:7, the readers are to remember their leaders, their lives, and imitate their faith. Elders in 1 Pet 5:3 are not to lead by domination, but by "being examples to the flock."

Suffering

Suffering is a big theme in Hebrews. Jesus was crowned with glory and honour because of his suffering to the point of death for the sake of all people (Heb 2:9). He was made complete through suffering as the founder of salvation (Heb 2:10). He was tempted in every way, learned obedience through suffering, but was without sin and able to bring salvation for the world (Heb 2:18; 5:8; 9:26). The readers too, in earlier times, had suffered greatly, being publicly humiliated, imprisoned, their property confiscated. The current readers are to persevere in what they are facing. They are to emulate the prophets and others of Heb 11 who suffered but held firm (Heb 11:36).

James recognises the reality of suffering. He also considers suffering educative, bringing faith tests that produce perseverance and maturity. Consistent with Paul's teaching in Rom 5:3–5, James urges readers should rejoice in suffering for it produces growth (Jas 1:2–4). They are to be patient in suffering for the Lord is coming. The patience of Job is given as an example (Jas 5:7–11).

Suffering is a huge theme in 1 Peter. His readers are facing persecution, perhaps an echo of what Nero was doing in Rome at the time to Christians. Believers are to see this positively as a faith test and rejoice (1 Pet 1:6–8). He cites the example of Christ who suffered unjustly yet did not retaliate as an example. We are to endure suffering as he did, while not resorting to bitterness and retaliation (1 Pet 2:19–25, s.a. 1 Pet 3:18). If we experience suffering from the world around us, we must do so through being good not evil (1 Pet 3:17; 4:15). In 1 Pet 4:12–19, Peter speaks into the present suffering of the Asians urging them not to be surprised or ashamed at suffering, but as does James and Paul, to rejoice in it for they are blessed through the Spirit (1 Pet 4:13–14). As they suffer, they are to entrust themselves to God and do good (1 Pet 4:19).

Impartiality

James 2 speaks of all who come to a church being treated equally. It is easy to be drawn to the gifted, wealthy, and influential. James warns us not to privilege such people. All are made in God's image; all are to be equally honoured. This is the culture of the Kingdom. For him, love leads to impartiality and if one does show favouritism, one is convicted by the law as a transgressor.

Godliness not Worldliness

James also rejects worldliness which is enmity to God including such things as quarrelling, lustful passions, murder, and covetousness. Believers are to submit to God and draw near to him in humility, resisting Satan and the pull of the world, and God will be with them. They are to repent of such things and humble themselves before God (Jas 4:1–10). Toward the conclusion of his second letter, Peter summons readers to godliness in the face of the worldliness of false teachers (2 Pet 3:11).

John also warns of worldliness urging readers not to love the world and its stuff, such as the desires of the flesh, for it is passing away (1 John 2:15–17).

Shepherding the Lost

James ends with mission in Jas 5:19–20. When we see a brother or sister wandering from the truth, we are to seek to bring them back. If we do, we save his soul from eternal death and sin. The mission of the church is to make disciples and sometimes they wander, so like the shepherd Jesus, we should seek to bring them back (Luke 15:1–10).

As an elder and witness of Christ's sufferings, Peter has injunctions for elders. They are to shepherd the flock, overseeing them, willingly, not for material gain, but by being examples to those under their care. They are not to dominate them (1 Pet 5:1–3).

A Missional People

Bringing the lost home was mentioned above in James' epistle. One of the themes of Peter's first letter is the way we are to conduct ourselves in the world. We are to declare God's excellencies in the world (1 Pet 2:9). As exiles in a foreign land, we are to abstain from the passions of the flesh warring against our souls, patterns of life the world finds normal. We are to maintain honourable conduct in the world, so that even when they malign us, our good deeds are seen (1 Pet 2:11–12). In 1 Pet 4:1–3, Peter again stresses transformed minds, not living by the patterns of the Gentiles with sensuality, passions, drunkenness, orgies, and so on.

Peter includes one of the most interesting verses in Scripture concerning evangelism. Knowing there were women in the churches married to unbelievers who have rejected the gospel, he urges them not to seek to evangelise them with words, but to seek to win them with good conduct. This has interesting repercussions for us who live in contexts where people have heard the gospel and rejected it. There is a time not to verbalise the gospel but show it to win them (1 Pet 3:1–6).

Where evangelism is concerned, he also stresses the need to always be prepared to give an answer to those who enquire concerning our faith. This means ensuring we are equipped to answer the sorts of questions people love to ask. We are to respond with gentleness and respect (1 Pet 3:15–17).

Jude ends his letter by appealing to the readers to "have

mercy on those who doubt; save others by snatching them out of the fire; to others show mercy with fear, hating even the garment stained by the flesh" (Jude 22–23). This is a wonderful statement encouraging us to be missional toward one another and the lost.

Resistance of Sin

James stresses the need to resist temptation, cutting it off at the knees, and not letting it grow into desire and then sin and death (Jas 1:12–15).

John stresses that sin is lawlessness and those who abide in him must stop sinning (in relative terms,1 John 4:5). Those who are born of God, do not continue to abide in habitual sin (1 John 4:9).

Love

Love is all-important across the NT. The writer of Hebrews tells readers to "let brotherly (and sisterly) love continue" (Heb 13:1). This includes hospitality to strangers, remembering those in prison and the mistreated (Heb 12:2–3).

Similarly, James calls the love of one's neighbour (Lev 19:18) the royal law (Jas 2:8) and law of liberty (Jas 2:12) which is the sum of all laws (Jas 2:11). It should lead us to impartiality (Jas 2:10) and radical concern for those at the margins, the widows, orphans, and the poor and needy (Jas 1:27; 2:14–16). Mercy triumphs over judgment (Jas 2:13). Indeed, without loving works, faith is dead (Jas 2:17).

Faith leads to love and without concrete love for those in material need, faith is dead. True faith leads to loving works such as feeding and clothing the needy. Mere platitudes are useless (Jas 2:14–15).

Peter makes the excellent point that true holiness is love for one another as family, a love that comes from a pure heart (1 Pet 1:22, s.a. 1 Pet 3:8). He tells them to keep loving one another solemnly, for love covers a multitude of sins (1 Pet 4:8). In his second letter, he urges readers to add to their armoury of virtue, brotherly affection and love (2 Pet 1:7).

Of all NT letters, 1 John above all emphasises love, especially in chs. 3 and 4. God is love (1 John 4:8, 16). He first loved us (1 John 4:19). Love comes from the Father and makes us his children (1 John 3:1; 4:7). It is evidence in the sending of Christ (1 John 4:9). As such, we should love one another (1 John 3:11; 4:1, 11). This love is the emulation of Christ's love in his self-giving (1 John 3:16). This must be love not merely in words but helping others in need (1 John 3:16–18). This love casts out fear (1 John 4:18). It is an essential mark of a Christian and especially a leader.

2 John urges readers to live out of what is now not a new commandment, but an old one, to love one another (2 John 5).

Hope

Leaders give people hope for a better future. In Hebrews 3:6, as Jesus is faithful over God's household, we can hold fast our confidence and boast in our hope . We have a full assurance of hope in Heb 6:11. We are to hold fast to the hope set before us anchored in the heavenlies in Christ (Heb 6:18–19; 10:23). Hebrews 12:18–29 both warns of God as a consuming fire but equally excites us with a spectacular vision of God's kingdom the heavenly Mt Zion and Jerusalem, the city of the living God, with innumerable partying angels, God's people, God himself King and Judge, Jesus the mediator of the new covenant. In Heb 11:1, faith is defined as "the assurance of things hoped for, the conviction of things not seen." A Christian leader paints pictures of the future God has for us, in keeping with God's will. This sustains us as we run our race for him.

The hope of Christ's coming is found in Hebrews (e.g. Heb 10:37), James (e.g. Jas 5:7–8), and Peter stresses the hope of eternal inheritance (e.g. 1 Pet 1:3–9). Peter urges readers to put their hope on the grace of Christ (1 Pet 1:13) and on God (1 Pet 1:21). The hope within us is to be defended as we are confronted with questions (1 Pet 3:15).

Sexual Purity

A feature of the false teachers of 2 Peter and Jude is their sexual immorality (2 Pet 2:2, 10, 13–14; Jude 4, 7). The author of Hebrews warns readers to "Let marriage be honoured among all, and let the marriage bed be undefiled, for the sexually immoral and adulterous will be judged by God" (Heb 13:4). Peter counsels his readers not to live in sensuality, passions, and alcohol abuse—things linked together in the world of the Romans and in our contexts today (1 Pet 4:3).

Beware the Love of Money

The author of Hebrews tells his readers plainly, "keep your life free from the love of money, being content with what you have" (Heb 13:5).

James powerfully warns the rich that their wealth is short-lived, unable to be taken with them. Those who have people in their employment, as in Christian organisations and churches, must not underpay them, especially if they themselves are living opulently. Such a person will face judgement (Jas 5:1–6).

Peter urges elders to shepherd their flock not for "shameful gain" but willingly (1 Pet 5:2).

Prayer

James emphasises the need for prayer. If one lacks wisdom, and every leader needs it, they should ask God with faith and not express doubt, and he will give it (Jas 1:5–7). Toward the end of his letter, James urges the suffering to pray, the cheerful to praise, the elders to lay hands on the sick, and to confess sin and pray for one another. He notes the example of Elijah who prayed against rain and was heard. As the prayer of the righteous has power, Christian leaders must first and foremost be people of prayer. Jude also calls for people to pray in the Spirit (Jude 20).

Humility

James stresses the need for believers to be humble. He sees in Christ a reversal; the lowly exalted, the rich humiliated (Jas 1:9–11). Peter too urges readers to have a humble mind (1 Pet 3:8). He tells all his churches to clothe themselves with humility toward one another. Both James and Peter warn readers that God opposes the proud but gives grace to the humble (James 4:6; 1 Pet 5:5). As such, they must humble themselves before the Lord and he will exalt them in his time (Jas 4:10; 1 Pet 5:6).

Listening, Thoughtful Non-angry Responses

A good leader is quick to listen, slow to open their mouth and respond, and slow to become angry (Jas 1:19–20). This is one of the great leadership ideas in Scripture. A good leader learns the art of listening deeply, hearing what is being said and what is behind what is said. They are very thoughtful and considered in their responses. They do not quickly turn to anger, for anger does not produce the righteousness of God. Nor does it build people up, it tears down.

Speech that Edifies

James discusses the tongue. Those who want to teach are judged strictly. The tongue has the power to control the direction of a life, as a bridle or bit for a horse, and the rudder of a ship. It is like a spark that set ablaze a forest. It can destroy life and stoke the fires of hell. It must be tamed as it has the power of evil and the power to poison. Leaders must be in control of their speech to ensure it edifies (Jas 3:1–12). In Jas 4:11–12, believers are not to speak evil against one another, which is judgmentalism. It is God's place to judge. Peter similarly urges believers to speak as if speaking God's word—this suggests serious effort to speak well (1 Pet 4:11).

Wisdom

Knowledge is good, but wisdom is better. Wisdom is practical knowledge, the capacity to apply knowledge and made good decisions for the betterment of oneself and others. James urges the readers to pray for wisdom (Jas 1:5–8). He encourages them to seek the wisdom from above that is humble and repudiates demonic "wisdom" that includes jealousy, selfish ambition, boasting, and falsehood which lead to disorder and corruption. Wisdom from above is pure, seeks peace, gentle, reasonable, merciful, impartial, sincere and produces a harvest of righteousness and peace (Jas 3:13–18).

Keeping One's Word

James echoes Jesus' teaching in Matt 5:33–37 in the Sermon on the Mount, urging readers not to swear oaths but to simply let one's "yes" be a "yes" and their "no" a "no." This summons Christians to be people of their word; people who can be trusted. As such, Christian leaders are to be very careful as they speak, and not make false promises, and throwing around visions that are unrealistic. They should speak carefully and follow through.

Joy

In Hebrews, Jesus endured the cross for the "joy set before him" (Heb 12:2). The writer of Hebrews urges us to run our race with the same mindset. He directly addresses leaders, urging them to watch their flocks with "joy and not with groaning" (Heb 13:17). Christian leadership is hard, but when we find ourselves groaning, we need to come back to this text and remind ourselves that we should serve with joy, remembering what awaits us.

James considers it a joy to suffer for it produces Christian growth (Jas 1:2, cf. Rom 5:3). Peter begins his first letter with a magnificent blessing speaking of the marvellous benefits received from God in Christ. Because of these blessings, despite temporary suffering, we are to rejoice (1 Pet 1:6, 8). As with Paul and James, he urges his readers to rejoice that in their suffering they participate in those of Christ (1 Pet 4:13). John speaks of completing joy through obedience (1 John 1:4; 2 John 12). He gains joy that converts are walking in truth (3 John 4). Jude speaks of that day when we stand before God as a time of joy (Jude 24).

Holiness

Peter cites the recurring OT phrase, "Be holy, because I am holy" (1 Pet 1:15; Lev 11:44–45). Holiness is not defined by separation from the world and external uncleanness through touching defiled things, but holiness of heart in relationships. We are to be ever prepared for action, hopeful, sober-minded, no longer conformed to our past sins and ignorance. As God is holy, so are we to be holy in our conduct. We are like those in exile in Babylon as we live in a fallen world. We are not to take on the lifestyles of the pagans who surround us. We are to conduct ourselves with lives shaped by the fear of the Lord knowing who we are and what God has done for us in Christ (1 Pet 1:12–21). True holiness is obedience and love. In 2 Peter 3:11, readers are summoned to holiness as they await and hasten Christ's coming.

Seeking Maturity

Paul bemoaned the Corinthians for their failure to mature, stuck on drinking milk and not solid food (1 Cor 3:1–4). Peter uses the same motif in a slightly different manner, urging readers to put away false attitudes of malice, deceit, hypocrisy, envy, and slander. They are to be like new-borns seeking pure spiritual milk from God to grow up into salvation (1 Pet 2:1-3). This is the image of God as a mother, and believers drinking her milk for growth.

Submission to the State

This is an important theme in Paul (Rom 13:1–7; Tit 3:1). Similarly, 1 Peter 2:13–18 stresses that we are to live within the Kingdoms of the world recognising that while fallen, God orders his world through governments. Without ever compromising our first allegiance to God and his Son, we are to be subject to the institutions of our nation (central and local governments, police, masters [over slaves], and other law). God has appointed them to maintain order. These passages are stunning when we consider that the world of the recipients and writer was ruled by Nero who was at this time, beginning to severely persecute Christians. We change the world not by revolution but a reloveution.

Hospitality

It has been noted that the ancients delighted in hospitality, especially the provision of food and welcome into the home. The author of Hebrews puts an interesting twist on this, urging readers to show hospitality, as in so doing, some may be welcoming angels (Heb 13:2). This calls to mind Abraham's welcome of the three strangers in Gen 18. Peter also stresses showing hospitality to one another without grumbling (1 Pet 4:9).

Exercising Gifts

Paul develops the idea of spiritual gifts, each person contributing to the church and world through gifts granted by God. Peter too mentions this. He assumes everyone has a gift and it is to be used to serve one another, using what God has given us through his grace (1 Pet 4:10).

Service

Hebrews stresses service. Angels are ministering spirits sent to serve us (Heb 1:14). The High Priest serves God (Heb 2:17; 10:11), as does Moses (Heb 3:5) and priests in general (Heb 13:10). He commends the recipients for their love of God and service on behalf of the saints (Heb 6:10). We are saved by the blood of Jesus to serve God (Heb 9:14). James begins his letter describing himself as a slave of God and Christ, recalling Paul doing the same (Jas 1:1, s.a. Rom 1:1; Phil 1:1; Tit 1:1). Peter does the same in his second letter (2 Pet 1:1), as does Jude (Jude 1).

Perseverance

In a sense, the whole letter of Hebrews is a summons to persevere in the faith and not desert it (e.g. Heb 2:1, 6:9–12; 10:19–25; 12:1–17). James also stresses perseverance, which is produced by the testing of faith and leads to maturity (Jas 1:3–4). He declares a person blessed for remaining steadfast under trial, for they will receive an eternal reward (Jas 1:12). Jude ends his letter with a call to persevere. The readers are to build themselves up in their faith, pray in the Spirit, keep themselves in the love of God, and wait for Christ (Jude 17–20).

Conclusion

Hebrews and the General Epistles are as important to our theology as the writings of the Gospels, Acts, Paul, and Revelation. The early church in its wisdom, informed by the Holy Spirit and its desire to ensure that the gospel is preserved, included these letters in the NT. As such, we must work to handle these texts of Scripture well and build our theology with the whole canon of Scripture. We must resist the tendencies today to create a canon within the canon, privileging the Gospels or Paul over other parts of the NT. We need to grapple with these other books and their messages.

Particularly, they help us understand: the OT better (esp. Hebrews), the dangers of false teaching and how to respond (esp. 2 Peter, Jude), perseverance (esp. Hebrews), the need to live lives that conform to the gospel we preach (esp. 1 Peter), the emphasis of love expressed in concrete action for those in need (esp. James, 1 and 2 John), the certainty of suffering and need for perseverance (Heb, James, 1 Peter), that Jesus is returning in judgement, the certainty of eternal life for God's people and eternal destruction for those who reject God and corrupt his gospel (esp. 2 Peter, Jude).

They also help us with our own communication of the gospel. They read like sermons. They draw on the OT creatively. They all have their own style and fit their contexts. Combined with Jesus' use of parables, Paul's use of metaphor, and the amazing drama of Revelation, we should be excited about using them to be more creative in our preaching and gospel sharing.

12

Chapter Twelve: Revelation

We come now to the final NT book, Revelation. Arguably, this is the most difficult book to interpret with its symbols and controversial history of interpretation. However, when considered in its context and genre, this difficulty is somewhat reduced although a full and final understanding is beyond any reader.

More Detail
Keown, *Discovering the New Testament*, Vol 3, ch. 8.
Suggested Bible Readings
Revelation 1–7, 13, 19–22

Revelation: Background Issues

Place in the Canon

There was a lot of debate concerning the inclusion of Revelation in the Canon of Scripture. In the western churches of the Roman world, it was excluded by Marcion, who rejected any NT book with strong allusions to the OT. It was also rejected by Gaius (Rome at the beginning of the second century), and the sect called the *Alogoi*. In the eastern churches, the Egyptian Bishop Dionysius questioned its apostolic authorship in order to minimize its authority. A number of other Eastern thinkers were influenced by this and the Council of Laodicea (360) did not recognize it as canonical.

However, there are also significant voices in the west and east that did support Revelation's authority. In the west, it is possible that it was known to Ignatius (ad 110–117), Barnabas (ad 135), and it was quite probably used by the author of the Shepherd of Hermas (ca. ad 150). It was accepted as authoritative by Papias (d. 130), Justin Martyr (mid-second century), and Irenaeus (180). It is found in the Muratorian Canon at the end of the second century. In the east, Clement of Alexandria and Origen supported its authority. As such, the majority did want it included.

Authorship

Revelation is written by John (Rev 1:1, 4, 9; 22:8). Traditionally, this is John the Apostle but as with many NT books, the identity of this particular John is questioned. This is supported by the style of the Greek which is much inferior to the Gospel and letters. The ideas are also regarded to be very different. However, a strong case can be made for John the Apostle. The way the name is simply placed in the text suggests that it is a well-known person. John traditionally lived his later life in Ephesus and ministered to Asia Minor. This fits with Revelation which is sent to the seven churches of the area. The different Greek can be accounted for by either John penning it himself whereas his Gospel and letters were written down by an amanuensis, or vice versa. The different ideas are likely due to the different purpose. The Gospel looks back and tells the story of Jesus. The letters are communiques to a moment in time. Revelation looks forward to events to come and so focuses on history and its climax, the return of Christ.

Date

The date is unclear. Some opt for an earlier date not long after Nero's death in ad 68. They see Nero as the prototype for the book. There was a myth of Nero's return (*Nero Redivivus*) that circulated. Some consider that the beast is modelled on him. If this is the case, it is written in the 70s. The majority view though is that Emperor Domitian's persecution of Christians and Jews is a better setting. He ruled from ad 81 to 96, and this would place Revelation in this period.

Setting and Recipients

We know from Rev 1:9 that John was at the time imprisoned for preaching the gospel on the island of Patmos, a small island around 50 km SE of Ephesus off the coast of Asia Minor (western Turkey). There is a cave there, purportedly where he was imprisoned, although this is uncertain.

We also know who the recipients were, the seven churches of Revelation planted in the main urban centres of Asia Minor (remembering that Colossae was destroyed in the earthquake in ad 60–61 and not rebuilt): Ephesus,

Smyrna, Pergamum, Thyatira, Sardis, Philadelphia, and Laodicea.

Apocalyptic Genre

The key to understanding Revelation is to recognise its genre. Revelation is written as a letter with an epistolary prologue in Rev 1:4–8 in which the writer is identified: John; the recipients are named: to the seven churches that are in Asia; and a greeting and blessing are given. This tells us that it was written by John.

However, while it is a letter, it also labelled in Rev 1:1 as *Apokalypsis Iēsou Christou*, "the revelation of Jesus Christ." This identifies Revelation as an example of apocalyptic literature. Apocalyptic literature is found in Judaism and early Christianity from around 200 bc to ad 200. There are many other examples in the Pseudepigrapha (e.g. Apocalypses of Abraham, Adam, Baruch, Ezra, among many others) and in early Christian writings (e.g. The Shepherd of Hermas).

These are a particular kind of writings which are written by someone in the first person, often using the name of a great saint (which may support it not being written by John), to people suffering great persecution. They often involve an angel or seer who takes the writer on a journey, giving them visions often of heaven and of things that are to happen on earth. They are full of symbolism such as numbers (e.g. 666), fierce animals (beasts, dragons, locusts), and people (e.g. a harlot). They often involve cataclysmic events like wars, earthquakes, plagues, and other natural and supernaturally caused disasters. They usually revolve around a conflict between God with his angels and the Devil and his demons. The people of God are also swept up into this conflict, the children of light versus the children of evil. They are really ramped up good versus evil battles. They involve governments and politics and war. They usually resolve into a cataclysmic victory of God and his angels, the vindication of the faithful, and the Shalom that God's people yearn for.

Apocalypses are notoriously difficult to interpret because they are full of symbolism that is drawn from the context and cannot be interpreted literally with any certainty. They are really like sci-fi or fantasy dramas that point to realities behind their symbolism but are not necessarily to be taken directly.

The ideas and symbolism must first be understood in relation to the context. In the case of Revelation, written sometime under Roman rule, the Roman Empire and its emperors loom behind it. It is also full of Old Testament allusions and imagery. It draws on some of Jesus' teaching. It has Greek ideas behind some of it. In many cases, there are multiple possibilities for interpretation that leave us looking at meanings that are probabilities more than certainties.

Bible readers who have not really looked into the genre of Revelation and the idea of apocalyptic literature can get into real trouble trying to interpret it literally and directly. They can start to find contemporary historical people and events foreseen in it. What they don't know is that people have been doing this and finding such people and events for centuries and have all been wrong. We have to think very carefully about the point each part of Revelation is making and not simply transport it directly to our world. However, as Scripture, it does have meaning and importance, and we need to read it carefully and consider its message.

Revelation: Methods of Interpretation

At the end of the day working out what Revelation is about is the critical question. What does Revelation mean? To what do the visions of John refer? What are we to learn from them? There are four main perspectives on Revelation.

The Preterist Approach

The View

Preterists read Revelation in its own context and do not read it as a prophecy of future events. It is written to and for the first readers only. It is the most commonly held view among biblical scholars today.

In this approach, the visions of John relate primarily to John's time and world. They grow out of and describe events happening then and are not to be read as futuristic. Hence, they are like other apocalypses which speak to the events happening at the time, usually, times of terrible evil and persecution. They were written to encourage people in great suffering, reminding them of the impending triumph of God.

The purpose of Revelation then is to show the first readers how God will bring his judgment on those who are oppressing them in their world, and how God is triumphing over the forces of their age and delivering them from their suffering. It is not to be taken literally and applied to history. Revelation then is a kind of pseudo-prophecy speaking of God's triumph in the present.

Those who take this view interpret the book against the Neronian persecution, the destruction of Jerusalem, the

Domitian persecution which was threatening the church in Asia, and the persecution of the church generally, at the time. They rigorously apply the symbolism to that time only.

So, the beast is one of the Roman emperors (Domitian or Nero) and the false prophet is the cult of the worship of the emperor. Revelation assures the readers of Christ's imminent return to destroy Rome and establish his Kingdom on earth.

Assessment

There is an element of truth to this view. Revelation was written out of, and speaks into, a time of persecution. However, there are significant differences from Jewish apocalypses, which were to be interpreted against the contexts in which they were written. In particular, is the concern in Revelation for the history of salvation running from OT to NT. John employs a rich array of OT imagery to prophesy into the future. In addition, this view misunderstands the nature of OT prophecy. While the OT prophetic oracles related to their own day, they also had a futurist emphasis, e.g. they predicted the return from exile and the ultimate hope of the new heavens and new earth (Isa 65–66). It is doubtful that Revelation should be considered to have *no* futuristic dimension, whether it is general and symbolic, or specific. However, Revelation *must* first be understood in relation to its original setting. So, the descriptions of the future grow out of the present experience of John and his readers. For example, it is possible that the Fall of Jerusalem is a pattern for the culmination and that both the historical event and some future catastrophe are in mind. If so, reading Revelation through a preterist lens can be useful in discerning the pattern.

The Historical Approach

The View

In this view, the symbolism speaks to human history at the time of interpretation. So, in the Middle Ages, there was a belief that the millennium was about to begin. To support this view, thinkers interpreted the events of Revelation as a sketch of *church history* from the time of Christ to their own day. In this way of interpreting Revelation, events in church history are found which correlate to the seals, trumpets, bowls, and so on, in Revelation. This approach was popular among the Reformers like Luther and Calvin, as it enabled them to interpret the beast in Revelation as the Catholic Church and Papacy. The historical approach has been used for a variety of schemes including those who accept a literal millennium (e.g. Isaac Newton) or those who don't (e.g. Luther) and postmillennialism.

Assessment

This view has little merit. Its problem is that each interpreter can make any symbol in Revelation correlate to anything they suppose in history, making the whole enterprise rather spurious. This has happened in our time as people find a modern state in Revelation and it turns out to be wrong. On the other hand, if the events of Revelation are future-orientated, the symbols may have some legitimate correlations in human history.

The Idealist or Symbolic Approach: The symbolism is general, not specific.

The View

In this perspective, the symbolism in Revelation is not to be taken literally but points to something in a general sense. This is another common view in biblical scholarship. So, the symbolism of Revelation is designed to help us understand God's person and plan in a general way; that is, Revelation does not give us specific incidents, rather the principles or ideals at work in history. The symbols then reflect spiritual powers in the world. Hence, Revelation is generally predictive, not specifically predictive, i.e. the message assures the readers that God will triumph without going into specifics. The things described are apocalyptic descriptions of suffering and struggle without necessarily correlating them to specific historical situations. However, all apocalyptic is based around a correlation between the symbols and events in history, so one would expect some correlation in Revelation.

Assessment

This approach is helpful because Revelation is highly symbolic, and this should be recognised. It also helps us to read Revelation non-chronologically, i.e. it can be understood as parallel rather than consecutive sections.

The Extreme Futurist Approach, i.e. Classical Dispensationalism

The View

In this view, the symbolism speaks of Israel, the Church, and the end of the world. Until the mid to late twentieth century it was popular to interpret Revelation through the lens of Classical Dispensationalism, that is, that there are two divine programs; one for Israel and one for the church. All the seals, trumpets, and bowls that belong to the Great Tribulation relate only to Israel and not the church (which has been raptured).

In ch. 2-3, the church is on earth. However, the word "church" never occurs again until 22:16. The twenty-four elders (Rev 4:4) are the church, raptured and rewarded. The rapture occurs at 4:1 and the 144,000 people of God on earth who remain are Jews, 12,000 from each of the twelve tribes (Rev 7:1–8), who proclaim the "gospel of the Kingdom" during the tribulation and win many Gentiles to God (Rev 7:9–17). The Beast is the head of the restored Roman Empire (cf. Dan 9:27). The final seven years begins with a covenant between the Beast (antichrist) and Israel that will be broken after three and a half years (forty-two months) and then the Beast will turn on the Jews. The great conflict in Revelation is between the antichrist and Israel, not the antichrist and the church. Chapters 4-19 have to do with the tribulation period and chapters 2 and 3 alone are for the church and the church age. The seven churches represent seven successive periods of church history; the final period (Laodicea) is one of apostasy and spiritual apathy. Chapter 19 to the end speaks of the events that will occur beginning with Jesus' return. There will be a millennium, final conflict, judgment, and the new heavens and earth.

Assessment

This view remains popular among many Christians because of the *Left Behind* books and movies that have popularised it, especially in the USA. However, this extreme futurist view, to a large degree, died out in the mid to late twentieth century in scholarship, even among many classical dispensational scholars. It is certainly a flawed view, as Rev 4:1 says nothing about a rapture. Rather, the church remains on earth and experiences the period of suffering, something consistent with the rest of the NT.

The Moderate Futurist Approach

The View

Some do not accept the Classical Dispensational perspective but do believe that the symbolism of Revelation does speak to a yet unfulfilled future but in a general and sweeping way. This is sometimes called a *consistent* futurist approach which holds that everything from chs. 4-22 in Revelation finds its fulfilment in the last days of human history. Adherents reject seeing a secret rapture in 4:1 and consider that the events foreseen in chs. 4-22 concern all humanity, Christian or otherwise. Revelation thus depicts the consummation of God's redemptive purposes involving salvation and judgment.

One variation of this is a more *moderate futurist approach* which believes that *some* of the events in these chapters, particularly the earlier ones, take place in history before the end. This blends the idealist and futurist viewpoint taking out the ideas of dispensationalism.

Assessment

This view, however, faces the problem of which ones should be taken literally, and which ones not. Often such a view will not hold to a secret rapture at some point. They anticipate that events on earth will be dire leading to Christ's return. They leave room for a millennium after Christ's return or before he returns (postmillennialism or amillennialism).

Note: Put simply, postmillennialists hold we are in the millennium now and expect the world to get better and better until the Kingdom is consummated. Christ's return is minimalised. Amillennialism similarly argues we are in the millennium now and it will consummate with Jesus' return. Most agree there will be a period of horrific strife prior to Jesus' return, although some would disagree.

Conclusion

It is probably best to take an eclectic approach and include dimensions of the preterist, idealist, and moderate futurist views when approaching the interpretation of Revelation.

The seven churches of Asia are most likely literal churches with real problems that are addressed by John, albeit in a stereotypical form. They do not refer to eras in history but are genuine words from God to John for these churches. This is supported by specific places (e.g. Ephesus, Smyrna), names (e.g. Antipas), groups (e.g. Nicolatians, Jews), and situations described. For example, the reference to the lukewarmness of the Laodiceans fits our understanding of the water supply in the town. Whereas the water at Hierapolis was warm and healing, and that at Colossae cool and refreshing, the water at Laodicea was undrinkable and generally useless. The description of Pergamum as Satan's throne fits with the importance of the Temple of Zeus or Asklepios to this city.

In ch. 4–22, John describes, in highly symbolic terms, the events surrounding the end of the age when God will establish his Kingdom and evil will be vanquished. The backdrop is life in the persecuted church under the tyranny of Rome and the Emperor Cult (preterist). That being the case, the vision of the future is to be interpreted through a first-century lens so that the situation of the churches at the time gives the first layer of meaning of the symbols used. While the orientation is future, clearly the message has present appeal to the first readers, giving them great encouragement as they face struggles and persecution; particularly the assurance of God's ultimate victory over evil and the vindication of his people (generally futurist).

Having said that, interpretation remains highly contentious and I would take a conservative and tentative general line in seeking to interpret events. For example, when considering the millennium, there seem to be two options that can work. First, that one takes a post-tribulation premillennialist approach, with Jesus returning and restoring his world in an interim millennial period. Second, that one takes the amillennial position, seeing the millennium as concurrent with history, with Jesus returning at some point to complete the work of restoration.

To be frank, anyone who really wants to interpret Revelation cannot do it without the aid of excellent commentaries. This is because each verse is a literal repository of links and connections that require assistance in understanding.

Some examples include:

Grant R. Osborne, *Revelation*, BECNT (Grand Rapids, MI: Baker Academic, 2002).

Leon Morris, *The Revelation of St. John*, TNTC (Grand Rapids: Eerdmans, 1969).

Robert H. Mounce, *The Book of Revelation*, NICNT (Grand Rapids, MI: Eerdmans, 1997).

Revelation: The Beast of Revelation 13

A very helpful book to enable readers to come to grips with the different ways that scholars interpret Revelation is Steve Gregg, *Revelation, Four Views: A Parallel Commentary* (Nashville, Tenn.: T. Nelson Publishers, 1997). His interesting commentary reads each passage demonstrating the different approaches to the text. Here I will summarize the different approaches to the mark of the beast to illustrate how the four approaches work regarding the mark of the beast (Rev 13:16–18).

In Revelation 13:16–18 a second beast working on behalf of the first causes all people to receive a mark on the right hand or forehead without which no-one can buy or sell. The number of this beast is 666 and the reader is challenged to interpret this. It needs to be remembered when interpreting this that the letters of the Greek, Hebrew, and Latin alphabets also served as numbers.

Preterism

Many *Preterists* identify the beast with Nero. Caesar Nero in Hebrew is *Nrwn Osr* (pronounced *"Nerōn Kaiser"*) which includes seven Hebrew letters adding up to 666 (50, 200, 6, 50, 100, 60, and 200). This is thus code used to avoid the Roman authorities. The ban on trading is the economic boycott of Christians by Nero. Christians should not yield to his rule. As such, the beast is not a future figure, but Nero. Revelation tells the story of his eventual defeat and God's victory (not literally).

Idealistic (or Symbolic, Spiritual)

The *spiritual* (*symbolic or ideal*) interpretation does not consider the mark literal any more than the "seal" in 7:3 or the 'name" in 14:1. The mark is symbolic of their selling out to the false idolatrous system. The forehead symbolizes the mind and the hand the act of trade. Thus, to receive the mark is to yield to the false system. This can apply to any age in which Christians are drawn to false systems. There is thus no need to work out who 666 is, as it symbolizes false religion.

One can see in these interpretations differing approaches. As noted above, many moderate futurists would hold that there may well be a future final empire with a despotic ruler with the same sort of mindset as Nero, Domitian, or other despots (cf. Matt 24:15; 2 Thess 2:3–10; 1 John 2:18). Christians will be forced to yield to that empire either through literally taking a mark, or as is more likely, yielding to its idolatrous rule (taking 666 symbolically). However, they will resist associating every literal element of the vision with certain figures and a particular.

Historical

The historicist solutions include that of Irenaeus who believed the name to be *Lareinous* (Greek for "Latin"), and so this is the name of the last of Daniel's four kingdoms (the Roman Empire). Others with a historicist perspective accepted this as the Roman Catholic Church, i.e. the *Latin* (Roman) church patriarch. This is thus a reference to the Papacy. The mark of being Catholic is Latin worship. The mark on hands or foreheads may refer to slaves and soldiers wearing the name of their owner or emperor on their hands or foreheads. The ban on buying and selling relates to banning commercial engagement with Protestants or heretics. Others who read it this way find the number appropriate for the Latin *Basileia* (kingdom), *apostaths* (apostate), the Hebrew for 'Roman,' the pope's title *Vicarius filii Dei* ("vicar of the Son of God"). Few would accept this today.

Futurists

As with much popular Christianity, many *Futurists* see here a worldwide empire with an associated cashless economy which requires a mark on the body for trade. Others take this non-literally referring to pledging allegiance to the ruler, the beast. To take the beast is to yield to his rule, and without doing so, one is shut out of the system. The number 666 has been variously interpreted. Some notice that six Roman numerals (I, V, X, L, C, D) add up to 666 and so suggests a Roman antichrist. The word "beast" occurs thirty–six times in Revelation, which is 6 times 6. Names have been associated with it including on some popular websites, Donald Trump and Vladimir Putin! Another possibility is that the number six represents humankind, and so 666 could be symbolic of humanity's rebellion against God.

Conclusion

While Revelation is a difficult book, apocalyptic in form, and full of difficult imagery, we must grapple with it. It forms a brilliant *inclusio* with Genesis, completing the story of God's creation, the Fall, God's redemption through Israel and Jesus, the mission of the church in the world, and the return of Christ and the new heavens and earth.

We must beware of reading it literally as this assumes the writer wants us to do this. Rather, as Jacob wrestled with God (Gen 32), we must struggle to understand what its rich symbolism is pointing to. We must resist reading past and future specific history into it. This leads to misreading the signs of the times and falsely predicting the return of Christ. Yet, we must also avoid making it a book without meaning for the present and future. It does summon us to be faithful to the end, even prepared to die for our faith. It tells us that while we submit to the State (Rom 13; Tit 3:1; 1 Pet 2:13–18), there is a time to resist the Beast non-violently, refusing to join it in its corporate evil (Rev 13). We must not bear its marks and instead must be clothed with Christ.

Revelation also gives us great hope, for Jesus will win! He is at work in the world amidst the carnage of sin. He is bringing redemption. People from every nation will be among his people, joined together in worship of God. Praise him!

He will return. He will judge the world. Evil will be destroyed. Heaven and earth will be merged. God, his Son, and his people will be together forever. The world will be recreated. Then, as eternal beings, with our eternal God, we will get to participate in his next works. What a fantastic thought and privilege! We should use our imaginations and let this vision motivate us to the end. Amen!

13

Works Referenced

Berchman, Richard. "Pagan Philosophers on Judaism in Ancient Times." Pages 1038–1051 in *The Encyclopedia of Judaism*. Edited by Jacob Neusner, Alan J. Avery-Peck, and William Scott Green. Leiden; Boston; Köln: Brill, 2000.

Davids, Peter H. *The Letters of 2 Peter and Jude*, PNTC. Grand Rapids, MI: Eerdmans, 2006.

Dunn, James D. G. *The Epistles to the Colossians and to Philemon: A Commentary on the Greek Text*, NIGTC. Grand Rapids, MI; Carlisle: Eerdmans; Paternoster Press, 1996.

Steve Gregg, *Revelation, Four Views: A Parallel Commentary*. Nashville, Tenn.: T. Nelson Publishers, 1997.

Keown, Mark J. *Discovering the New Testament*. 3 Vols. Bellingham, WA: Lexham, 2018, 2020.

Metzger, Bruce Manning, United Bible Societies. *A Textual Commentary on the Greek New Testament, Second Edition a Companion Volume to the United Bible Societies' Greek New Testament (4th Rev. Ed.)*. London; New York: United Bible Societies, 1994.

Moo, Douglas J. *The Letters to the Colossians and to Philemon*, PNTC. Grand Rapids, MI: Eerdmans, 2008.

Morris, Leon *The Revelation of St. John*, TNTC. Grand Rapids: Eerdmans, 1969.

Mounce, Robert H. *The Book of Revelation*, NICNT. Grand Rapids, MI: Eerdmans, 1997.

Osborne, Grant R. *Revelation*, BECNT. Grand Rapids, MI: Baker Academic, 2002.

Osburn, Carroll D. "Discourse Analysis and Jewish Apocalyptic in the Epistle of Jude." Pages 287–319 in *Linguistics and New Testament Interpretation: Essays on Discourse Analysis*. Edited by David A. Black. Nashville: Broadman, 1992.

Patzia, A. G. & A. J. Petrotta, *Pocket Dictionary of Biblical Studies*. Downers Grove, IL: IVP, 2002.

Snodgrass, K. R. "Parable," *DJG* 591

Watson, JoAnn Ford. "Thaddaeus." Page 435 Volume 6 in *AYBD*.

See also

"The Seven Churches in Asia Minor: Mentioned in the Book of Revelation." https://www.bible-history.com/new-testament/seven-churches-of-asia.html.

Lightning Source UK Ltd.
Milton Keynes UK
UKHW022039010221
378054UK00010B/2204